The Nicene Option

The Nicene Option

An Incarnational Phenomenology

James K. A. Smith

BAYLOR UNIVERSITY PRESS

© 2021 by Baylor University Press
Waco, Texas 76798

All Rights Reserved. No part of this publication may be reproduced, stored in a retrieval system, or transmitted, in any form or by any means, electronic, mechanical, photocopying, recording, or otherwise, without the prior permission in writing of Baylor University Press.

Cover and book design by Kasey McBeath
Cover art by Daniel Domig, *Prayer Invites Chaos* (2019). Used with permission.

Library of Congress Cataloging-in-Publication Data

Names: Smith, James K. A., 1970- author.
Title: The Nicene option : an incarnational phenomenology / James K. A. Smith.
Description: Waco : Baylor University Press, 2021. | Includes bibliographical references and index. | Summary: "A collection of essays spanning Smith's career that examines the prospects for a renewed continental philosophy of religion, while making a constructive case for Smith's own vision of the "Nicene option" and incarnational theology as conversation partner"-- Provided by publisher.
Identifiers: LCCN 2021015534 (print) | LCCN 2021015535 (ebook) | ISBN 9781481313728 (hardcover) | ISBN 9781481314220 (pdf) | ISBN 9781481313742 (epub)
Subjects: LCSH: Philosophy and religion. | Philosophical theology. | Derrida, Jacques. | Phenomenology.
Classification: LCC BL51 .S5724 2021 (print) | LCC BL51 (ebook) | DDC 210--dc23
LC record available at https://lccn.loc.gov/2021015534
LC ebook record available at https://lccn.loc.gov/2021015535

Printed in the United States of America on acid-free paper with a minimum of thirty percent recycled content.

For Merold Westphal,
exemplar

Contents

Acknowledgments	ix
Introduction God on the Left Bank? Prospects for a Continental Philosophy of Religion	1
I Outline of an Incarnational Continental Philosophy of Religion	9
1 The Philosophy of Religion Takes Practice A Methodological Manifesto	11
2 Secular Liturgies Prospects for a "Post-Secular" Study of Religion	29
3 Continental Philosophy of Religion Prescriptions for a Healthy Subdiscipline	53
4 A Logic of Incarnation The Nicene Option in Continental Philosophy of Religion	63
II Derrida, Marion, and the Possibility of a Christian Phenomenology	93
5 Determined Violence Derrida's Structural Religion	95

6	Re-Kanting Postmodernism? Derrida's Religion within the Limits of Reason Alone	111
7	Determined Hope A Phenomenology of Christian Expectation	127
8	Beyond Epistemology Derrida and the Limits of the "Limits of Knowledge"	153
9	A Principle of Incarnation in Derrida's *(Theologische?) Jugendschriften* Towards a Confessional Theology	171
10	Deconstruction—an Augustinian Science? Augustine and Derrida on the Commitments of Philosophy	189
11	Picturing Revelation Idolatry and the Aesthetic in Marion and Rosenzweig	201
12	The Call as Gift The Subject's Donation in Marion and Levinas	223

Afterword 235
    An Incarnational Phenomenology

Author Index 239

Acknowledgments

Gathering work from the past twenty-five years, this volume represents scholarship nourished by several academic communities whose support I want to acknowledge. Villanova University was an incubator of almost every trajectory coursing through this book, and the mentorship and encouragement of John Caputo have left an indelible mark on my own work, even if we fundamentally disagree. I will always be grateful for his kindness to me. My time at Loyola Marymount University was a source of lasting friendships and the site of a crucial encounter with the Jesuit tradition that has continued to shape and prod me. My long-term home, however, has been the storied halls of the Philosophy Department at Calvin College (now University). It was the work of an older generation of philosophers from Calvin who played a critical role in my own sense of calling to philosophy; but it has been my contemporary colleagues who have shaped me most. As someone trained in continental philosophy and phenomenology, Calvin has been a crucible for learning how to "speak analytic," and my work has been better for it. I also appreciate the long leash they give me to reinvent myself every once in a while, and for appreciating that it's not only writing laden with footnotes and technical jargon that counts as scholarship. That said: here is the book with all the footnotes just as reassurance (I hope).

I dedicate this volume to Merold Westphal, a doyen of continental philosophy of religion before we ever called it that. Though I was never his official student, I have learned much from him, particularly a kind of philosophical ecumenism that refuses to retreat to an enclave. When students ask me how to improve the clarity of their writing as they try to expound philosophers who are notoriously opaque, I always give them essays by Merold to read. Above all, Merold's work has always been suffused with a discerning Christian wisdom that was neither reactive nor dismissive. He is a sage who refused any mantle of the guru. I remain grateful for his work and witness.

A number of these chapters first appeared elsewhere in earlier versions. I am happy to acknowledge permission to include material here.

Chapter 1 was first published as "Philosophy of Religion Takes Practice: Liturgy as Source and Method in Philosophy of Religion," in *Contemporary Practice and Method in the Philosophy of Religion: New Essays*, ed. David Cheetham and Rolfe King (London: Continuum, 2008), 133–47. Used by permission of Bloomsbury Publishing Plc.

Chapter 2 was earlier published as "Secular Liturgies and the Prospects for a 'Post-Secular' Sociology of Religion," in *The Post-Secular in Question*, ed. Philip Gorski, David Kyuman Kim, John Torpey, and Jonathan VanAntwerpen (New York: NYU Press, 2012), 159–84 and is here included with the permission of NYU Press.

Both chapters 3 and 6 first appeared in the journal of the Society of Christian Philosophers and are here included with permission: "Continental Philosophy of Religion: Prescriptions for a Healthy Subdiscipline," *Faith and Philosophy* 26 (2009): 440–48, and "Re-Kanting Postmodernism?: Derrida's Religion within the Limits of Reason Alone," *Faith and Philosophy* 17 (2000): 558–71.

Chapter 4 was first published as "The Logic of Incarnation: Towards a Catholic Postmodernism," in *The Logic of Incarnation: James K. A. Smith's Critique of Postmodern Religion*, ed. Neal DeRoo and Brian Lightbody (Eugene, Ore.: Wipf & Stock, 2008), 3–37. Used by permission of Wipf & Stock Publishers. www.wipfandstock.com.

Chapter 5 was first published as "Determined Violence: Derrida's Structural Religion," *The Journal of Religion* 78, no. 2 (April 1998): 197–212. © 1998 by The University of Chicago. Reprinted with permission.

Chapter 7 was first published as "Determined Hope: A Phenomenology of Christian Expectation," in *The Future of Hope: Essays on Christian Tradition amid Modernity and Postmodernity*, ed. Miroslav Volf and William Katerberg (Grand Rapids: Eerdmans, 2004), 200–227. Reprinted by permission of the publisher.

Chapter 9 earlier appeared as "A Principle of Incarnation in Derrida's (*Theologische?*) *Jugendschriften*," *Modern Theology* 18 (2002): 217–30, and is reprinted with permission.

Chapter 10 was originally published as "Is Deconstruction an Augustinian Science? Augustine, Derrida, and Caputo on the Commitments of Philosophy," in *Religion with/out Religion: The Prayers and Tears of John D. Caputo*, ed. James H. Olthuis (London: Routledge, 2001), 50–61, and is included here with the permission of Taylor & Francis Informa UK Ltd.

Chapter 12 is excerpted from *The Hermeneutics of Charity*, ed. James K. A. Smith and Henry Venema (Grand Rapids: Brazos, 2004). © 2004. Used by permission of Brazos Press, a division of Baker Publishing Group.

Introduction

God on the Left Bank? Prospects for a Continental Philosophy of Religion

We now take for granted something that was virtually unthinkable just seventy-five years ago: that serious philosophical engagement with religion, even work that could be described as philosophical theology, is undertaken within the mainstream of the philosophical academy in North America. While religion was a persistent theme of philosophical reflection from Plato up through Hegel and even Nietzsche in the nineteenth century, the brief hijacking of Anglo-American philosophy by logical positivism had the effect of withering this subdiscipline in philosophy.[1] But in the mid-twentieth century, after the implosion of logical positivism (whose shaky foundations couldn't sustain critique), there was a movement of analytic philosophers that, in the course of challenging the epistemological assumptions of positivism, also cleared space for serious philosophical attention to God and religious phenomena. In different ways and in different streams, Elizabeth Anscombe, Alvin Plantinga, William Alston, Marilyn McCord Adams, Nicholas Wolterstorff, and many others began to unapologetically turn their philosophical tools to religious questions, while also letting their religious commitments inform their work on broader, mainstream philosophical

---

1   This story is recounted, for example, by Nicholas Wolterstorff in "Analytic Philosophy of Religion: Retrospect and Prospect," in *Inquiring about God: Selected Essays*, vol. 1, ed. Terence Cuneo (Cambridge: Cambridge University Press, 2009), 17–34.

issues in epistemology, metaphysics, ethics, and aesthetics. The result was not only a renaissance in philosophy of religion but also a burgeoning movement of Christian philosophy. It is telling, and encouraging, that several of these figures would be appointed (and honored) as presidents of the American Philosophical Association and would, in 1978, found the Society of Christian Philosophers.

As most will concede, this is largely an "analytic" story; that is, this is a story about the demise and reemergence of religion in analytic philosophy, which is the dominant mode or style of philosophy in the Anglo-American academy, and also the stream that was most derailed by logical positivism.[2] It explains why the so-called "renaissance" in philosophy of religion and Christian philosophy has been centered in analytic philosophy.

But the reason some philosophy is tagged as "analytic" is to distinguish it from another stream that we often call "continental" philosophy.[3] And with respect to religion, it is important to note that the continental stream was never hoodwinked by logical positivism and thus doesn't have the same "Ichabod" episode in the twentieth century that it needed to overcome. To take just one example, questions about God, faith, and theology leave their mark across Heidegger's corpus, from his early 1927 lecture on "Phenomenology and Theology" to his later critique of "onto-theo-logy"

---

2   I do not have any great stake in the distinction between "analytic" and "continental" philosophy except as a helpful description for different styles or streams of philosophical reflection. I appreciate Wolterstorff's suggestion that "the identity of the analytic tradition is a narrative, rather than a purely systematic, identity. What makes a philosopher an analytic philosopher is that he places himself within a certain story line of philosophy in the twentieth century" (*Inquiring about God*, 17). I would happily describe "continental" philosophy in the same way: there is no "essential" identity; only a historical, contingent, narrative identity insofar as the continental philosopher locates herself in a story of philosophical questions and debates that tracks onward from Edmund Husserl rather than, say, Frege. And none of this precludes philosophers becoming conversant in both conversations. See, for example, Samuel C. Wheeler, *Deconstruction as Analytic Philosophy* (Stanford: Stanford University Press, 2000), or the way Paul Ricoeur engages analytic discussions of identity in *Oneself as Another*, trans. Kathleen Blamey (Chicago: University of Chicago Press, 1992).

3   There is something of an apples-to-oranges problem in these two adjectives, the first being conceptual and the second being geographical ("continental" Europe vs. England and the English-speaking United States). The problem with any geographical description, of course, is that no region is monolithic. On the other hand, to describe continental philosophy as, say, "phenomenological" philosophy is also too narrow since there are important figures in French and German philosophy who eschew the phenomenological heritage of Husserl and Heidegger. We are left to live with all of these adjectives as fuzzy as best—which, per Wittgenstein, does not mean they do not serve a function.

in *Identity and Difference*.[4] And French philosophers working in Heidegger's wake—what Alain Badiou calls "the 'German move'" that is a feature of twentieth-century French philosophy[5]—continued to grapple with questions of God and religion, particularly in the work of Emmanuel Levinas, Paul Ricoeur, and Jean-Luc Marion, but also in more surprising thinkers such as Jacques Derrida.[6] So when phenomenologist Dominique Janicaud pointed out (and criticized) what he described as a theological "turn" in phenomenology, the justifiable retort was that theology had been woven into phenomenology almost since the beginning.[7]

In that sense, questions about faith, religion, and God were never *verboten* in continental philosophy the same way they were functionally outlawed by logical positivism's hegemony in early twentieth-century analytic philosophy. However, insofar as the field of philosophy of religion (and Christian philosophy) congealed in response to analytic debates, the newly energized field of philosophy of religion tended to be synonymous with *analytic* philosophy of religion. Both the parameters of debate and

4 Martin Heidegger, "Phenomenology and Theology," trans. James G. Hart and John C. Maraldo in *Pathmarks*, ed. William McNeill (Cambridge University Press, 1998), 39–54; idem, "The Onto-Theo-Logical Constitution of Metaphysics," in *Identity and Difference*, ed. Joan Stambaugh (New York: Harper & Row, 1969), 42–74.

5 See Alain Badiou, *The Adventure of French Philosophy*, trans. Bruno Bosteels (London: Verso, 2012), liv–lv. For further explication that bears directly on phenomenology of religion, see Jason W. Alvis, *The Inconspicuous God: Heidegger, French Phenomenology, and the Theological Turn* (Bloomington: Indiana University Press, 2018).

6 Levinas' *Totality and Infinity*, trans. Alphonso Lingis (Pittsburgh: Duquesne, 1969), is an extended mediation on ethics on a religious register, but see more directly, Emmanuel Levinas, "God and Philosophy," in *Basic Philosophical Writings*, ed. Adriaan T. Peperzak, Simon Critchley, and Robert Bernasconi (Bloomington: Indiana University Press, 1996), 129–47. A representative collection of Paul Ricoeur's contributions can be found in *The Conflict of Interpretations: Essays in Hermeneutics*, trans. Don Ihde (Evanston, Ill.: Northwestern University Press, 1974). Marion's breakout book in this respect was *God without Being*, trans. Thomas A. Carlson (Chicago: University of Chicago Press, 1991), but much of his corpus, including early historical work on Descartes, attends to theological and religious questions. For one of Derrida's earliest direct and sustained confrontations with theology (though it is also broached in early work from 1967–1972), see Jacques Derrida, "How to Avoid Speaking: Denials," trans. Ken Frieden in *Derrida and Negative Theology*, ed. Harold Coward and Toby Foshay (Albany: SUNY Press, 1992), 73–142. (This Derrida essay was, in many ways, my entrée into the project that comprises the present book.)

7 This debate in France in the late 1980s and early 1990s is now helpfully catalogued in a volume that includes both Janicaud's critique and responses from Jean-François Courtine, Paul Ricoeur, Jean-Louis Chrétien, Jean-Luc Marion, and Michel Henry. See Dominique Janicaud et al., *Phenomenology and the "Theological Turn": The French Debate* (New York: Fordham University Press, 2000).

methods for tackling the questions simply assumed the analytic story. But if Wolterstorff is correct (and I think he is) that what defines analytic philosophy is contingent—a particular history, even a particular bibliography, one might say—then philosophy of religion certainly shouldn't be the exclusive province of analytic philosophy.

While the history of continental philosophy across the twentieth century testified to this, we can also admit that in the 1990s there came a more concerted effort to constitute continental philosophy of religion (and philosophical theology) as a field and subdiscipline within the North American academy. This included the launch of the Theology and Continental Philosophy Group within the American Academy of Religion and the founding of the Society for Continental Philosophy and Theology, leading, eventually, to the establishment of the *Journal for Continental Philosophy of Religion*.[8]

This book is at once a reflection of the emergence of this field as well as, I hope, a contribution to its future. Gathering some of my work at the intersection of phenomenology and faith over the past twenty-five years, the book is organized into two parts. The first part is what we might describe as the "meta" section. The first three chapters address methodological questions about how to undertake philosophy of religion. Animated by the conviction that a philosophy of religion needs to be a philosophical reflection on the *practice* of religion (religion as a "form of life," Wittgenstein would say), I make a case for the distinct contributions that a phenomenological approach can make to philosophy of religion (and religious philosophy).

The second part of the book is then a series of what we might describe as case studies that enact this methodological vision, tracking a sustained engagement with the work of Jacques Derrida and Jean-Luc Marion—not because I think they deserve more attention than others, but simply because my own itinerary as a specialist has been forged by the discipline of attending carefully to their work.[9] My point in this section is not to extol Jacques Derrida as the patron saint for continental philosophy of religion (if anything, I am a bit iconoclastic in this regard, especially

---

8   These developments of the field are discussed in more detail in chs. 1 and 3 below.
9   Elsewhere I have argued that, even though Jacques Derrida first gained attention in North America as an import through English departments and literary theory, it is important to situate him as a phenomenologist. See James K. A. Smith, *Jacques Derrida: Live Theory* (London: Continuum, 2005), ch. 1.

vis-à-vis some other trends in continental philosophy of religion). Rather, the hope is that this sustained engagement with one or two philosophers in the continental tradition could provide a model for what critical, Christian engagement can look like in this field.

The thread (and, I hope, distinct contribution) that holds together the chapters in part 2 is laid out programmatically in chapter 4. In these critical studies I aim to demonstrate the curious way in which Derrida's explicit reflections on religion replay rather predictable, Kantian claims about (embodied) particularity and (rational) universality. In other words, many of Derrida's particular claims about religion fall into decidedly modern binaries, which is particularly ironic since Derrida was so often invoked as heralding a "postmodern" account. When we attend carefully to a range of texts, Derrida's later distinctions look like replays of Kantian, even Platonic binaries.

In particular, while Derrida extols a religious sensibility about matters of justice—what he calls "the messianic"—he divorces this from any of the particularities of embodied, particular religions ("messianisms," as he calls them). In this respect, particularity and embodiment are construed as contaminations of a "pure" religion, a messianic distinct from the messy particularity and history of any identifiable messian*isms*. While many were intrigued that a French philosopher would seem to take religion seriously, upon closer examination Derrida's appropriation turns out to be a more predictable dismissal, invoking a form of religious discourse but denying the substance thereof. In this sense, Derrida's project looks like one more instance of the modern penchant for "excarnation," as Charles Taylor puts it.[10] And insofar a certain appropriation of Derrida has been especially influential in continental philosophy of religion, particularly through the popularity of John Caputo's work, much that trafficked under the banner of a "postmodern" philosophy of religion was more like a French extension of modern thought. While the unenlightened devote themselves to particular religions, the Enlightened have escaped such parochial particularity for the purity of "the messianic" itself. This is a story Kant was telling himself in the eighteenth century.

---

10 Charles Taylor, *A Secular Age* (Cambridge, Mass.: Harvard University Press, 2007), 288–94. I have discussed this in more detail in James K. A. Smith, *How (Not) to Be Secular: Reading Charles Taylor* (Grand Rapids: Eerdmans, 2014), 57–59.

For those with any theological sensibility, this move by Derrida to eschew particularity and embodiment and point to a "pure" ideal has the feel of a Gnostic aspiration—one that deserves critique and hence calls for an alternative. That critique and alternative are the substance of part 2 of this book. Across a number of Derrida's influential texts, I track the way he devalues and demonizes embodied particularity. The pattern that emerges is what I call his "logic of determination" that sees particularity and embodiment as inherently violent, faulting creatures for being finite.

If we run with the analogy to Gnosticism, then the early church's confrontation with Gnostic heresies becomes *philosophically* interesting. It was just this sort of demonization of finitude and embodiment that motivated the early councils of the church refused when they confronted heretical understandings of Christ that tried to make him less than human (even if they thought this made Christ more divine). In contrast, the church's articulation of Christology at Nicea and Chalcedon refused this binary logic, affirming that humanity and divinity are not mutually exclusive—that, in fact, they both fully inhere (and cohere) in Christ ("consubstantiality"). Most significantly, vis-à-vis Derrida's logic, in the Nicene understanding of the Incarnation, the divinity of the Son was not "violated" or "contaminated" by becoming flesh. It was Gnostics who saw finitude as an impurity, a contamination. The theological imagination of orthodox Christology imagined finitude and embodiment very differently.

So, in contrast to the binary logic of determination, in Nicea and Chalcedon we see a very different logic at work—what I describe below as a "logic of incarnation" which affirms the goodness of finitude and particularity. In this way, I hope these chapters exhibit not only critical work in continental philosophy of religion but also an example of how *Christian* philosophy can be carried out, drawing on distinct insights of revelation as a conceptual lens, not in an apologetic mode but as a kind of theoretical offering staked on the conviction that the theological lens better illuminates phenomena when considered philosophically.[11] This intuition informs the work of Catholic phenomenologist Jean-Luc Marion, whom I engage in the final two chapters, and Marion was an early critic of Derrida

---

11   I take this to be in the spirit of Alvin Plantinga's veritable manifesto, "Advice to Christian Philosophers," *Faith and Philosophy* 1 (1984): 253–71, in which he recommends research programs that begin unapologetically from "what we know as Christians," not as a sectarian or parochial endeavor but in the mainstream of the academy.

in this respect. However, as I will show in chapters 11 and 12, there is still a strange way in which Marion's work remains beholden to a dichotomous account of difference, which makes it all the more surprising that a Jewish philosopher like Franz Rosenzweig is closer to my "incarnational" account.

This constructive proposal—the "logic of incarnation"—ties together part 2. I make no claims to its being either a comprehensive or an exhaustive working out of implications for philosophy of religion and philosophical theology. The hope is that a proposal along these lines sketches possibilities for future work. I think the logic of incarnation, for example, would prove especially illuminating in aesthetics, and hope to be able to tease out some of those implications in future work.

The specialist studies that comprise this book cohere internally around the logic of incarnation. But they also cohere with my wider corpus, which includes a number of books intended for an audience beyond specialists in philosophy. Since the publication of my book *Who's Afraid of Postmodernism? Taking Derrida, Lyotard, and Foucault to Church*, alongside my scholarly work I have tried to concurrently publish work I describe as "translation" scholarship.[12] Writing for these wider audiences, yet still drawing on philosophical expertise, I have endeavored to marshal philosophical sources, tools, and insights to elucidate everyday experience, religious observance, and cultural criticism. Key insights of Heidegger's phenomenology, for example, animate the core thesis of my book *Desiring the Kingdom*, just as the work of Maurice Merleau-Ponty and Pierre Bourdieu is the spine of *Imagining the Kingdom*.[13] Ludwig Wittgenstein, Charles Taylor, and Richard Rorty are key conversation partners in *Who's Afraid of Relativism?*, and *On the Road with Saint Augustine* includes a sustained conversation with Heidegger, Derrida, Albert Camus, and other philosophers.[14]

---

12 James K. A. Smith, *Who's Afraid of Postmodernism? Taking Derrida, Lyotard, and Foucault to Church*, The Church and Postmodern Culture Series (Grand Rapids: Baker Academic, 2006).
13 See James K. A. Smith, *Desiring the Kingdom: Worship, Worldview, and Cultural Formation*, Cultural Liturgies 1 (Grand Rapids: Baker Academic, 2009), and *Imagining the Kingdom: How Worship Works*, Cultural Liturgies 2 (Grand Rapids: Baker Academic, 2013).
14 James K. A. Smith, *Who's Afraid of Relativism? Community, Contingency, and Creaturehood* (Grand Rapids: Baker Academic, 2014), and *On the Road with Saint Augustine: A Real-world Spirituality for Restless Hearts* (Grand Rapids: Brazos, 2019).

But the nature of such non-specialist writing means forgoing the level of analysis and detail expected of properly scholarly work. This book, then, could be read as the extended footnote to those semi-academic books of "translation" scholarship. In a sense, this book is meant to "show the work," so to speak—to provide a glimpse of the more careful analyses underlying the claims in my books for wider audiences. In the spirit of incarnation and embodiment, this book provides a peek into the skeleton that upholds the wider body of work. If those other books have been gateways to philosophy for some readers, this book is an invitation to a new depth of reflection.

Gathering these studies into a book, looking back across twenty-five years of scholarship, I also see paths not chosen, trajectories I glimpsed but never chased. There is a sense in which the production of a book like this is a work of mourning. I have had to reckon with the finitude of my own capacities and what time has afforded. Some of these essays carry a whiff of youthful energy and aspiration of which the older man can be both envious and embarrassed. Encountering articles written while Jacques Derrida was still alive, I was confronted by the very tense of the verbs, recalling a time (now passed) when Derrida was still writing. Changing those verbs, editing as finality, pitched me into an unexpected sadness—a reminder that scholars and scholarship are "entangled," Derrida would say, with other human concerns. But that, I claim in this book, has long been the argument of phenomenology: that our being-in-the-world is bound up with our bodily immersion. There is no philosopher who is not incarnate; this book is a proposal for a philosophy of religion that embodies this truth.

I
Outline of an Incarnational Continental Philosophy of Religion

1

The Philosophy of Religion Takes Practice

A Methodological Manifesto

Limits of the "Renaissance" in Philosophy of Religion

There has been much discussion of the "renaissance" in the philosophy of religion since the last several decades of the twentieth century.[1] After the last gasp of positivism and the final attempt to police philosophical discourse through ordinary language philosophy, there emerged the space for a renewed consideration of religion within the halls of philosophy in two senses: on the one hand, religious themes and questions once again became legitimate topics for philosophical reflection; on the other hand, and perhaps more radically, a critique of the supposed neutrality and objectivity of philosophical reason opened the space for *religious* philosophy—that is, philosophical reflection undertaken from a perspective and orientation that was unapologetically religious and confessional. The "of" in this renewed philosophy *of* religion was both an objective and subjective genitive: religion was reintroduced as a legitimate mainstream topic of consideration (objective genitive), and religion was admitted as a legitimate orienting perspective for philosophical research and reflection (subjective genitive).

---

1 For a report from a firsthand contributor to this development, see Nicholas Wolterstorff, "Analytic Philosophy of Religion: Retrospect and Prospect," in *Inquiring about God: Selected Essays*, vol. 1, ed. Terence Cuneo (Cambridge: Cambridge University Press, 2009), 17–34.

Work along the former lines included renewed interested in religious phenomena such as miracles, the perennial problem of evil, as well as the conditions of possibility of religious language or "God-talk."[2] This developed into a more robust renewal of "philosophical theology" now exemplified in the work of Eleonore Stump, Marilyn Adams, Stephen Davis, Brian Hebblethwaite, Brian Leftow, and many others working on the project described as "analytic theology."[3]

Developments along the latter lines of a *religious* philosophy were closely connected with the development of "Reformed epistemology" as articulated by Nicholas Wolterstorff and Alvin Plantinga—a distinctly non-foundationalist epistemological project that sought to contest the criteria of "rationality," which had been marshaled to exclude religious belief from both the halls of philosophy and the sphere of public discourse.[4] Articulating a critique of the supposed neutrality and autonomy of reason, Wolterstorff and Plantinga argued that religious belief was *just as* "warranted" as other presuppositions in philosophy that, in fact, shared the same epistemic status.[5] Thus Reformed epistemology undercut the

2   As an example of this development, consider, for instance, the work of Antony Flew: *Hume's Philosophy of Belief* (London: Routledge, 1961); *God and Philosophy* (New York: Dell, 1966); and Antony Flew and Alasdair MacIntyre, eds., *New Essays in Philosophical Theology* (London: SCM Press, 1955).
3   For just a sample of representative work in this vein, see Kelly James Clark, ed., *Our Knowledge of God: Essays on Natural and Philosophical Theology* (The Hague: Kluwer, 1992); Eleonore Stump, ed., *Reasoned Faith: Essays in Philosophical Theology in Honor of Norman Kretzmann* (Ithaca, N.Y.: Cornell University Press, 1993); Marilyn McCord Adams, *Horrendous Evils and the Goodness of God* (Ithaca, N.Y.: Cornell University Press, 2000); Brian Hebblethwaite, *Philosophical Theology and Christian Doctrine* (Oxford: Blackwell, 2005); Stephen T. Davis, *Christian Philosophical Theology* (Oxford: Oxford University Press, 2006); and Oliver D. Crisp and Michael C. Rea, *Analytic Theology: New Essays in the Philosophy of Theology* (Oxford: Oxford University Press, 2009).
4   There is an earlier European and Catholic story that runs parallel to this American Protestant movement in the work of Maurice Blondel and later Gilson's claims regarding a "Christian philosophy." As usual, at stake here is how we receive the legacy of Thomas Aquinas—a debate that has come to the fore again with contemporary retrievals of *nouvelle théologie*. However, I cannot do justice to these issues here. For relevant discussion, see Francesca Aran Murphy, "Gilson and Chenu: The Structure of the *Summa* and the Shape of Dominican Life," *New Blackfriars* 85 (2004): 290–303; D. Stephen Long, "The Way of Aquinas: Its Importance for Moral Theology," *Studies in Christian Ethics* 19 (2006): 339–56; and Adam C. English, *The Possibility of Christian Philosophy: Maurice Blondel at the Intersection of Theology and Philosophy*, Radical Orthodoxy Series (London: Routledge, 2006).
5   Most famously, Plantinga pointed out the analogy between the epistemic status of belief in "other minds" and belief in God. See Alvin Plantinga, *God and Other Minds: A Study of Rational Justification of Belief in God* (Ithaca, N.Y.: Cornell University Press, 1967).

foundationalist rationalism of philosophy and thereby opened a path of legitimacy for philosophical reflection oriented and informed by religious presuppositions.[6] This critique of foundationalism and neutrality resonated with other developments in philosophy, including Alasdair MacIntyre's account of the "traditioned" nature of rationality,[7] as well as the tradition of "hermeneutic" philosophy associated with Heidegger and Gadamer, which also emphasized the constitutive role of presuppositions in shaping rationality—anticipating the shape of a "postmodern" critique foundationalist reason.[8] This other, "continental" critique of secular reason could be seen as culminating in the work of John Milbank.[9] While these different schools of thought are not often associated (indeed, Reformed epistemology remains virulently allergic to "postmodernism"), I would suggest that, in fact, these tensions represent a kind of sibling rivalry.[10]

These developments represent a flourishing renaissance in philosophy of religion, and the work of this preceding generation has made it possible for those who follow to further imagine what the future of philosophy of religion might look like. In this chapter, I want to offer an appreciative

---

6 For classic statements of this project, see Nicholas Wolterstorff, *Reason within the Bounds of Religion* (Grand Rapids: Eerdmans, 1976); Alvin Plantinga and Nicholas Wolterstorff, eds., *Faith and Rationality: Reason and Belief in God* (South Bend: University of Notre Dame Press, 1984); Plantinga, *Warranted Christian Belief* (Oxford: Oxford University Press, 1999). For a succinct introduction to Reformed epistemology, see Kelly James Clark, *Return to Reason: A Critique of Enlightenment Evidentialism and a Defense of Reason and Belief in God* (Grand Rapids: Eerdmans, 1990).
7 MacIntyre, *Whose Justice? Which Rationality?* (South Bend: University of Notre Dame Press, 1989).
8 For a summary of this related to philosophy of religion, see James K. A. Smith, *The Fall of Interpretation: Philosophical Foundations for a Creational Hermeneutic* (Downers Grove, Ill.: InterVarsity Press, 2000), and idem, "The Art of Christian Atheism: Faith and Philosophy in Early Heidegger," *Faith and Philosophy* 14 (1997): 71–81.
9 John Milbank, *Theology and Social Theory: Beyond Secular Reason* (Oxford: Blackwell, 1990). In *Introducing Radical Orthodoxy: Mapping a Post-Secular Theology* (Grand Rapids: Baker Academic; Carlisle: Paternoster, 2004), I try to suggest some overlap between the project of Reformed epistemology and Radical Orthodoxy.
10 Much work remains to be done on this score, and I can't pursue it further here. Suffice it to say that Plantinga's critique of "postmodernism" (*Warranted Christian Belief*, part 3) is a rejection of a straw man, and that, in fact, his non-foundationalist account of warranted belief has much in common with Heidegger, Rorty, and perhaps even Derrida. For some hints along this line, see the discussion of Plantinga and Rorty in G. Elijah Dann, *After Rorty: The Possibilities for Ethics and Religious Belief* (London: Continuum, 2006). I have discussed this in more detail in James K. A. Smith, *Who's Afraid of Relativism? Community, Contingency, and Creaturehood* (Grand Rapids: Baker Academic, 2014), 25–29.

critique of these developments in philosophy of religion. Recognizing my own indebtedness to this earlier work, I nonetheless want to suggest a significant lacuna or blind spot, viz., the absence of any rigorous attention to worship, liturgy, or the practices of religious communities. In sum, one could argue that philosophy of religion has been attentive to beliefs but not believers. It has been characterized by a kind of epistemological fixation that myopically focuses on either the epistemic status of religious belief or an explication of the propositional content of specific beliefs (e.g., the goodness of God, God's eternity, or resurrection). But philosophy of religion has given relatively little attention to how embodied, flesh-and-blood believers experience religion primarily as a form of life. A formative and usually central aspect of that form of life—across religious traditions—is participation in corporate worship, liturgical practices, and other forms of shared spiritual disciplines. In other words, believers tend to focus on faith as a way of life ("what we *do*") whereas contemporary philosophy of religion tends to treat faith as a way of thinking ("what we *believe*").[11]

In this chapter, I will sketch a way forward for philosophy of religion that seeks to overcome this blind spot and direct the attention of philosophy of religion to *practice*, and liturgical practice in particular. More specifically, I want to consider liturgy[12] as both a "source" and "method" in

---

11   Though over the past decade (since this chapter was originally published) there have been encouraging developments in the direction I am suggesting. Notable examples of philosophical reflection on religious practice include Terence Cuneo, *Ritualized Faith: Essays on the Philosophy of Liturgy* (Oxford: Oxford University Press, 2018), and Christina M. Gschwandtner, *Welcoming Finitude: Toward a Phenomenology of Orthodox Liturgy* (New York: Fordham University Press, 2019).

12   I will employ the term "liturgy" in a broad and generous sense (in order to see some kind of "liturgy" as integral to different religions), without diluting its meaning (such that any and all "ritual" would constitute liturgy). As a baseline definition, liturgy could be said to include not all ritual, but specifically *rituals of ultimate concern*: rituals that are *formative* for identity in a way that trumps other ritual formations. This is not Tillichian (or Hickian) insofar as it is informed by a genuine pluralism; I don't mean to suggest that all rituals of ultimate concern are, at the end of the day, concerned with the same ultimate. Rather, embedded in the practices are very different, antithetical understandings of the ultimate.

Admittedly, this might include rituals not associated with "traditional" religions (e.g., rituals of Nazi fascism, other rituals of totalizing nationalism). I want to leave the door open for a consideration of these "secular" liturgies, but will not consider them in this chapter. Here I will be assuming liturgies associated with identifiable religions. And while I will tend to privilege examples of Christian liturgy, I think my account provides a framework for considering Jewish, Muslim, Buddhist, and other liturgies in the same way. For further discussion, see ch. 2 below.

philosophy of religion. This roughly correlates with the two trajectories of philosophy of religion I have sketched above in terms of two modes of the genitive "of": on the one hand, worship and liturgical practice needs to be made a more central object of philosophical consideration; on the other hand, in league with the critique of secularity sketched above, liturgical participation might be understood as a unique condition of possibility for philosophical reflection.

Cartesian Ghosts: The Lingering Rationalism in Philosophy of Religion

Levinas famously remarked that Dasein is never hungry.[13] And yet, does Dasein ever eat? In the same vein we might ask: Does Dasein ever worship? Or more pointedly, do the believers countenanced in contemporary philosophy of religion ever kneel or sing?[14] Do they ever pray the Rosary? Do they ever respond to an altar call, weeping on their knees? In fact, do *believers* ever really make an appearance in philosophy of religion? Judging from the shape of the conversation in contemporary philosophy of religion, one would guess that "religion" is a feature of brains-in-a-vat, lingering in a particularly spiritual ether but never really bumping into the grittiness of practices and community. Indeed, one wonders whether such "believers" really even need to go through the hassle of getting up on Sunday morning. Once the beliefs are "deposited," it is hard to see what more is needed to be faithful.[15]

The renaissance in philosophy of religion in the past thirty years has been beholden, I would contend, to a lingering rationalism which remains at least haunted (if not perhaps *governed*) by a Cartesian anthropology that tends to construe the human person as, in essence, a "thinking thing." Because it assumes a philosophical anthropology that privileges the cognitive and rational, philosophy of religion thus construes religion as a

---

13   Emmanuel Levinas, *Totality and Infinity*, trans. Alphonso Lingis (Pittsburgh: Duquesne University Press, 1969), 134.
14   To his credit, it should be noted that in the later Heidegger, believers dance and pray. See Martin Heidegger, "The Onto-Theo-logical Constitution of Metaphysics," in *Identity and Difference*, trans. Joan Stambaugh (San Francisco: Harper & Row, 1969), 72. For further discussion, see Merold Westphal, "Overcoming Onto-Theology," in *God, the Gift, and Postmodernism*, ed. John D. Caputo and Michael Scanlon (Bloomington: Indiana University Press, 1999), 146–63.
15   One might legitimately wonder whether this is an indication of the overwhelmingly Protestant influence in contemporary philosophy of religion.

primarily epistemological phenomenon. As a result, the "religion" in philosophy *of religion* is a very cognitive, "heady" phenomenon—reduced to beliefs, propositions, and cognitive content, which are the only phenomena that can make it through the narrow theoretical gate that attends such rationalism. Believers, insofar as they appear, seem to be little more than talking heads. The result is a reductionism: religion, which is primarily a "form of life" and lived experience, is slimmed down to the more abstract phenomena of beliefs and doctrines. The rich, dynamic, lived experience of worshiping communities is reduced to propositions that can be culled from artifacts produced by these communities (e.g., documents, creeds, Scriptures). If philosophy of religion pays any attention to liturgy or other religious practices, it is usually only in order to mine the "artifacts" of liturgy for new "ideas."

Thus philosophy of religion as currently practiced tends to reflect a working (or at least functional) assumption that doctrine is prior to liturgy and thus ideas and propositions trump practices. Practiced in this rationalist mode, philosophy of religion finds a ready-made proportionality to theological doctrines, ideas, and propositions. Hence what has flourished in philosophy of religion has been philosophical theology of a particular sort.[16] At best, this amounts to a reduction of "religion" to propositional thinking, a narrowing of the richness of religious lived experience. At worst, the result is not just a "thinning" of religion, but a falsification of it, insofar as religion construed as primarily a cognitive or propositional or epistemological phenomenon fails to discern the heart of religion as practice.

What one works on is often a reflection of one's tools. If all I have is a hammer and nails, I'm not equipped to work on an electric circuit. In

---

16 For instance, when philosophers of religion turn to a consideration of prayer, it is primarily the epistemological challenges that are focused upon, or issues of how prayer can be reconciled with the doctrines of God's omniscience and omnipotence. See, for example, Eleonore Stump, "Petitionary Prayer," *American Philosophical Quarterly* 16 (1979): 81–91, and Lawrence Masek, "Petitionary Prayer to an Omnipotent and Omnibenevolent God," in *Philosophical Theology: Reason and Theological Doctrine*, Proceedings of the American Catholic Philosophical Association 74 (2000): 273–83. For a contrasting philosophical engagement with prayer, see Peter Ochs, "Morning Prayer as Redemptive Thinking," in *Liturgy, Time, and the Politics of Redemption*, ed. C. C. Pecknold and Randi Rashkover (Grand Rapids: Eerdmans, 2006): 50–90. Cp. D. Z. Phillips, *The Concept of Prayer* (London: Routledge, 2014 [1965]), a Wittgensteinian analysis of the significance of what people *do* when they pray.

that vein, contemporary philosophy of religion is equipped with a toolbelt made for thinking about thinking—analyzing concepts of a certain sort. As a result, the philosopher of religion is only equipped to "work on" religion insofar as it can be made (and thus cut down) to the measure of conceptual, cognitive thinking.[17] Attention to aspects of religion as a form of life and set of practices would require a different, or at least expanded, toolbelt.[18] A new renaissance in philosophy of religion could be sparked by reversing this assumption and taking seriously the priority of liturgical practices over doctrinal formulations. Otherwise, we would be in a situation akin to theatre studies, which is absorbed with texts and forgets that these are scripts for performance.[19] It should also point us to the priority of liturgy and practice vis-à-vis the artifacts of religious traditions. Before the creeds were "creeds," and thus documents to be mined, they were *prayers* enacted by a community in the context of confession in worship.[20]

If we are going to reverse the assumption, and recover the priority of liturgy to doctrine—that is, recover a sense of religion as a form of life and embodied experience—this will require challenging the rationalist philosophical anthropology that underlies contemporary philosophy of religion. And in fact, religion itself does this: religious faith—and the ways of life associated with religious communities—resist rationalist reduction and exhibit a way of being-in-the-world that manifests the fundamentally affective nature of the human person. In sum, it is precisely the phenomenon of religious life that points up the paucity and thinness of the Cartesian "thinking thing" as a very *un*natural beast. It's not that a cognitivist philosophical anthropology is just too narrow or selective, but that it actually falsifies the engaged, embodied character of our being-in-the-world. So attention to religion as a form of life and nexus of liturgical practices

---

17   I do not think this is a phenomenon unique to "analytic" of Anglo-American philosophy. Much "continental" philosophy of religion also exhibits an epistemological fixation. See my discussion of Derrida in ch. 8 below.
18   In *Speech and Theology: Language and the Logic of Incarnation* (London: Routledge, 2002), I argue that this was precisely the project of the young Heidegger: to come up with a new "concept" that could do justice to the richness of lived experience, and *religious* lived experience in particular (see 67–113).
19   For a related discussion, see Ben Faber, "Ethical Hermeneutics in the Theatre: Shakespeare's *Merchant of Venice*," in *Hermeneutics at the Crossroads*, ed. Kevin Vanhoozer, James K. A. Smith, and Bruce Ellis Benson (Bloomington: Indiana University Press, 2006), ch. 11.
20   One could perhaps describe my approach as a "postliberal" philosophy of religion, per Lindbeck et al. See Smith, *Who's Afraid of Relativism?* 151–82.

brings us up against a phenomenon that challenges and deconstructs the lingering rationalist anthropologies that continue to shape method in philosophy of religion. There is, one could say, a very different, non-rationalist philosophical anthropology implicit in liturgical practice such that liturgy becomes a catalyst, even a "revelation," that unsettles overly cognitivist pictures of the human person. In sum, it is the very phenomenon of religion as liturgical practice which functions as a shot in the arm to philosophy of religion by calling for a philosophical anthropology that honors our primarily affective, precognitive, communal, and "practiced" mode of being-in-the world. Thus there is a dialectical relationship envisioned between philosophy and liturgy: on the one hand, the lived religious experience embodied in liturgical practice points to the necessity of an affective (non-rationalist) philosophical anthropology; on the other hand, the development and assumption of an affective philosophical anthropology enable philosophy of religion to be primed for dealing better with the more fundamental phenomena associated with religion, viz., practices rather than doctrines.

In fact, it was just this impetus—this interjection of embodied, lived religious experience as a "shock" to regnant philosophical method—that was the prompt for the young Heidegger's critique of the lingering Cartesian rationalism that characterized Husserl's early phenomenology.[21] The trajectory I am suggesting is, in important ways, latent and internal to early phenomenology, particularly in the critical reception of Husserl in the work of Heidegger, Levinas, and Merleau-Ponty. Thus we can find the resources for retooling philosophy of religion by considering an analogous critique in the rudimentary elements of Heidegger's critique of Descartes and Husserl. A central aspect of Heidegger's project in *Being & Time* was to call into question the rationalist anthropology assumed by Husserl, who still tended to construe human beings as primarily perceiving things—as if we inhabited the world as observers and spectators who spend time *thinking* about the world. In contrast, Heidegger argued that primarily and for the most part, we do not *think* about a world of objects; rather, we are *involved* with the world as traditioned actors. The world is

---

21 Another impetus was the messiness of lived ethical experience as analyzed by Aristotle. For a discussion of Aristotle in these terms, see Martin Heidegger, "Phenomenological Interpretations with Respect to Aristotle: Indications of the Hermeneutic Situation [1922]," trans. Michael Baur in *Man and World* 25 (1992): 355–93.

the environment in which we swim, not a picture that we look at as distanced observers.[22]

Careful phenomenological attention to the dynamics of religious life—that is, religion as a way of life (Hadot) or form of life (Wittgenstein)—manifests something about the nature of human being-in-the-world that is missed by the overly cognitivist paradigms that currently govern philosophy of religion. In particular, the communal practices that shape religion show us that human being-in-the-world is oriented more fundamentally by desire than thinking, and manifests itself more in what we do than what we think.[23] As such, it is precisely religious life that calls for a revision of the philosophy at work in "philosophy of religion."

The Critique of Secular Reason

The Heideggerian critique of Cartesian rationalism—a critique that was directly generated by engagement with religious sources—yields a more supple philosophical anthropology that is primed to think about religion as a lived, embodied phenomenon rather than merely a set of beliefs, doctrines, or ideas. A philosophy of religion that methodologically adopts this affective philosophical anthropology will be poised to consider "religion" in a way more proportionate to how it is lived "on the ground," so to speak. In short, it will be a philosophy of religion enacted as a philosophy of liturgy, a philosophy of lived religious practices.

However, that is only half of the methodological revolution I am advocating. In arguing for a more robust engagement between philosophy and liturgy, I am not only advocating that philosophy of religion make liturgical practice an object of more sustained reflection; I also want to make the further suggestion that liturgical practice and formation do and ought to function as the condition of possibility for

---

22 I have unpacked this in more detail in *Speech and Theology*, 67–82.
23 Religion as a form of life ("what we *do*") also confirms important developments in philosophy of mind, cognitive science, and neuroplasticity, which emphasizes the ways and extent to which our comportment to the world happens at the level of the bodily, tactile, and preconscious. Philosophy of religion has yet to engage these conversations, but a turn to liturgy provides the catalyst for such explorations. For relevant discussions, see Timothy D. Wilson, *Strangers to Ourselves: Discovering the Adaptive Unconscious* (Cambridge, Mass.: Harvard University Press, 2002), and Shaun Gallagher, *How the Body Shapes the Mind* (Oxford: Clarendon Press, 2005). This just comes down to requiring that philosophy of religion take embodiment seriously. For an important beginning, see Sarah Coakley, ed., *Religion and the Body* (Cambridge: Cambridge University Press, 2003).

properly *religious* philosophy. So the complete picture will include not only a philosophy *of* liturgy, but a liturgical philosophy.

On this score, the vision of a liturgical philosophy is simply a more radical development of existing models that advocate for the integrity of religious philosophy—that is, philosophical reflection that unapologetically begins from and is informed by a specific religious worldview. As such, it extends existing critiques of foundationalism and Enlightenment dreams of a "secular reason" as neutral, objective, and autonomous. This has been articulated in several different ways over the past century:

- A philosophical tradition stemming from the Dutch Reformed tradition, embodied in Abraham Kuyper's vision of Calvinism as a "world-and-life view"—which included the claim that all thinking about the world begins from *some* world-and-life view and that such worldviews have the same epistemic status as identifiably "religious" worldviews.[24] This was further developed in Herman Dooyeweerd's critique of the pretended autonomy of theoretical thought, articulated in explicit dialogue with the phenomenological tradition of Husserl and Heidegger.[25]

- A related but somewhat different development of this Kuyperian critique of Enlightenment objectivity is articulated in the "Reformed epistemology" of Alvin Plantinga and Nicholas Wolterstorff. Rejecting the foundationalism that would rule out religious presuppositions as a contamination and compromise of objectivity, Reformed epistemology is a non-foundationalist account of rationality which secures warrant for religious starting points for thought. Furthermore, Reformed epistemology

---

24 For a succinct statement, see Abraham Kuyper, *Calvinism: Six Stone Foundation Lectures* (Grand Rapids: Eerdmans, 1943). These were presented as the Stone Lectures at Princeton Theological Seminary in 1898. Thus Malcolm Bull once described Kuyper as "the first postmodern" (Bull, "Who Was the First to Make a Pact with the Devil?" *London Review of Books*, May 14, 1992, 22–24).

25 See Herman Dooyeweerd, *In the Twilight of Western Thought: Studies in the Pretended Autonomy of Philosophical Thought*, Collected Works B/4, ed. James K. A. Smith (Lewiston, N.Y.: Edwin Mellen Press, 1999). For exposition, see Roy Clouser, *The Myth of Religious Neutrality: An Essay on the Hidden Role of Religious Belief in Theory*, rev. ed. (South Bend: University of Notre Dame Press, 2005); and James K. A. Smith, "Dooyeweerd's Critique of 'Pure' Reason," introduction to Dooyeweerd, *In the Twilight of Western Thought*, v–xiii.

argues that all rational reflection begins from *some* ultimate presuppositions, though it is pluralist about this, arguing that theoretical thought can begin from very different, and even incommensurate "control beliefs."[26] In any case, there is no such thing as a "neutral" or presuppositionless Reason of the sort promised by Enlightenment accounts of rationality.

- The same critique of Enlightenment models of rationality—particularly Cartesian and Kantian—was articulated by Heidegger (as already discussed above) and further developed by his student Hans-Georg Gadamer, who pointed out the "Enlightenment prejudice against prejudice."[27] A similar mid-century critique of objective ("scientific") rationality was articulated by Michael Polanyi.

- Alasdair MacIntyre offered an allied critique of "secular" or supposedly "objective" rationality with a specific attention to ethics. In particular, MacIntyre has been concerned to point out the way in which reason is always already *traditioned*—indebted to and shaped by particular narratives generated by particular communities. Thus there is a significant sense in which rationality is "relative to" these stories, communities, and traditions—and there is no rationality which is not tethered to *some* story, community, and tradition.[28]

- Building on the work of MacIntyre and Hauerwas, and marshaling the resources of post-Heideggerian continental philosophy (while also offering a trenchant critique of

---

26 See Wolterstorff, *Reason within the Bounds of Religion*, 67–70 and passim. As such, Reformed epistemology could be read as a kind of "standpoint" epistemology and thus would be akin to recent developments in feminist epistemology. For a discussion, see Victoria S. Harrison, "Feminist Philosophy of Religion and the Problem of Epistemic Privilege," *Heythrop Journal* 48 (2007): 685–96, and Janet Wesselius, "Points of Convergence Between Dooyeweerdian and Feminist Views of the Philosophic Self," in *Knowing Other-wise: Philosophy at the Threshold of Spirituality*, ed. James H. Olthuis (New York: Fordham University Press, 1997), 54–68.

27 Hans-Georg Gadamer, *Truth and Method*, rev. ed., trans. Joel Weinsheimer and Donald G. Marshall (New York: Continuum, 1993), 270.

28 This is most fully articulated in MacIntyre, *Whose Justice? Which Rationality?* but for a succinct statement, see Alasdair MacIntyre, "Epistemological Crises, Dramatic Narrative, and the Philosophy of Science," *Monist* 60 (1977): 453–72.

the latter), John Milbank's critique of supposedly "secular" social theory is a dense microcosmic challenge to the very notion of a neutral "secular reason" as the basis for theory of any sort, philosophy included. Milbank radicalizes MacIntyre's critique by suggesting that so-called "secular" reason always assumes a covert theology, and that in the context of Western modernity, the operative "theology" undergirding secular reason is a kind of bastardized, heretical version of Christianity.[29] As such, theorizing about any sphere of human life and culture—including sociology, economics, and philosophy—always already begins from an operative (albeit covert) theology. As such, it is no longer possible to exclude explicitly Christian theological starting points from the space of the academy on the grounds that such "theological" presuppositions contaminate the purity of secular theory. There is no pure secular reason; there are just certain theologies which get to pass themselves off as universal and objective. Once the emperor's nakedness is pointed out, however, then other theological starting points should be admitted to an academic space which is pluralist, not secularist.[30]

While I have not reproduced the arguments here, cumulatively these diverse critiques of secular reason and the myth of objectivity opened the space for the legitimacy of *religious* philosophy—philosophical reflection that is informed and oriented by explicitly confessional starting points (whether Jewish, Christian, Muslim, Hindu, etc.). Having debunked the "myth of religious neutrality" (Clouser), religious starting points could no longer be ruled as violations of academic orthodoxy. (It is perhaps an irony that American departments of "religious studies" are often the last bastions for this passé secular orthodoxy.)

However, while these critiques of secular reason spawned much distinctively religious philosophy, the "religion" that informs such philosophy still tends to be a religion of *ideas*. The way religion contributes to

29 The boldest statement of this remains Milbank, *Theology and Social Theory*. For an exposition of this project, see Smith, *Introducing Radical Orthodoxy*, esp. chs. 4–5.
30 This sort of critique is not just offered by Christian theologians. See, for instance, William Connolly, *Why I Am Not a Secularist* (Minneapolis: University of Minnesota Press, 1999). For a Christian theological engagement with Connolly's non-Christian anti-secularist pluralism, see Kristen Deede Johnson, *Theology, Political Theory, and Liberalism: Beyond Tolerance and Difference* (Cambridge: Cambridge University Press, 2007).

philosophy is by means of a conceptual jumpstart: distinctive special revelations give to philosophy concepts and propositions that would not otherwise have been available for reflection. We might describe this as a "revelational" or "illuminative" model of religious philosophy whereby what religion provides is a unique storehouse of ideas and concepts that would not otherwise be available to philosophical thought. Religious revelation offers a unique deposit of wisdom that is then mined and refined by philosophical reasoning. This revelational model characterizes otherwise diverse modes of religious philosophy, from Gilson's understanding of Catholic philosophy to Plantinga's account of Reformed epistemology to Levinas' account of the genius of the Torah.[31]

But such a model for the influence of religion on philosophy continues to reflect the rationalism criticized above. It still takes religion to be a set of beliefs which provide content for propositional thought, a result of assuming believers are primarily "thinking things" or "believing animals" for whom faith is more about the right propositional content than an embodied comportment to the world and the neighbor. Religious philosophy just argues that such "ideas" are not only legitimate *objects* of philosophical reflection, they constitute legitimate *starting points* for philosophical reflection. But whether under the microscope (objective) or in the mind of the perceiver (subjective), "religion" in this picture remains a largely conceptual, heady phenomenon. In sum, though the critique of secular reason that underwrites contemporary religious philosophy has challenged the myth of neutrality associated with Enlightenment reason, it has not properly countered the rational*ism* that attended this, construing human beings primarily as thinking things and solitary[32] "perceivers" of the world. In short, believers are construed as if they were more down-to-earth versions of academics,

---

31 See Gilson, *The Spirit of Medieval Philosophy*, trans. A. H. C. Downes (Toronto: PIMS, 1993 [1933]), which is a series of meditations on truths shown to philosophy by revelation; Alvin Plantinga, "Augustinian Christian Philosophy," *Monist* 75 (1992): 291–320; on Levinas' conception of the relation between religion and philosophy, see Jill Robbins, *Prodigal Son / Elder Brother: Interpretation and Alterity in Augustine, Petrarch, Kafka, Levinas* (Chicago: University of Chicago Press, 1991), 100–32.
32 This aspect of the regnant paradigm should not be underestimated. A survey of the literature in philosophy of religion will yield a picture of religion as something that one does largely on one's own (again, I think a certain Protestantism is at work here). If philosophy of religion stands in need of a turn to liturgy, it also stands in need of a communitarian shot in the arm via a more robust ecclesiology. Indeed, one might suggest that ecclesiology is one of the theological loci most ignored by the renewal of philosophical theology.

and religious faith is treated as the sort of thing one does at academic conferences. In this picture, religion is reduced to a matter of seeing, not loving.

The versions of this critique of secular reason offered by MacIntyre and Milbank, however, point toward another, more integral understanding of religious philosophy precisely because they recognize the central place of practices and liturgy in the formation of human identity, and thus the role of both in the very shaping of rationality. In sum, one can already see in MacIntyre and Milbank an alternative philosophical anthropology that understands human persons not as thinking things but as practicing animals—even liturgical animals of a sort. This is both a result of and feeds into a more fulsome postliberal understanding of religion as a set of communal practices—a "form of life."

A Way Forward: Philosophy of Liturgy and Liturgical Philosophy

I would suggest that the renaissance in philosophy of religion stands in need of another renaissance—that Reformed epistemology stands in need of further reformation (*semper reformanda!*). In particular, the future of philosophy of religion—while agreeing that religion is both a legitimate topic and starting point—must also contest the reductionism and lingering rationalism that remain operative in philosophy of religion. I suggest that the future for a properly post-foundationalist, postliberal, and post-secular philosophy of religion requires that philosophy turn to liturgy—both as topic and fount for reflection.

This requires a twofold methodological reorientation. First, as I have been arguing, philosophy of religion must eschew philosophical anthropologies of the Cartesian variety, which still tend to construe even religious believers as thinking things. This leads to a second reorientation, viz., recovering a sense of religion as a way of life or form of life. By "religion" I do not mean some universal phenomenon or generic type (I am not advocating a return to "phenomenology of religion" as articulated by Otto, VanderLeuw, and others); rather, attention to religion as a form of life will require grappling with religion as inescapably *particular* and thus tied to particular practices. This shift in orientation should then give us a new angle of vision, putting a different set of phenomena in our philosophical sights, particularly the communal practices of religious communities and traditions that constitute the formative liturgies of the faith. We will then be in a position to appreciate that, for the faithful, religion in a matter of practice.

What's at stake here is a refusal of still lingering theory/practice dualisms. While contemporary philosophy of religion has recovered religion as a legitimate topic of philosophical investigation, and even recovered religious faith as a warranted starting point for philosophical reflection, it still tends to assume a priority of ideas over practices, and thus a priority of doctrine over liturgy. It thus gives the impression that doctrines are not inextricably tethered to practices. So philosophical theology distills the "doctrines" of, say, Christian faith and then sets them under the philosophical microscope with little if any consideration of their origins in a confessing, worshiping community. Before the Trinity was crystallized as a doctrine, it was expressed in prayer, and the liturgical milieu out of which doctrine emerges is crucial for understanding what is at stake for the religious community. For instance, the community's baptismal confession that "Jesus is Lord" is not a matter of merely theoretical knowledge and "getting it right." It is a political *act* that contests the reigning practice of confessing Caesar as Lord.[33] As such, conversion to Christian faith and baptismal profession was not seen as the adoption of merely a new "paradigm" or set of propositions, but rather a transformation of one's allegiances embodied in a unique set of practices inscribed by participation in the liturgy. There is an irreducibility of faith's liturgical enactment that cannot be simply translated or exhausted by articulation of doctrines. Thus, if we are to try to do justice to religion philosophically, we will need to honor this irreducible and primary liturgical moment of religion.

We might find a way to conceptualize this in Charles Taylor's notion (adopted from Benedict Anderson) of the "social imaginary." Taylor emphasizes that all societies and communities are animated by a social imaginary, but this does not mean that all are oriented by a "theory." The social imaginary is "much broader and deeper than the intellectual schemes people may entertain when they *think* about social reality in a disengaged mode."[34] Rather, the social imaginary is meant to indicate "the ways people *imagine* their social existence, how they fit together with

---

33 N. T. Wright, "Paul's Gospel and Caesar's Empire," in *Paul and Politics: Ekklesia, Israel, Imperium, Interpretation*, ed. Richard A. Horsley (Harrisburg, Pa.: Trinity Press International, 2000), 161–62.
34 Charles Taylor, *Modern Social Imaginaries* (Durham: Duke University Press, 2004), 23, emphasis added.

others, how things go on between them and their fellows, the expectations that are normally met," etc.[35] Taylor describes this as an "imaginary" in order to refer to "the way ordinary people 'imagine' their social surroundings," which is "not expressed in theoretical terms, but is carried in images, stories, and legends."[36] Most importantly, Taylor emphasizes a dynamic relationship between understanding and practice: "If the understanding makes the practice possible, it is also true that it is the practice that largely carries the understanding."[37] Or, to put it otherwise, the understanding is "implicit in practice." As Taylor remarks, "Humans operated with a social imaginary well before they ever got into the business of theorizing about themselves."[38] I am suggesting that philosophy of religion could attend to the richness of religion as practice if we considered it in terms of a social imaginary. By analogy, then, we could say that humans were religious well before they ever developed a theology, and for most "ordinary people," religion is rarely a matter of theology. Rather, there is an understanding of the world—a horizon for inhabiting the world—that is carried in and implicit in the practices of religious worship and devotion. These rituals form the imagination of a people who thus construe their world as a particular kind of environment based on the formation implicit in such practices. If philosophy of religion is going to take religion seriously, then it needs to attend to religion as a social imaginary—a set of liturgical practices in which a unique understanding is implicit.

We see examples of this sort of reorientation of philosophy of religion in work associated with Radical Orthodoxy. For example, the work of Catherine Pickstock and Graham Ward has paid close attention to Christian liturgy, specifically the Eucharist. Pickstock's *After Writing* is an extended analysis of the distinctive ontology and philosophy of language embedded in the Roman rite.[39] Similarly, Ward has taken seriously the

---

35   Taylor, *Modern Social Imaginaries*, 23, emphasis added.
36   Taylor, *Modern Social Imaginaries*, 23.
37   Taylor, *Modern Social Imaginaries*, 25. It should be noted that "understanding" here refers to something akin to Heidegger's notion of "understanding" (*Verstehen*) which is not to be equated with theoretical or propositional "knowledge." See *Being and Time*, §31. This "understanding" is still distinct from, and irreducible to, "theoretical" or propositional knowledge. So not even the "understanding" implicit in practice is to be identified with the sorts of "ideas" that tend to be the currency of contemporary philosophical theology.
38   Taylor, *Modern Social Imaginaries*, 26.
39   Catherine Pickstock, *After Writing: On the Liturgical Consummation of Philosophy* (Oxford: Blackwell, 1998).

words of institution ("this is my body") to generate a unique participatory or analogical ontology.[40] These are clear examples of a shift in topic, looking to liturgy as a resource for philosophy. However, one could suggest that this mode of philosophical engagement with liturgy still remains within the "illuminative" model described above. In both cases, the liturgy is taken to be a resource for new *ideas* which can generate a distinctly Christian philosophy. The liturgy is construed as a space for a thought project. This is significant and legitimate; however, it still tends to treat liturgy as a fund for ideas rather than a practice of formation. Thus, engagements with liturgy tend to be mining expeditions for ideas and concepts otherwise unavailable.[41]

A further reorientation of philosophy to liturgy would not just look to liturgical practice as another place to find ideas, but would be attentive to the central dynamics of *formation* that are at the heart of liturgical practice. And an even further radical reorientation would then consider how liturgical participation would contribute to the formation of philosophical imagination itself—not just philosophical reflection on how liturgical practices shape our comportment to the world, but how liturgical practices shape our *philosophical* comportment to the world. On this account, the condition of possibility for a properly *religious* philosophy is not just access to a unique set of ideas unveiled by revelation, but participation in the liturgical practices of the community as a means of shaping the philosophical imagination and what constitutes "rationality." One can see something like this anticipated in MacIntyre's account of rationality as traditioned, but the explicit link to liturgy is only beginning to be developed.

Such a thorough reorientation of philosophy of religion can be seen in a couple of promising examples. The first is recent work by Jewish philosopher Peter Ochs on Jewish Morning Prayer. In particular, Ochs carefully explicates the way in which immersion in the ritual of Jewish Morning Prayer is a mode of "training in how to make judgments."[42] More specifically, he shows how participation in Jewish Morning Prayer is a practice of redemptive thinking which "redeems the way we ordinarily misjudge

---

40   See Graham Ward, *Cities of God* (London: Routledge, 2001), esp. 81–96.
41   George Vandervelde offers a nuanced critique of Ward's tendency to see the Eucharist as a "privileged ontological site." See Vandervelde, "'This is My Body': The Eucharist as Privileged Theological Site," in *Radical Orthodoxy and the Reformed Tradition*, ed. James K. A. Smith and James H. Olthuis (Grand Rapids: Baker Academic, 2005), 263–76.
42   Ochs, "Morning Prayer as Redemptive Thinking," 50.

the world"—a way of undoing our socialization into propositional ways of judging the world, which tend to be absolutized, and thus fail to do justice to the richness of the world. Jewish Morning Prayer, then, is a way to "nurture actual, everyday habits of thinking that are not dominated by this logic"—which translates into a new *philosophical* orientation when they are undertaken by the philosopher.[43] Second, I find William Abraham's articulation of "canonical theism" to be an example of a "thicker" philosophical vision that draws on the liturgical specificity of Catholic confession and liturgy as both resource and condition for insightful philosophical reflection. Abraham emphasizes the importance of drawing on the "deep content" of Christian belief—the canonical theism "dispersed in the scriptures, the Nicene Creed, the iconography, and the liturgy"—in contrast to the "minimalist theism" of current philosophy of religion, which cannot "do full justice to the way in which a host of Christian believers actually believe."[44]

In this space I have been able to provide only a programmatic survey of the current landscape and sketch a suggestion of further agendas for research. Promising developments give an indication and hope that a new renaissance in philosophy of religion is possible—one in which we finally appreciate that philosophy of religion takes (liturgical) practice. The chapters that follow fill out some of the details for how we might practice such a philosophy of religion.

---

43 Ochs, "Morning Prayer as Redemptive Thinking," 50, passim. Ochs' work is indicative of a promising developing practice in postliberal philosophical theology called "Scriptural Reasoning." See Peter Ochs, "Philosophic Warrants for Scriptural Reasoning," *Modern Theology* 22 (2006): 465–82, as well as the essays collected in Pecknold, ed., *Liturgy, Time, and the Politics of Redemption*. For further discussion, see James K. A. Smith, "How Religious Practices Matter: Peter Ochs' 'Alternative Nurturance' of Philosophy of Religion," *Modern Theology* 24 (2008): 469–78.
44 See William J. Abraham, *Crossing the Threshold of Divine Revelation* (Grand Rapids: Eerdmans, 2006). For further discussion see James K. A. Smith, "Epistemology for the Rest of Us: Hints of a Paradigm Shift in Abraham's *Crossing the Threshold*," *Philosophia Christi* 10 (2008): 353–61.

2

Secular Liturgies

Prospects for a "Post-Secular" Study of Religion

Imagining Religion at the End of the World

In his landmark work *Ideas Pertaining to a Pure Phenomenology*, Edmund Husserl undertook a thought experiment intended as a kind of limit case that would help elucidate the nature of consciousness. The strategy is suggestive: Imagine, Husserl (rather blithely) suggested, the complete annihilation of the world. Imagine the utter destruction of materiality: not just buildings and trees, but animals and planets. Imagine the obliteration of the earth, the eradication of material stuff, and the annihilation of our bodies. What would be left? Could consciousness survive such a catastrophe? Oddly enough, Husserl answered "yes" to such a question: "while the being of consciousness, of any stream of mental processes whatever, would indeed be necessarily modified [!] by an annihilation of the world of physical things, its own existence would not be touched."[1]

I would like to invite you to consider some analogous thought experiments, not in order to distill the essence of consciousness, but in order to press the traditional or received ways we think about "religion" and its correlate, "the secular."

- Let's begin with Husserl's own scenario: If the entire physical universe evaporated, would religion survive? If there were no

1 Husserl, *Ideas Pertaining to a Pure Phenomenology and to a Phenomenological Philosophy*, book 1, trans. F. Kersten (The Hague: Nijhoff, 1983), §49 (110, italics eliminated).

bodies, no buildings, and no bread, could there still be "religion?" Just what sort of religion could survive such an evisceration of materiality?

- Second, let's try something a little less drastic but no less catastrophic: Imagine the harrowed world of Cormac McCarthy's novel *The Road*. Imagine what's left of a world after a disastrous incineration of almost all that we know as nature and culture. Imagine a world of unspeakable cruelty and the degradation of the human race to a cannibalistic war of all with all. Would that be a "secular" world? When humanity is reduced to "bare life" (Agamben), exposed and vulnerable and just fixated on the quotidian task of *surviving*—reduced to animality—is humanity then reduced to something less than religious? Are animals "secular?"

- Finally, let's try a slightly different, less harrowing, thought experiment: imagine the whole world looked like the Upper West Side. Imagine that, by some catastrophe (or *eu*catastrophe, depending on your perspective), the whole world looked like the enclaves of what Peter Berger calls a "globalized elite culture."[2] Or, if you like, imagine a different kind of "destruction" of the world where everyone is converted by the gospel of Sam Harris and Christopher Hitchens—a veritable secular eschaton, if you will, that leaves us solidly ensconced in immanence. Would "religion" survive that annihilation/transformation? Would the global triumph of secularism—in which everyone reflected the ideal, cultivated, "secular" citizen—signal the obliteration of religion?

---

2 Peter Berger, "The Desecularization of the World: A Global Overview," in *The Desecularization of the World: Resurgent Religion and World Politics*, ed. Berger (Grand Rapids: Eerdmans, 1999), 10. As Berger puts it, "There exists an international subculture composed of people with Western-type higher education, especially in the humanities and social sciences, that is indeed secularized. This subculture is the principle 'carrier' of progressive, Enlightened beliefs and values. While its members are relatively thin on the ground, they are very influential, as they control the institutions that provide the 'official' definitions of reality, notably the educational system, the media of mass communication, and the higher reaches of the legal system."

I think our received (modern) categories and conceptions of both "religion" and "the secular"—the very categories and conceptions that tend to inform both philosophy of religion and the social sciences—yield predictable answers to the questions posed by these thought experiments. For instance, recall the first Husserlian scenario: could "religion" survive the utter annihilation of matter and bodies? Well, surprisingly enough, the religion of modernity wouldn't really miss a beat. Sure, it might be "modified," as Husserl puts it. But the "religion" of modernity—and the "religion" that is considered by sociology of religion, philosophy of religion, and much of theology—*is* a religion for disembodied minds. It is a religion of "beliefs" and "values," of representations, the stuff of minds and souls.

But the odd thing is that a lot of believers wouldn't know how to believe if they didn't have bodies. That's because they wouldn't know what to *do*. For those who *practice* faith, faith *takes practice*. And such practice is embodied and material; it is communal and liturgical; it involves eating and drinking, dancing and kneeling, painting and singing—all of which are impossible delights for a disembodied mind. Such embodied, practiced religion could never survive the annihilation of the world of bodies. Our "secular" paradigms, in this respect, are largely "intellectualist":[3] they impose on religion a picture of human persons that reflects a distinctly modern emphasis on the cognitive—a top-heavy emphasis on beliefs, ideas, and doctrines. But why should modernity get to define the human person, and hence the shape of "religion?" Perhaps it's time for a *post-secular* account of religion, along with a post-secular account of religion, whether philosophical or sociological.

Rethinking the shape of religion, however, also invites us to reconsider our received assumptions about "the secular." If "religion" is not primarily defined by a set of beliefs, ideas, values, or doctrines, but rather by particular, charged, identity-forming[4] practices, then could it be the case that

---

3   This is Charles Taylor's term to describe models which "see the human agent as primarily a subject of representations." See Taylor, "To Follow a Rule . . . ," in *Bourdieu: Critical Perspectives*, ed. Craig Calhoun, Edward LiPuma, and Moishe Postone (Chicago: University of Chicago Press, 1993), 45–60, esp. 45–49.

4   As will become clear below, my project has resonances with Saba Mahmood's recent account of "secular religion" as articulated in "Secularism, Hermeneutics, and Empire: The Politics of Islamic Reformation," *Public Culture* 18 (2006): 323–47, esp. 341–47. For just this reason, I will be contesting Stathis Gourgouris' defense of the "secular" as areligious. Gourgouris wants to starkly distinguish religion and secularism, and yet further muddies the waters by construing Mahmood's "post-secular" approach as inherently *anti*-secular

there are practices and institutions which have that same function and force, but have slipped under our "religion-detecting radar"? Even in our third "end of the world" scenario above (where Dawkins is pope, Hitchens is in charge of the Congregation for the Doctrine of Disbelief, and Sam Harris is president of Notre Dame), might it be the case that "religion" is still at work? Granted, certain sets of doctrines, beliefs, and ideas have been eliminated, replaced by cold, hard scientific rationality and, I take it, a universal global democracy (and I'm guessing capitalism is doing just fine in this secular eschaton). But why should we thereby conclude that there's no *religion* in this wholly "secular" world? Will there not still be powerful, identity-forming practices that implicitly articulate what counts as human flourishing? Would there not still be rituals that "carry," as Taylor suggests, a fundamental orientation to the world and what matters? Indeed, wouldn't such secular rituals still function as "liturgies"—those rituals and practices that shape our attunement to what is ultimate?[5] What if humans are inescapably liturgical animals? Will a secular eschaton really be able to eliminate *liturgies*? Might "secular" liturgies be no less religious?[6]

(see Gourgouris, "Detranscendentalizing the Secular," *Public Culture* 20 [2008]: 437–45). I will suggest this stems from the fact that he fails to appreciate (1) that religious ("nonsecular") practices are *political* practices and (2) that secular practices, *because* they are identity-forming, amount to *religious* practices. In short, he too tightly identifies the religious with the transcendent—as essentially "otherworldly." See Gourgouris, "Antisecularist Failures: A Counterresponse to Saba Mahmood," *Public Culture* 20 (2008): 453–59. I will be arguing that the "religious" is not essentially tied to the transcendent or the otherworldly but to the *modes* of identity-formation and the *status* of the practices that engender such.

5   I am using the term "liturgy" here in a way analogous to Christian Smith, *Moral, Believing Animals: Human Personhood and Culture* (New York: Oxford University Press, 2003), 16: "Liturgy ritually reenacts a tradition, an experience, a history, a worldview. It expresses in dramatic and corporeal form a sacred belief system in words, music, imagery, aromas, tastes, and bodily movement. In liturgy, worshipers both perform and observe, act out truth and have the truth act on them, remember the past and carry it into the future. Liturgy expresses, professes, performs, and informs. This is what religious liturgies do. It is *also* exactly what human social life more generally does with cultural moral order. All of the social practices, relations, and institutions that comprise human social life generally themselves together dramatize, ritualize, proclaim, and reaffirm the moral order that constitutes social life. Moral order embodies the sacred story of the society, however profane it appears, and the social actors are believers in social congregation."

6   This is not to say that every practice is religious; however, it does entail that a number of practices we consider "secular" function religiously precisely because they form ultimate desires—that is, they function as formative rituals of ultimacy. See my distinction between practices, rituals and liturgies in James K. A. Smith, *Desiring the Kingdom: Worship, Worldview, and Cultural Formation* (Grand Rapids: Baker Academic, 2009), 85–88. For an anal-

Religion is not (just) where we have been looking for it. We need a new theoretical radar to "pick up" religion where we don't usually see it, in two senses: first, we need to appreciate that religion "takes practice," so to speak—that religion is an embodied, material, liturgical phenomenon that shapes our desire and imagination before it yields doctrines and beliefs. Precisely because of that, we also need to recalibrate our theoretical radar in order to pick up secular religion, in order to appreciate the force of secular liturgies.[7] Thus my goal is twofold: First, I want to propose a methodological shift in both philosophy of religion and sociology of religion that rejects what Taylor calls "intellectualism." The inherited intellectualist model bears all the marks of the "hermeneutical project" criticized by Mahmood: it yields "a secularized conception of religion in which religion is understood to be an abstracted category of beliefs and doctrines"; as a result, "religion's phenomenal forms—its liturgies, rituals, and scriptures—are understood to be inessential to it."[8] In contrast, I will sketch an essentially "liturgical" account of religion, drawing on Taylor, Wittgenstein, Heidegger, and Bourdieu. Second, as an implication of this, I will argue that such a paradigm is "post-secular" in two senses: (1) it rejects the intellectualist anthropology and epistemology that informs "secular" social sciences; and (2) it will be primed to see certain "secular" practices *as* religious, thus expanding the purview of both sociology of religion and philosophy of religion. I want to sketch a methodological paradigm for a "post-secular" study of religion that is attuned to worship rather than (just) belief, and is thus primed to recognize religion in practices and institutions that we generally consider "secular."[9] In short, I want to propose a methodological paradigm[10] that has the theoretical radar, so

---

ysis of "secular liturgies," see pp. 89–129. My use of "secular" appears in scare quotes here precisely because I am employing the term in its folk usage, we might say. This will be nuanced in the next section.

7   Though I cannot develop it here, I also think this helps us to account for the overwhelming force of American civil religion; basically, in (Protestant) America, the devil gets all the best liturgies.

8   Mahmood, "Secularism, Hermeneutics, and Empire," 341.

9   I do so, cognizant of Gourgouris' admonition that "we have to be equally careful with ascribing to secularism a religious quality in a straightforward sense" ("Detranscendentalizing the Secular," 441). I will argue that Gourgouris, in addition to clinging to the ideal of "autonomy," also equivocates on the features of "the secular." Taylor's taxonomy will help us bring clarity to the issue.

10   As will become clear below, I share Saba Mahmood's thesis that what's at stake in "normative secularism" is an "attendant anthropology of the subject"—that is, an assumed

to speak, to pick up on "secular liturgies." Insofar as exclusive humanism has its liturgies, it remains religious.[11]

Whose "Secular?" Which "Post-Secular?"

The "secularization thesis" has fallen on hard times. Only a generation ago social scientists confidently predicted the withering of religion in public life. Just as social scientists were offering descriptive accounts of secularization, political theorists were articulating normative doctrines of secular*ism* which carved out the public sphere as a realm of "pure reason"—a space for "rational actors" who would have to leave religious belief (and other irrationalities) at the door. But of late, experience has proved otherwise. Two movements contest both descriptive secularization and normative secularism: On the one hand, a so-called resurgence of religion in domestic and global politics has disproven the prognostications of secularization theorists. On the other hand, a postmodern and post-liberal critique of Enlightenment models of rationality (allegedly neutral and objective—and therefore "secular") has called into question the theoretical impetus of normative secular*ism*. The latter critiques (such as Nicholas Wolsterstorff's critique of Rorty and Audi,[12] Jeffrey Stout's critique of Rawls,[13] or John Milbank's critique of "secular" social theory[14]) have called into question the epistemological foundations of secularism, suggesting—perhaps even calling for—a "*post*-secular" age.

But is "post-secular" a descriptive term or a normative program? If it is a *de*scriptive term, countering the secularization thesis, then we encounter some empirical questions: Is it the case that we are entering a post-secular "era?" Is "post-secular" a name for an era which has "got

---

picture of just what sorts of animals we are. See Mahmood, "Secularism, Hermeneutics, and Empire." I think the same point is discerned (albeit from very different quarters) in Smith, *Moral, Believing Animals*.

11 Thought not, *pace* Gourgouris, "in a straightforward sense" ("Detranscendentalizing the Secular," 441).

12 Nicholas Wolterstorff, "An Engagement with Rorty," *Journal of Religious Ethics* 31 (2003): 129–39; Robert Audi and Nicholas Wolterstorff, *Religion in the Public Square: The Place of Religious Convictions in Political Debate* (Lanham: Rowman & Littlefield, 1997).

13 Jeffrey Stout, *Democracy and Tradition* (Princeton: Princeton University Press, 2004), 64–76.

14 John Milbank, *Theology and Social Theory: Beyond Secular Reason* (Oxford: Blackwell, 1990). For further articulation, see James K. A. Smith, *Introducing Radical Orthodoxy: Mapping a Post-Secular Theology* (Grand Rapids: Baker Academic, 2004).

religion" (back), so to speak—having recovered from an "era" of secular backsliding as it were? Is that an apt or warranted description of our contemporary situation? Are we more religious? Have we ever really been secular?

Perhaps "post-secular" is less a descriptor and more a normative ideal, a *pre*scription for how society or the sciences ought to be ordered and conducted, countering normative doctrines of secularism. But what is being advocated under the banner of the "post-secular?" Does this amount to a covert *anti*-secularism which itself amounts to a covert theocratic project?[15] If the sciences are essentially secular, then wouldn't the post-secular be anti-scientific, a worrisome retreat back into irrationality and tribal narratives?

Before taking up my constructive project, I want to utilize Charles Taylor's analysis of our "secular age" in order to clarify and make sense of "post-secular" as both a descriptive and normative term. Taylor's nuanced analysis of our "secular age" reconnoiters these debates by noting the equivocation of the term "secular." As Taylor notes, "secular" can have several connotations.[16]

(1) In classical or medieval accounts, the "secular" amounted to something like "the temporal"—the realm of "earthly"[17] politics or of "mundane" vocations. This is the "secular" of the purported sacred/secular divide. The priest, for instance, pursues a "sacred" vocation, while the butcher, baker, and

---

15   As Stathis Gourgouris seems to assume in "Detranscendentalizing the Secular" and "Antisecularist Failures."
16   Charles Taylor, *A Secular Age* (Cambridge, Mass.: Harvard University Press, 2007), 2–4, 12–15, 425–26 (henceforth cited in the text as SA). I have discussed this in more detail in James K. A. Smith, *How (Not) to Be Secular: Reading Charles Taylor* (Grand Rapids: Eerdmans, 2014).
17   It should be noted that this is more complicated in Augustine. For Augustine, the *saeculum* is primarily a *time*: the "age" between the Fall and the consummation of the Kingdom (the eschaton). So technically (and Augustine is not entirely consistent on this point), the *saeculum* is not coincident with creation and temporality as such; it would represent a disfiguration of temporality after the Fall. In short, "the secular" is not equivalent with "this world" if by "this world" we mean *creation*. For instance, one could imagine the work of baking and candlestick making as vocations in a *good* creation—in a prelapsarian world. In that case, such "mundane" work would not be "secular." But if, instead, "this world" refers to the current fallen configuration of creation (per 1 John 2:15-17; 5:19), then the *saeculum* is identical to "this world."

candlestick maker are engaged in "secular" pursuits.[18] Following Taylor, let's call this secular$_1$.

(2) In modernity, "secular" refers to a non-sectarian, neutral, and *a*religious space or standpoint. We'll refer to this as secular$_2$. It is this notion of secular$_2$ that is assumed both by the secularization thesis and normative secularism. According to secularization theory, as cultures experienced modernization and technological advancement, the (divisive) forces of religious belief and participation would wither in the face of modernity's disenchantment of the world. According to secularism, political spaces (and the constitutions that create them) should carve out a realm purified of the contingency, particularity, and irrationality of religious belief and instead be governed by universal, neutral rationality. Secular*ism* is always secularism$_2$.

(3) But Taylor helpfully articulates a third sense of the secular (secular$_3$): a society is "secular$_3$" insofar as religious belief or belief in God is understood to be one option among others, and thus contestable (and contested). At issue here is a shift in "the conditions of belief," or what Peter Berger would call the "plausibility structures" of a society. As Taylor notes, the shift to secularity "in this sense" indicates "a move from a society where belief in God is unchallenged and indeed, unproblematic, to one in which it is understood to be one option among others, and frequently not the easiest to embrace" (SA 3). It is in this sense that we live in a "secular age" even if religious participation might be visible and fervent. And it is in this sense that we could still entertain a certain "secularization$_3$ thesis." But this would be an account, not of how religion will wither in late modern societies, but rather of how and why the plausibility structures of such societies will make religion contestable (and contested).[19]

---

18 One can thus read the Reformation as refusing and obliterating the distinction by sacralizing what had been previously construed as merely "secular" (SA 265–66). In short, all is sacred, or at least has the potential of being a sacred vocation if it is rightly ordered.
19 In fact, this seems to be very similar to what Jeffrey Stout—a critic of secular*ism*—describes as the "secularization" of political discourse: "What makes a form

Now, given Taylor's taxonomy, what would it mean to speak of a "post-secular" age? First, it seems clear that what must be meant is post-secular$_2$, not post-secular$_3$. There's no turning back the clock on the shift of plausibility structures occasioned by the advent of modernity; in short, secular$_3$ is here to stay. Indeed, it is precisely an appreciation of our pluralistic situation of contested plausibility structures which engenders the critique of secularism$_2$. One might say that secularism$_2$ is a standpoint which fails to recognize the contestability of its own plausibility structures—a standpoint which just takes its standpoint to be axiomatic, "the way things *really* are." Paradoxically, secularism$_2$ fails to own up to the secular$_3$.[20]

However, while the secularization$_2$ thesis has been rightly challenged, normative secularism$_2$ remains influential in public discourse (with renewed vigor in Europe) and perhaps particularly in the methodology of the social sciences. This lingering secularism is loaded into the very category of "religion" as analyzed by the social sciences and humanities, particularly when the "religious" is distinguished from or contrasted with "the political" or "the public." So while affirming Taylor's claim that we live in a "secular$_3$ age," I am arguing for a normative post-secular$_2$ methodology. This will require articulating a more dynamic and nuanced anthropology to undergird social scientific study. And on this "attendant anthropology," as Mahmood describes it, Taylor can also be a guide.

---

of discourse secularized, according to my account, is not the tendency of the people participating in it to relinquish their religious beliefs or to refrain from employing them as reasons. The mark of secularization, as I use the term, is rather the fact that participants in a given discursive practice are not in a position to take for granted that their interlocutors are marking the same religious assumptions they are." Thus participants in such "secularized" discourse "cannot reasonably . . . expect a single theological perspective to be shared by all of their interlocutors" (*Democracy and Tradition*, 97). Unfortunately, Stout seems to think that those he calls "new traditionalists" (MacIntyre, Hauerwas, and Milbank) "resent" this situation (99), as if they all longed for the reinstitution of the plausibility conditions of the Holy Roman Empire. This is a serious misreading that can't distract us here. For further discussion of Stout, see James K. A. Smith, "The Politics of Desire: Augustine's Political Phenomenology," in *Augustine and Postmodern Thought: A New Alliance against Modernity?* ed. Lieven Boeve and Mathijs Lamberigts (Leuven: Peeters, 2009), 211–35.

20   This may help clarify Gourgouris' worry that Mahmood's critique of secularism is, in fact, an anti-secularism. Parsing this is difficult, but I would suggest that, yes, Mahmood is rejecting secularism$_2$ (to which Gourgouris may remain "committed"), but she is not rejecting "the secular$_3$."

We Have Never Been Secular[21]

Because we live in a secular$_3$ age, we need a post-secular$_2$ religious studies.

Now, if we were focused on matters of epistemology and the conditions of knowledge in the sciences, I might make the claim even stronger: there never has been a secular$_2$ social science precisely because there is no unbiased, a-traditioned, neutral, universal standpoint.[22] Our theorizing, and even our observation, begins from and is shaped by pre-theoretical commitments and is indebted to traditions of rationality. Since I have articulated this epistemological critique of "secular" social science elsewhere,[23] here I would like to take a different tack.

I suggest that our social scientific accounts of our being-in-the-world need to be "post-secular$_2$," by being attuned to the fact that humans are inescapably religious animals. That claim does not mean to suggest that humans inescapably believe in God, gods, or even transcendence. Rather, in claiming that humans (including social scientists!) are inescapably religious animals, I mean that humans are *liturgical* animals whose orientation to the world is shaped by rituals of ultimacy: our fundamental commitments are inscribed in us by ritual forces and elicit from us orienting commitments that have the epistemic status of belief. So to suggest that we are liturgical animals is not just to claim that we are all *believers* at some fundamental level; it is to also claim that we *become* believers through ritual formation—and such formative rituals have the status of "liturgies." This identification of "religion" with liturgy effects a double-displacement: it displaces the "site" of religiosity from beliefs to

---

21 I am playing a bit on Bruno Latour, *We Have Never Been Modern*, trans. Catherine Porter (Cambridge, Mass.: Harvard University Press, 1993). According to Latour's analysis, the "modern" is a kind of impossible ideal of purity (10). But in fact, "modernity" is characterized by "practices" which yield hybrids rather than the desired purities. Thus "we have never been modern." I am going to suggest something analogous about the ideal of the "secular."

22 I suppose that Gourgouris might concede that social science could never be unbiased, neutral, etc.—and yet still affirm that social science be "secular" by being radically "immanent," by shutting down any reference to transcendence. Whereas I am suggesting that critique or social science might be radically immanent (or exclusively humanist) and still be *religious*, and hence not "secular." I am not exactly sure how to mediate these different stipulations of what's loaded into the meaning of "secular" except to say that the conditions I'm noting here—something like pure Kantian rationality—were taken to be the conditions for shutting down reference to the religious/transcendence. If Gourgouris rejects these "Kantian" criteria, I think he loses the ground for excluding the religious.

23 See Smith, *Introducing Radical Orthodoxy*, 125–42.

practices, and it displaces the identification of religion with only transcendent or "other-worldly" models.

Religion as a "Heady" Affair: The "Intellectualism" of the Secular

Saba Mahmood, in a provocative essay, has recently suggested that secularism is attended by a distinct philosophical anthropology—an implicit picture of the human person.[24] And this standard, assumed picture of human persons sees "religion" (1) as a basically optional phenomenon and (2) as a primarily cognitive phenomenon.

The standard picture, we might say, sees religion as a sort of addendum to being human: *all* humans eat, sleep, breathe, have sex, are citizens of some nation, engage in play, etc. Then, in addition to that, *some* (perhaps even *many*) *Homo sapiens* are "religious": they are "believers" who participate in religious rituals and practices, identify with religious communities, and hold religious beliefs. These beliefs and practices are generally taken to be tied to certain established traditions and institutions (Buddhism, Christianity, Islam, etc.).[25] Those who study "believers" are often those without this extra-human supplement: they are "just" human, i.e., "secular." "Believers," to them, are kind of exotic; they have conspicuous growths, like two heads. From the perspective of the secular scientist, who lacks such growths (who has been "healed" of such lesions, as it were), this religious "addendum" is a curious supplement to being human—a kind of deformation.

But implicit in this picture and assumed in this anthropology is a microcosmic version of what Taylor calls a "subtraction story": some humans have managed to excise the religious addendum that has clung to humanity for so long, and continues to cling to so many. The enlightened "secular" observers have pared down to only what is essentially human. To return to our opening thought projects, because secularism assumes this sort of anthropology, it assumes that the Upper West Side is *not* religious. But what grounds this anthropological commitment? What is the warrant for this model of the human person and its attendant understanding of religion? What if the warrant for these anthropological assumptions actually has the epistemic status

---

24 Mahmood, "Secularism, Hermeneutics, and Empire," 330.
25 Recent research on "new religious movements" stretches this somewhat, perhaps; but our catalogue of NRMs doesn't include, say, capitalism. So the R in NRM is still circumscribed by the "traditional" religions in some sense.

of a kind of *faith*? How does one come to believe this model? What if such anthropological assumptions are absorbed through identity-forming practices that inscribe in these "secular" observers a particular, normative vision of human flourishing—an implicit understanding of what is ultimate?[26] Then, I want to suggest, even those who *are* "secularized" (Berger's global intelligentsia) are *still* religious—and not just in some banal, Tillichian sense. I would argue that even the secularized academic who spends Sunday morning reading the *New York Times Magazine* is still shaped and formed by liturgies—what I will call, somewhat grudgingly, "secular liturgies." But in order for such a claim to have any possible viability, we need to articulate an alternative philosophical anthropology.[27]

Social Imaginaries and Liturgical Animals

The "standard (secularist) picture" of the human person is top-heavy: it still construes religion as primarily a cognitive-propositional phenomenon, as a set of beliefs or "values" (as in "the values voter"). It is this sort of epistemological fixation which makes it possible for secularist anthropologies to see religion as an addendum, an optional supplement: clearly not all people have *those sorts* of beliefs or values, thus "religion" is not an essential feature of being human.

But what if "religion" were not viewed primarily through the cognitive lens of beliefs, values, and propositions but rather through attention to rituals, practice and liturgy? What if we "located" religion, as it were, not in the head but in the body? And what if our identities—our desires, our

---

[26] As Christian Smith wryly comments, "Sociologists not only make stories but are animals who are made by their stories. . . . No one, not even the statistics-laden sociologist, escapes the moral, believing, narrative-constituted condition of the human animal" (Christian Smith, *Moral, Believing Animals*, 87).

[27] I do not think this is just a matter of dueling, stipulative anthropologies; that is, I don't think that we're in an utterly relativist situation where the secularist arbitrarily articulates her anthropology and the post-secularist merely offers an alternative, competing anthropological model, and now we are left in a position of indifference and have to make some sort of unmotivated "choice" between them. Rather, I think such alternative anthropologies have to "prove themselves," as it were, by how they can account for the phenomena of human social behavior. And my wager is that the post-secular model I am sketching does a better job of doing this, and that the secularist model is inadequate not just because it is secular but because it cannot do justice to the data, so to speak. For a robust articulation and defense of a similar thesis, see Christian Smith, *What Is a Person? Rethinking Humanity, Social Life, and the Moral Good from the Person Up* (Chicago: University of Chicago Press, 2010).

loves, our allegiances, our visions of the good life—were shaped through such embodied rituals? Then our "thickest," identity-forming rituals would have an *ultimacy* about them that we might legitimately call religious.

Thus I want to offer a general definition of liturgies as *rituals of ultimate concern*: rituals that are formative for identity; that inculcate particular, normative visions of "the good life"; and do so in a way that means to trump other ritual formations. Admittedly, this might include rituals not associated with traditional religions (e.g., rituals of Nazi fascism or other rituals of totalizing nationalism); indeed, expanding our conception of what counts as "worship" is precisely the point.[28] Our thickest practices—which are not necessarily linked to institutional religion—have a *liturgical* function insofar as they are a certain species of ritual practice that aim to do nothing less than shape our identity by shaping our desire for what we envision as the ideal of human flourishing. Liturgies are the most loaded forms of ritual practice because they are after nothing less than our hearts, our most fundamental motivations. They want to determine what we *love* ultimately. By "ultimately" I mean what we love "above all," that to which we pledge allegiance, that to which we are devoted in a way that overrules other concerns and interests. Our ultimate love is what defines us, what makes us the *kind* of people we are. In short, it is what we *worship*.[29]

Consider, for example, the ritual power of the opening of a NASCAR race or an NFL football game: In a massive space thronging with people, eager for the beginning of the event, a crowd of one hundred thousand people can be brought into remarkable placidity by the exhortation "Please stand for the national anthem." Like parishioners who know all the motions of the Mass by heart, these fans instinctively and automatically

---

28 See also Philip Kenneson, "Gathering: Worship, Imagination, and Formation," in *The Blackwell Companion to Christian Ethics*, ed. Stanley Hauerwas and Samuel Wells (Oxford: Blackwell, 2006), 53–67. Kenneson notes that since the basic feature of "worship" is "ascribing worth," then all sorts of human gatherings are "fundamentally formative" insofar as they train us to ascribe worth to certain ends (53–54). This doesn't mean that *everything* is religious or constitutes "religion." I would reserve the category "religious" (and "liturgy") for identity-forming rituals that aim to trump others and hold a status of ultimacy.

29 Another way of putting this is to say that liturgies are ritual practices that function as pedagogies of ultimate desire. I develop this "pedagogical" theme more fully in Smith, *Desiring the Kingdom*. For relevant discussion, see Robyn Barnacle, "Gut Instinct: The Body and Learning," *Educational Philosophy and Theory* 41 (2009): 22–33.

rise together. They remove their caps and many place a hand over their heart as an artist or group sings a rendition of one of the world's most affecting national anthems, laden with military themes such that those singing it are transposed into battle, the identity of the nation being wrapped up in its revolutionary beginnings and legacy of military power. Perhaps even more importantly, this rehearses and renews the myth of national identity forged by blood sacrifice. The sounds of the anthem are usually accompanied by big, dramatic sights of the flag: a Star-Spangled Banner the size of a football field is unfurled across the field by a small army of young people whose movements make it undulate as if blowing in the winds of battle, proudly defiant, but almost dripping with blood in those red lines across it. And almost always, the concluding crescendo of the anthem—announcing that this is the "land of the free" and "home of the brave"—is accompanied by a flyover from military aircraft, whether the searing slice of F-15 fighter jets across the sky or the pulsating presence of Apache helicopters chugging across the air space of the stadium. The presence of the aircraft has a double effect: it concretizes the militarism of the anthem and the flag while also making the scene something that is *felt*, as the sounds of the jets or choppers is a kind of noise one picks up in the chest more than the ears. A crowd larger than many American cities then erupts in cheers and applause as this ritual of national unity has united even fans of opposing teams. I'm suggesting that this constitutes a liturgy because it is a material ritual of ultimate concern: through a multisensory display, the ritual both powerfully and subtly moves us, and in so doing implants within us a certain reverence and awe, a learned deference to an ideal which might someday call for *our* "sacrifice." But this isn't conveyed as a "message" to be disseminated; it is not even the communication of "beliefs"; it is more the ritual enactment and enforcement of a story the seeps into the imagination. Such liturgies don't just, or even primarily, interact with the intellect; they operate on the level of desire.

This focus on *liturgies* stems from appreciating the centrality of *love*; and it is a focus on love which grows out of an alternative, non-intellectualist anthropology. Our current theoretical radar in the study of religion—whether in philosophy or sociology—is calibrated to register the propositional: thoughts, beliefs, ideas, "values." This assumes a cognitivist or intellectualist picture of the human person as the sort of animal that is moved to act on the basis of cognition and conscious deliberation.

But accumulating research in philosophical anthropology (and, increasingly, in the neurosciences[30]) suggests that this intellectualist model is not the best picture for explaining human behavior, including religious behavior. Rather, an alternative paradigm indicates that precognitive modes of intentionality much more significantly shape and drive our relation to, and action in, the world. Drawing on Heidegger, Taylor, and Bourdieu, I want to sketch the shape of this affective anthropology and then go on to indicate how it ought to recalibrate our model of "religion."

Feeling Our Way Around the World
The Hermeneutics of Love in Heidegger

In light of the Gourgouris/Mahmood debate about the "anthropology" assumed by secularism, I think the early work of Martin Heidegger can be seen in a new light precisely because, almost a hundred years ago, Heidegger was already contesting the "rationalist" or "intellectualist" picture bequeathed to us by modernity (and more immediately, by his teacher Husserl). For Heidegger, we are never simply spectators of what is "given." Heidegger saw in Husserl's phenomenology a lingering, implicit picture of the human person as a kind of swiveling brain on a stick: an unengaged mind that scanned the world like a lighthouse, simply "perceiving" things as "objects." In contrast, Heidegger emphasized that (1) our relation to the world is always already a *construal*, a "take" on the world; and (2), more importantly for us here, that such construal happened at a precognitive level. The first point emphasizes that to be in the world is to always already *interpret* the world; indeed, there is no "world" without interpretation. The world never simply appears as something given but rather is construed *as* a world on the basis of presuppositions or background "horizons" which condition (and make possible) our construal of the world.[31] But the second point emphasizes that such construal and interpretation happens on

---

30 I have in mind increased conversation between phenomenology and cognitive science as seen in Shaun Gallagher, *How the Body Shapes the Mind* (New York: Oxford University Press, 2006), Mark Okrent, *Rational Animals: The Teleological Roots of Intentionality* (Athens: Ohio University Press, 2007), Mark Johnson, *The Meaning of the Body: Aesthetics of Human Understanding* (Chicago: University of Chicago Press, 2007), and Timothy Wilson, *Strangers to Ourselves: Discovering the Adaptive Unconscious* (Cambridge, Mass.: Belknap Press of Harvard University Press, 2002).
31 See Heidegger, *Being and Time*, trans. John Macquarrie and Edward Robinson (Oxford: Blackwell, 1962), §32.

a register that is not discursive or intellectual—a register that is not even, in a way, "*conscious*."[32] Thus Heidegger can suggest that the world is construed on the order of "mood." It is this strange claim that I would like to unpack a bit.

Almost struggling for words, Heidegger argues that we find ourselves to be essentially "mooded": "Dasein always has some mood."[33] But this is not just a psychological ("ontic") matter—e.g., that I find myself happy or sad, disturbed or elated. Rather, such different moods are possible because I am fundamentally *attuned* to the world on a register more akin to mood than thought. Thus he describes this as an "attunement"[34] to the world—a mode in which the world is "disclosed" but by a disclosure that eludes "knowledge." As Heidegger puts it, in attunement one understands something of the world that "one does not *know*. And Dasein cannot know anything of the sort because the possibilities of disclosure which belong to cognition reach far too short a way compared with the primordial disclosure belonging to moods."[35] So mood discloses the world for us in a primordial way; it effects a construal of the world *before* our cognitive, intellectual "knowledge" of the world comes into play. And we do an injustice to this "understanding" that is effected by mood/attunement if we require it to answer to our more familiar criteria for "knowledge." "[W]e would wholly fail to recognize both *what* mood discloses and *how* it discloses," Heidegger cautions, "if that which is disclosed were to be compared with what Dasein is acquainted with, knows, and believes 'at the same time' when it has such a mood."[36] And even if we do sometimes get a handle on our particular (ontic) moods by volitional and cognitive strategies, we shouldn't let this mislead us "into denying that ontologically mood is a primordial kind of Being for Dasein, in which Dasein is disclosed to itself *prior to* all cognition and volition, and *beyond* their range of disclosure."[37]

---

32 This claim has to be qualified since for Heidegger, as a phenomenologist, any mode of intending the world is a mode of consciousness. On the other hand, current parlance tends to associate "conscious" modes of intentionality with occurent, "chosen" acts. It's vis-à-vis the latter that Heidegger's account of mood points to a sort of "unconscious" construal of the world.
33 *Being and Time*, §29, 173.
34 Heidegger's term for this "existentiale" is *Befindlichkeit*, translated by Macquarrie & Robinson as "state-of-mind" and by Stambaugh as "attunement."
35 *Being and Time*, §29, 173.
36 *Being and Time*, §29, 175.
37 *Being and Time*, §29, 175.

So it's not just that mood is a kind of immature, prior disclosure that needs to be articulated and then superseded by cognitive disclosure; rather, such mooded disclosure is both primordial *and irreducible*. The heart, we might say, has reasons of which reason knows nothing.[38]

Attunement (*Befindlichkeit*, moodedness) is a precognitive mode of intentionality that discloses the world precisely because it construes the world. It effects an interpretation of the world before we even get around to "thinking" about it.[39] This mode of being in the world is "circumspective": I encounter the world not just as a collection of objects to be observed or perceived, but as a world that I am involved with. I am after something, up to something, care about something and am engaged in and with the world on the basis of that concern—even if I might not be able to articulate that for myself in a "cognitive" manner. In short, things *matter*.[40]

Recent work in cognitive theory on the emotions can elucidate Heidegger's intuition here. As Paul Griffiths has described it, the emotions work as "independent modular systems." In this picture, a "modular system" is one that "processes information from our senses though it remains isolated from our central cognitive system."[41] It functions as an independent "appraisal system operating below the level of consciousness," but such appraisals need to be distinguished from (cognitive) judgments. As such, they play "a central role in our orientation in the world," effecting an independent, noncognitive construal of the world. They are not dependent on beliefs; rather, they set the agenda for beliefs and desires.[42]

The upshot is something like this: humans construe the world—and thus orient their action and pursuits—primordially on the basis of an affective relation to what matters. We intend the world—and what matters within the world—not, first and foremost, in cognitive, intellectual ways, but more fundamentally in a way that is independent of, prior to, and fundamentally eludes cognition. And this, Heidegger emphasizes, is also

---

38 The Pascalian allusion is not out of place; Pascal had significant impact on Heidegger's *Being and Time*. See *Being and Time*, §29, 178.

39 *Being and Time*, §29, 176.

40 *Being and Time*, §29, 176. Heidegger goes on to summarize: "*Existentially, a state-of-mind implies a disclosive submission to the world, out of which we encounter something that matters to us*" (177, italics original).

41 As summarized by Kevin Sludds, *Emotions: Their Cognitive Base and Ontological Importance* (Bern: Peter Lang, 2009), 124.

42 Sludds, *Emotions*, 130. See also Robert C. Roberts, "What an Emotion Is: A Sketch," *The Philosophical Review* 97 (1988): 183–209.

true of our *theorizing*. Our theoretical and scientific investigation of the world—including the world of human behavior—is already, Heidegger says, a "dimming down" of the rich complexity of the world.[43] Our theoretical radar, calibrated to the cognitive and intellectual, lacks the nuance and complexity to register the sorts of precognitive, affective "drivers" that orient our being in the world. Furthermore, Heidegger emphasizes, our theoretical investigation cannot escape what we've just seen, viz., the fundamental and irreducible impact of "mood" on how we construe the world. "Even the purest *theoria* has not left all moods behind it. . . . Any cognitive determining has its existential-ontological Constitution in the state-of-mind of Being-in-the-world; but pointing this out is not to be confused with attempting to surrender science ontically to 'feeling.'"[44]

Now why is all of this of interest to us here? What does this have to do with the notion of a post-secular account of religion? There are three points of contact: First, I suggest that we think of religion more on the order of "mood" than cognition. That's not to say that there are no cognitive or intellectual elements of religion. But neither can religion be reduced just to its cognitive and intellectual artifacts. When we "dim down" religion to its cognitive and intellectual aspects—the parts of religion that can register on quantitative instruments—we can then easily restrict religion to certain kinds of beliefs and ideas, and thus sequester religion to a certain subset of the population. But if religion operates more on the order of mood—as a precognitive disclosure of the world and an affective construal of what matters—then Heidegger's account primes us to see something like religion operative beyond the confines of synagogue, church, or mosque.

Second, Heidegger's account also primes us to appreciate that philosophers of religion and social scientists are moody: what *matters* is determined by precognitive factors. Our theorizing cannot leave "mood" behind. In a similar way, our theorizing cannot leave behind the fundamentally affective ways that we construe what matters. And if that is to be identified as "religion," then all theorizing is religious.

Finally, Heidegger's analysis of Dasein—despite articulating a holistic anthropology that displaced the rationalism of his day—did not adequately articulate just *how* such attunement and understanding was acquired and

---

43 *Being and Time*, 177.
44 *Being and Time*, 177.

absorbed. While Heidegger's groundbreaking analysis emphasized the significance of history—that the ego was *made* more than born—his own analyses were inattentive to the material dynamics of *formation*, in part because even Heidegger was insufficiently attentive to the *body*. It was precisely into this lacuna that the work of Maurice Merleau-Ponty strode, now engendering a growing area of research at the intersection of phenomenology and cognitive science which is particularly attuned to the bodily basis of intentionality.[45] Such research is also attentive to the bodily means of formation: that our precognitive attunement and understanding is not (merely) a hardwired product of evolutionary "natural" development but is fundamentally inscribed in us by material practices that function as formative rituals.[46] And some rituals ratchet up to "liturgies" when they inscribe in us "trumping" construals of what matters. On this point, I think Charles Taylor provides further help as I try to make my case that we are "liturgical animals."

Love Takes Practice: Taylor on Bourdieu

Drawing on Heidegger and Wittgenstein, Taylor articulates his own critique of "intellectualism"—the working picture that sees "the human agent as primarily a subject of representations." This subject, he comments, "is a monological one. She or he is in contact with an 'outside' world, including other agents, the objects she or he and they may deal with, her or his own and others' bodies, but this contact is through the representations she or he has 'within.'" As a result, "what 'I' am, as a being capable of having such representations, the inner space itself, is definable independently of body or other." And it is just "this stripped-down view of the subject which has made deep inroads into social science" and "stands in the way of a richer, more adequate understanding of what the human sense of self is really like and hence of a proper understanding of the real variety of human culture

---

45   What Mark Johnson refers to as "the new sciences of embodied mind" (*Meaning of the Body*, xi). Cp. Francisco J. Varela et al., *The Embodied Mind: Cognitive Science and Human Experience* (Cambridge, Mass.: MIT Press, 1992).
46   I do not at all deny that there is an evolutionary basis for just how and why there is a bodily basis for "meaning." See MacIntyre, *Dependent, Rational Animals*, and Okrent, *Rational Animals*. I just mean to emphasize that "mood" and "understanding" are also inscribed by cultural systems of formation.

48   The Nicene Option

and so of a knowledge of human beings."[47] I would add that this especially stands in the way of an adequate understanding of religion.

"To obey a rule," on such an intellectualist account, involves an agent cognitively processing the rule, "knowing" what it means, knowing the reasons for obeying, then consciously and intentionally choosing to obey the rule—and if asked *why* one did that, one must be able to articulate reasons. In contrast, Taylor is intrigued by Wittgenstein's cryptic claim that "'obeying a rule' is a practice." At some point, Wittgenstein emphasizes, we can no longer give reasons for what we're doing.[48] But, Taylor emphasizes, that doesn't mean we lack *understanding*; this doesn't mean that there isn't a certain "sense" to our actions and practices. It's just that this "sense" is *unarticulated*, and even unarticul*able*. But, given the sorts of animals we are, even this "make[s] a kind of sense"—it constitutes "a kind of unarticulated sense of things."[49]

One can see how this "unarticulated sense" resonates with Heidegger's account of mood and precognitive understanding,[50] but Taylor's model is more attuned to the acquisition of such unarticulated understanding. In particular, he emphasizes that "this puts the role of the body in a new light. Our body is not just the executant of the goals we frame or just the locus of the causal factors which shape our representations. Our understanding itself is embodied." This constitutes a "bodily know-how" which is irreducible and which "encodes" our understanding of self and world.[51] Not surprisingly, Taylor here avails himself of Bourdieu's notion of *habitus* in order provide an account of how our "background understanding" is acquired, shaped, and formed. And like Bourdieu, Taylor is attentive to *rituals*, from "micro" rituals of saying "hello" to macro-rituals of "a political or religious movement."[52] On the one hand, such rituals

---

47   Taylor, "To Follow a Rule . . . ," 49. Interestingly, with respect to Taylor's particular account of emotions, Kevin Sludds criticizes Taylor's picture as still too cognitivist. See Sludds, *Emotions*, 131–35.
48   Sludds, *Emotions*, 47, citing *Philosophical Investigations*, §§202, 211, 217.
49   Taylor, "To Follow a Rule . . . ," 48.
50   Taylor explicitly invokes Heidegger's parallel account of "understanding" (*Verstehen*) in this context. See "To Follow a Rule . . . ," 50; cp. *Secular Age*, 172–73: social imaginaries constitute just this sort of "understanding."
51   Taylor, "To Follow a Rule . . . ," 50.
52   Taylor, "To Follow a Rule . . . ," 51–52. Taylor's conjunction of "political or religious" in this context hints at what I'm suggesting here: not only do religious rituals have similar features to "secular" (e.g., political) rituals, but secular rituals can also bear

have a "sense" about them which is absorbed through doing; the practices become ritualized. On the other hand, the rituals "carry" an understanding and thus we absorb this understanding through the ritual. One can see how this resonates with what Taylor will later describe as "social imaginaries." The social imaginary is "much broader and deeper than the intellectual schemes people may entertain when they *think* about social reality in a disengaged mode."[53] Rather, the social imaginary is meant to indicate "the ways people *imagine* their social existence, how they fit together with others, how things go on between them and their fellows, the expectations that are normally met," etc.[54] Taylor describes this as an "imaginary" in order to refer to "the way ordinary people 'imagine' their social surroundings," which is "not expressed in theoretical terms, but is carried in images, stories, and legends."[55] Most importantly, he emphasizes a dynamic relationship between understanding and practice: "If the understanding makes the practice possible, it is also true that it is the practice that largely carries the understanding."[56] Or, to put it otherwise, the understanding is "implicit in practice." As Taylor remarks, "Humans operated with a social imaginary well before they ever got into the business of theorizing about themselves."[57]

Returning to Bourdieu, Taylor emphasizes that to say that a practice or ritual "carries" an understanding within it is *not* to say that it houses a proposition that is just waiting to be articulated. The practice or ritual is not an "expression" or "application" of what is otherwise known by other means. When one "follows a rule," one is not "applying" what one cognitively knows. Rather, "the 'rule' lies essentially *in* the practice. The rule is what is animating the practice at any given time, not some formulation behind it, inscribed in our thoughts or our brains or our genes or whatever."[58] The rule only exists *in* the practice; it cannot be adequately distilled into some other cognitive, intellectual form. Similarly, a *habitus*

---

similarities to religious rituals, not in terms of transcendence but in terms of *ultimacy* and *identity formation*.
53   Charles Taylor, *Modern Social Imaginaries* (Durham: Duke University Press, 2004), 23, emphasis added.
54   Taylor, *Modern Social Imaginaries*, 23, emphasis added.
55   Taylor, *Modern Social Imaginaries*, 23.
56   Taylor, *Modern Social Imaginaries*, 25.
57   Taylor, *Modern Social Imaginaries*, 26.
58   Taylor, "To Follow a Rule . . . ," 58.

is a bodily disposition that "encodes a certain cultural understanding."[59] The ritual doesn't "contain" or "express" an interpretation; it *is* an interpretation, an irreducible "take" on the world that can never be adequately articulated otherwise.

How would this make a difference in the way we conceive "religion" in sociology of religion or philosophy of religion? I note just two implications: First, most obviously, we would do well to see religion as an "understanding" or "social imaginary" that is carried in rituals and practices and inscribed through bodily practices. But second, and going beyond Taylor, I suggest that we consider "religious" those rituals that carry a sense of *ultimacy* about them; that is, I think we might be able to demarcate rituals of *ultimate concern*. Rituals would be rituals of ultimate concern insofar as they carry within them a sense of "what matters" (Heidegger), which also mean to *trump* other, competing construals—and which therefore mean to be *identity-constituting*, to mark the practitioners as *those sorts of people*. To put it otherwise, we might simply say that some rituals are "thin" whereas others are "thick," where "thick" rituals are those that organize the plethora of thin, seemingly neutral practices we engage in. And if "religious" rituals are not just rituals that deal with the transcendent or the afterlife or the holy, etc., but those rituals which mean to be *trumping* rituals, then we will begin to see "religion" even in some aspects of "the secular."

In a way, I have been trying to displace our identification of religion with "transcendence" or "the otherworldly" and, instead, connect it to matters of *ultimacy*. In addition, I have tried to show that human behavior and practice is shaped and driven by a kind of teleology that is more fundamentally affective than intellectual: that we construe and interpret our world and our place within it on a register closer to love than logic—and such orientations are inscribed and absorbed through material, communal practices. In short, we learn to love something *as* ultimate ("trumping") through rituals of ultimate concern. And it's this nexus of ultimacy and its rituals that I want to describe as "religious." The reason to employ "liturgy" in this sense is to raise the stakes of what's happening in a range of cultural practices and rituals. Insofar as they aim to shape our desire and specify our ultimate concern, they function as nothing less than liturgies. Above we emphasized the importance of seeing what might appear to be

---

59 Taylor, "To Follow a Rule . . . ," 58.

"thin" practices (such as shopping at the mall, attending a football game, or taking part in "frosh week" at university) as, in fact, thick practices that are identity-forming and telos-laden. We need to then take that recognition one step further and recognize these thick practices as *liturgical* in order to appreciate their *religious* nature. Such ritual forces of culture are not satisfied with being merely mundane; embedded in them is a sense of what ultimately matters. Just because they are "worldly" doesn't mean that they don't function religiously. "Secular"[60] liturgies are fundamentally formative and constitute a *hermeneutic of ultimacy*.

Secular Formations

My task has been to consider the shape of a "post-secular" philosophy of religion or sociology of religion. This might simply require that these disciplines relinquish any Enlightenment claim to unbiased neutrality that is usually associated with the requirement of "secular" scholarship. In that sense, any philosophy or sociology that appreciated something like the "hermeneutic turn" would be, effectively, post-secular.[61] On this account, post-foundationalism entails post-secularism. But this seems insufficient.

I have intentionally decided not to run with this epistemological version of the argument (though I do think it is a viable approach). Instead, I am suggesting that a "post-secular" turn in the social sciences will not only be concerned with the conditions of "science"; it must also retool its conception of "religion." This stems from rejecting the intellectualist anthropology that attends secularism and opting instead for something like Heidegger and Taylor's affective, embodied anthropology which recognizes the central role of the precognitive and its embodied formation through ritual. Once we make that move, then even much that claims to be "secular" will be seen *as religious*—not in the sense that it is covertly concerned with transcendence or the gods or the afterlife, but insofar as we can discern secular rituals and practices which have an affective, formative power that shapes how

---

60 I use the term loosely since one of the implications of this analysis is that, in fact, there is no secular. If humans are essentially liturgical animals, and cultural institutions are liturgical institutions, then there are no "secular" (a- or non-religious) institutions. By describing them as "secular" liturgies I am heuristically conceding to some common habits of thought.
61 Cp. Christian Smith's account of a post-foundationalist *and therefore* post-secular social science in *Moral, Believing Animals* (New York: Oxford University Press, 2003), 45–61.

practitioners construe "what [ultimately] matters." Insofar as these constitute rituals of ultimate concern, I'm suggesting that we describe them as "secular liturgies." In short, I suggest that our accounts will be post-secular just to the extent that we relinquish the notion that "the secular" is *a*religious.

But what's the upshot of this admittedly contentious and provocative suggestion? What's to be gained? I see at least two potential gains from this move: (1) it critically unmasks the naïve conceit which posits any simple distinction between "the religious" and "the secular" on the basis of particular doctrines or beliefs (e.g., concerning gods or transcendence); and (2) it prompts sociologists of religion to train their eyes to see religion (i.e., formative liturgies) at work where we haven't previously been inclined to look, which should then also reshape current discussions regarding policy which naïvely posit a sphere of discourse or action that is areligious. Ultimately, I want to suggest that humans are essentially liturgical animals. What's at issue, then, is not *whether* we engage in rituals of ultimate concern, but *which*. In this sense, we have never been secular. The "post-secular" would be a recognition of this fact.

I grant that my suggestion of "secular liturgies" will not be enthusiastically received. Some will protest that this feels like a kind of theological colonialism: why can I not just let atheists be atheists and naturalists, naturalists? But of course, I am: I am just suggesting that atheists and naturalists are still *religious*, shaped and primed by rituals that amount to liturgies. I don't mean to thereby suggest that they are "anonymous Christians" or "implicit" Catholics. I just don't think they can escape being liturgical animals. Those who resist my thesis cling to a conception of "the secular" as *a*religious because, implicitly, they continue to operate with an "intellectualist" understanding of religion. They still tend to identify "religion" with particular beliefs and doctrines, especially beliefs and doctrines concerning gods and transcendence. But if this "attendant anthropology" is put into question, then this intellectualist picture of religion *and "the secular"* must also be put in question. It is this move, I think, that "secular" critics are unwilling to make.[62]

---

62 One thinks here of Gourgouris, but we might also consider Talal Asad's proposal in *Formations of the Secular: Christianity, Islam, Modernity* (Stanford, Calif.: Stanford University Press, 2003). See my critique in James K. A. Smith, "Secularity, Religion, and the Politics of Ambiguity: A Review Essay," *Journal of Cultural and Religious Theory* 6, no. 3 (2005): 116–21.

3

Continental Philosophy of Religion

Prescriptions for a Healthy Subdiscipline

As already discussed, over the past twenty years there has been a burgeoning of work in philosophy of religion that has drawn upon and been oriented by continental sources in philosophy—associated with figures such as Edmund Husserl, Martin Heidegger, Jacques Derrida, Emmanuel Levinas, Jean-Luc Marion, Gilles Deleuze, Gianni Vattimo, and many others. One could identify the rumbling of this thirty years ago in Jean-Luc Marion's landmark work *L'idole et la distance* (1977) or in the earlier and influential work of Jewish philosopher Emmanuel Levinas.[1] In fact, elements of such "continental" (or, more specifically, phenomenological) engagements with religious phenomena can already been seen in Husserl and Heidegger.[2] In North America, this continental impetus has generated a lively discourse and secondary literature. One might suggest that the 1997 publication of John D. Caputo's *The Prayers and Tears of Jacques Derrida* was something of a "coming out" party for a field or sub-discipline

---

1   For helpful discussion, see Jeffrey L. Kosky, *Levinas and the Philosophy of Religion* (Bloomington: Indiana University Press, 2001).
2   Rudolf Schmitz-Perrin notes the religious motivation behind Husserl's phenomenology in "La phenomenology et ses marges religieuses: la correspondance d'Edmund Husserl," *Studies in Religion/Sciences Religieuses* 25 (1996): 481–88. For a helpful overview of the early Heidegger on these matters, see Merold Westphal, "Heidegger's 'Theologische Jugendschriften,'" *Research in Phenomenology* 27 (1997): 247–61.

sometimes referred to as "continental philosophy of religion"[3]—though such discourse had already been sustained in the work of Robert Sokolowski, Edith Wyschogrod, Merold Westphal, Morny Joy, Carl Raschke, Adriaan Peperzaak, Pamela Sue Anderson, Mark C. Taylor, and others.[4] And it has only continued to grow.

I think this is a significant development and one that should be welcomed by the community of Christian philosophers. Continental figures provide unique theoretical frameworks and resources for "faith seeking understanding,"[5] not least because so many continental figures, such as Heidegger and Levinas, were significantly shaped by religious imaginations, even if their relationship to religious institutions was tenuous. There are important resonances, for instance, between the hermeneutic tradition stemming from Heidegger, Gadamer, and Ricoeur and both

---

3   I have no stake in defending this nomenclature, and grant that the category of "continental" is contested. Nonetheless, I think the term has a heuristic value and it has become a standard reference. See, for instance, Philip Goodchild, "Continental Philosophy of Religion: An Introduction," in *Rethinking Philosophy of Religion: Approaches from Continental Philosophy*, ed. Philip Goodchild (New York: Fordham University Press, 2002), 1–39; Deane-Peter Baker and Patrick Maxwell, eds., *Explorations in Contemporary Continental Philosophy of Religion* (Dordrecht: Rodopi, 2003); Merold Westphal, "Continental Philosophy of Religion," in *The Oxford Handbook of Philosophy of Religion*, ed. William J. Wainwright (Oxford: Oxford University Press, 2005), 472–93; Eugene Thomas Long, ed., *Self and Other: Essays in Continental Philosophy of Religion* (Dordrecht: Springer, 2007) [a reprint of *International Journal for Philosophy of Religion* 60, nos. 1–3 (2006)]; and Nick Trakakis, "Meta-Philosophy of Religion: The Analytic-Continental Divide in Philosophy of Religion," *Ars Disputandi* [http://www.ArsDisputandi.org] 7 (2007), esp. §§45–57. Cp. also John D. Caputo, ed., *The Religious*, Blackwell Readings in Continental Philosophy (Oxford: Blackwell, 2001).

4   John D. Caputo, *The Prayers and Tears of Jacques Derrida: Religion without Religion* (Bloomington: Indiana University Press, 1997); Robert Sokolowski, *Eucharistic Presence: A Study in the Theology of Disclosure* (Washington, DC: Catholic University of America Press, 1994); Merold Westphal, *Overcoming Onto-Theology*, Perspectives in Continental Philosophy (New York: Fordham University Press, 2001); Adriaan Peperzak, *Ethics as First Philosophy: The Significance of Emmanuel Levinas for Philosophy, Literature, and Religion* (London: Routledge, 1995). Without any hope of being comprehensive, one should also note the work of Carl Raschke, Charles Winquist, Mark C. Taylor, and many others. See particularly Raschke, ed., *Deconstruction and Theology* (New York: Crossroad, 1982), and idem, ed., *New Dimensions in Philosophical Theology* (Chico, Calif.: Scholars Press, 1982). One might argue, as Trakakis does (§46), that this flourishing of continental philosophy of religion represents the materialization of what Merold Westphal called for in an early essay, "Prolegomena to Any Future Philosophy of Religion Which Will Be Able to Come Forth as Prophecy," *International Journal for Philosophy of Religion* 4 (1973): 129–50.

5   Contra R. R. Reno, "Theology's Continental Captivity," *First Things*, April 2006, 26–33.

Catholic theological emphases on the role of tradition and Reformed epistemology's emphasis on "control beliefs" that govern knowing. Husserl's phenomenological framework provides helpful theoretical tools for considerations of religious experience.[6] And of late, voices in European philosophy have turned their attention to specifically religious figures and texts: from Derrida's engagements with Kierkegaard and Augustine, to Badiou's and Agamben's provocative readings of St. Paul.[7]

A scan of *Faith and Philosophy*, one of the gold-standard journals in philosophy of religion, or a skim of recent programs of the Society for Christian Philosophers might not (yet) indicate this, but this growing field has generated important alternative or specialized venues for scholarship and conversation. The Society for Continental Philosophy and Theology hosts stand-alone conferences and sessions in collaboration with the APA, ACPA, and SPEP.[8] In addition, the American Academy of Religion is home to the Theology and Continental Philosophy Group, and meetings of the Society of Christian Philosophers at both the APA and AAR have been increasingly open to continental philosophy of religion. Work in continental philosophy of religion has appeared in leading ("mainstream") journals such as *Faith and Philosophy* and *International Journal for Philosophy of Religion*,[9] as well as journals such as *Modern Theology* and the *Journal for Cultural and Religious Theory*. The field now touts its own journal, *The Journal for Continental Philosophy of Religion*. There are also several book series that have been primary venues for the field, particularly the Indiana Series in Philosophy of Religion (edited by Merold Westphal), Fordham University Press' Perspectives in Continental

---

6 In addition to Otto's classic work *The Idea of the Holy*, cp. more recent proposals in this vein such as James K. A. Smith, *Speech and Theology: Language and the Logic of Incarnation* (London: Routledge, 2002), and Anthony J. Steinbock, *Phenomenology and Mysticism: The Verticality of Religious Experience* (Bloomington: Indiana University Press, 2007).
7 Jacques Derrida, *The Gift of Death*, trans. David Wills (Chicago: University of Chicago Press, 1994); Giorgio Agamben, *The Time That Remains: A Commentary on the Letter to the Romans*, trans. Patricia Dailey (Stanford: Stanford University Press, 2005); Alain Badiou, *Saint Paul: The Foundation of Universalism*, trans. Ray Brassier (Stanford: Stanford University Press, 2003).
8 The fruit of SCPT conferences can be seen in books such as Bruce Ellis Benson and Norman Wirzba, eds., *The Phenomenology of Prayer*, Perspectives in Continental Philosophy (New York: Fordham University Press, 2005), and idem, *Transforming Philosophy and Religion: Love's Wisdom*, Indiana Series in Philosophy of Religion (Bloomington: Indiana University Press, 2008).
9 See Long, ed., *Self and Other*, for a selection of essays from *IJPR*.

Philosophy series (edited by John D. Caputo), and most recently the Columbia University Press series Insurrections: Critical Studies in Religion, Politics, and Culture (edited by Slavoj Žižek, Clayton Crockett, Creston Davis, and Jeffrey W. Robbins).

Suffice it to say, continental philosophy of religion is a lively and growing field. Furthermore, I think the field of continental philosophy of religion has enough of a history—and certainly enough momentum—that some critical reflection on "the state of the field" is warranted. Intending to stimulate dialogue, I want to briefly and selectively take stock of the field of continental philosophy of religion and suggest that the field is developing some unhealthy patterns that threaten to compromise its viability as a properly scholarly conversation. In particular, I worry that the field is becoming increasingly insular, reactionary, and (ironically)[10] monolithic.

The burden of this brief chapter is to suggest a bit of a prescription for the future health of this important field.[11] This is offered as an essay, and makes no claims to being comprehensive or exhaustive. Instead, it works from impressions of certain trends in the field as seen from the perspective of one immersed in the conversation. It is offered in the spirit of dialogue. In particular, I will address six areas of concern; more specifically, I will suggest that if continental philosophy of religion is to grow and advance—and be heard at the larger philosophical table—it is imperative that continental philosophers of religion develop six key habits or practices of scholarship.

---

10   I say "ironically" because so much of continental philosophy is taken with the notion of "difference," including continental philosophy of religion. And yet it seems to me that much of what we get in the name of difference is just more of the same; and in fact, the conversations tend to be inhospitable to approaches that call into question the regnant paradigms.
11   In doing so, I don't mean to take on the mantle of paternalistic physician (to which critics will no doubt reply, "Heal thyself!"). I recognize that even suggesting this critique seems to put me in the position of someone who thinks they have "authority" to speak to "the field." In fact, I do not presume such (I resisted the temptation to title this "Advice to Continental Philosophers"!). Instead, as a practitioner invested in the field I want to merely offer an anecdotal diagnosis of the field and suggest some practices in response. Both are offered in the spirit of "conversation starters." For some initial conversation, see Bruce Ellis Benson, "A Response to Smith's 'Continental Philosophy of Religion: Prescriptions for a Healthy Subdiscipline,'" *Faith and Philosophy* 26 (2009): 449–56, and my "The End of Enclaves: A Reply to Benson," *Faith and Philosophy* 26 (2009): 457–61.

(1) *Continental philosophers of religion should seek training and formation that is rigorous, pluralistic, and rooted in the history of philosophy.* The shape of scholarship in continental philosophy of religion is, to some extent, an effect of the training that continental philosophers of religion receive. So if continental philosophy of religion exhibits worrisome patterns, we do well to consider the formation and education of those working in the field. That is, we need to carefully consider the shape of the "curriculum," so to speak. In this respect, I think that some of the worst habits that are exhibited in continental philosophy of religion (insularity, a propensity to retreat to enclaves, and an ironic hostility to difference and critique) are to some extent products of graduate training that exhibit the same characteristics. Some continental philosophers of religion receive training in departments of religious studies that lack rigorous structures of accountability in philosophy, particularly the history of philosophy; the result can sometimes be a kind of philosophy without accountability.[12] Others (like myself) are trained in philosophy programs that are exclusively "continental" and thus insulated from (and often hostile to) broader discussions in (analytic) philosophy of religion. But it seems to me that philosophy of religion will profit from structures and education that brings together the resources and riches of both analytic and continental approaches. Granted, I think this also entails some revised habits and practices in analytic philosophy of religion (which is de facto the majority culture in philosophy of religion) learning to welcome continental philosophy of religion as a partner in its work. This should also be reciprocated: those engaged in continental philosophy of religion should be looking for training and formation that will enable them to engage philosophers of religion more broadly. This will require both learning a sort of "second language" as well as a stance that sees analytic philosophy of religion as a legitimate project (though not impervious to critique). Such collaboration will not be well-served by caricatures or stereotypes from either side.[13]

12 I owe this phrase to my colleague Lee Hardy (who, admittedly, was discussing much of the work that happens in "theory" programs in literature).
13 For example, I do not think it is constructive to denigrate logical or propositional analysis as such, even if continental philosophers of religion will worry about a reductionism that sometimes attends such models. Consider, for instance, this take on the situation from John D. Caputo: "The talk about God and religion in contemporary continental philosophy bears almost no resemblance to what passes for traditional 'philosophy of religion.' The latter has typically concerned itself with offering proofs for the immortality of the soul and for the existence of God. . . . This tradition, which goes back to the scholastic debates

And it seems to me that graduate school—a particularly intense period of formation where deep-grained habits take hold—is the place to form good, generous habits of collaboration and conversation. This requires an environment, resources, and curriculum to sustain such formation.

I would suggest that continental philosophy of religion would be strengthened and deepened if those seeking training in the field matriculated in graduate programs in philosophy that are intentionally pluralistic, providing training not only in continental philosophy but also the history of philosophy as well as the *lingua franca* of philosophy of religion today, which will require training in analytic philosophy as well. Graduate formation will be the first opportunity to enact study and conversation across the analytic-continental divide. Those being formed in graduate programs of religion or religious studies would do well to enter programs and departments which have constructive relationships with philosophy departments.

(2) *Continental philosophers of religion should consistently submit their work to the rigors of peer review and revalue the journal article as a central arena for discourse.* Here my concern is the proliferation of edited volumes of essays that increasingly seem to be the publishing venue of choice in continental philosophy of religion.[14] (And I say this as one who has both edited and contributed to such collections.) While such edited

---

of the high middle ages, is largely perpetuated today in the works of contemporary Anglo-American philosophers, who offer the old wine of metaphysical theology in the new bottles of analytic philosophy.... We on the continental side of this divide have sworn off that sort of thing" (Caputo, "Introduction" to *The Religious*, 2). Construals of the terrain in philosophy of religion such as Caputo's recent analysis are not particularly conducive to the kind of collaboration I am suggesting here. Nor are they encouraged by the caricatures of postmodern thought proffered by, say, Alvin Plantinga in *Warranted Christian Belief* (Oxford: Oxford University Press, 2000), 422–37.

14 In addition to work already cited above, see, for example, Phillip Blond, ed., *Post-Secular Philosophy: Between Philosophy and Theology* (London: Routledge, 1998); John D. Caputo and Michael J. Scanlon, eds., *God, the Gift, and Postmodernism* (Bloomington: Indiana University Press, 1999); John D. Caputo, Mark Dooley, and Michael J. Scanlon, eds., *Questioning God* (Bloomington: Indiana University Press, 2001); James H. Olthuis, ed., *Religion with/out Religion: The Prayers and Tears of John D. Caputo* (London: Routledge, 2002); Jeffrey Bloechl, ed., *Religious Experience and the End of Metaphysics* (Bloomington: Indiana University Press, 2003); Kevin Hart and Barbara Wall, eds., *The Experience of God: A Postmodern Response* (New York: Fordham University Press, 2005); John Panteleimon Manoussakis, ed., *After God: Richard Kearney and the Religious Turn in Continental Philosophy* (New York: Fordham University Press, 2006); and Conor Cunningham and Peter M. Candler, Jr., eds., *Transcendence and Phenomenology* (London: SCM Press, 2007).

volumes are published by university presses and include important, constructive work, as can be the case in any field, the process of peer review for such volumes seems to sometimes lack the same rigor and controls as journals.[15] Instead, such collections tend to be repetitions of the usual suspects—and also tend to be quite predictable, merely new riffs on an established line. In addition, the proliferation of edited volumes results in the loss of any "center of gravity" for the conversation in continental philosophy of religion. Because discussions are sequestered in books, we lose the opportunity to cultivate journals as "go-to" venues for ongoing conversations (as, for instance, *Faith and Philosophy* has "hosted" ongoing discussions of Reformed epistemology, *Religious Studies* has been the go-to venue for discussion of miracles, etc.). Furthermore, edited volumes lack the opportunity for continuing a critical conversation that publication in peer-reviewed journals offers. Continental philosophers of religion would serve the conversation by submitting to the rigors (and frustrations!) of peer-reviewed, journal-based publishing.

(3) *Continental philosophers of religion should seek to publish their work in more "mainstream" channels.* One of the most detrimental trends in continental philosophy of religion is a set of habits that encourages "preaching to the choir" (this is related to point 4 below). The field tends to retreat to enclaves, setting up alternative societies and meetings and publishing in "friendly" (read: "controlled") venues. The result is a sectarian insularity: continental philosophers of religion talk only to themselves. Granted, I think the same is true in the majority culture of analytic philosophy of religion, which is usually just as insulated from dissenting voices. The result on both sides is a kind of tribal insularity. As a result, they often encounter little resistance or critique—a state of affairs that is generally detrimental to good scholarship. But equally importantly, by working and publishing in such enclaves, continental philosophers of religion are also missing opportunities to encounter, challenge, and contribute to broader conversations in philosophy of religion.

By seeking to present their work in venues that are more broadly constituted (regional meetings of the Society of Christian Philosophers, the

---

15 For instance, peer review of edited volumes is almost never double blind; furthermore, it is more easily commandeered by networks of nepotism. (It's difficult for me to be more specific about this without compromising the peer-review process.) That said, I have no illusions about peer review as some kind of guarantee for quality scholarship. Granted, analytic philosophy is not immune to problems in this regard.

Philosophy of Religion Section of the AAR, etc.), and by aiming to publish in more mainstream journals (such as *Faith and Philosophy*, *Religious Studies*, *International Journal for Philosophy of Religion*, etc.), continental philosophers of religion will both open themselves to critique (which is a scholarly virtue) and create opportunities to contribute to the field as a whole (including the opportunity to critique regnant paradigms on their own turf, rather than getting away with caricatured critiques within a safe enclave that is little more than an echo chamber).[16] This will require doing some translation work, relinquishing the ease and comfort of in-house jargon, but without requiring that we relinquish the unique "genius" of continental sources and traditions of inquiry.[17]

(4) *Continental philosophers of religion should move beyond the "essay" and take responsibility for literature review as integral to their work.* As a continental philosopher of religion, I must to confess to one facet of "analytic envy": I have been deeply impressed by the tight sense of the "state of the field" that characterizes certain subfields of analytic philosophy. In particular, conversations in analytic philosophy always begin with a literature review that considers the *status quaestionis* for a particular question or problem. Every article must make an original contribution to the field, and in order to make an *original* contribution it needs to (a) take account of all earlier, relevant contributions and (b) make an argument that *advances* this contribution. Granted, for many philosophers this is standard practice, but I have been struck by the common absence of such a practice in continental philosophy of religion. In particular, "essays" in continental philosophy of religion offer "new" perspectives that often fail to take account of either (a) earlier contributions that make the same argument or (b) earlier arguments that have already demonstrated the paucity or faulty nature of the supposedly "new" contribution. Continental philosophy of religion could be revolutionized if we would just adopt

---

16 My criticism of certain trends in continental philosophy of religion is by no means intended to give a "free pass" to analytic philosophy of religion. Nor am I suggesting the continental philosophy of religion would "get it right" if it would just get in line with the analytic school.

17 When I review (and, sadly, often reject) "continental" articles for various philosophy of religion journals, I usually point authors to the work of Merold Westphal as an exemplar of just what I am describing here. For just two examples, see Merold Westphal, "Taking Plantinga Seriously," *Faith and Philosophy* 16 (1999): 173–81; and idem, "Christian Philosophers and the Copernican Revolution," in *Christian Perspectives on Religious Knowledge*, ed. C. Stephen Evans and Merold Westphal (Grand Rapids: Eerdmans, 1993): 161–79.

the literature review as a standard procedure—and if the peer review process required this for publication.

(5) *Continental philosophers of religion should move beyond "victimhood" and embrace critique.* Continental philosophers of religion—like continental philosophers in general—tend to construe certain types of criticism of their work as a kind of persecution for their "continental" commitments. As such, we tend to assume a "victim" mentality—which then drives our retreat into insulated enclaves and the comfort of the choir. Granted, the philosophical establishment in North America is governed by "analytic" practices and assumptions. And I would also grant that, at times, this does translate into biases and prejudices that ideologically reject continental discourse. However, not all critique is ideologically driven; some of it is *philosophically* warranted. And continental philosophers should welcome *that* kind of critique, for it is philosophical critique that advances the field.

(6) *Continental philosophy of religion should encourage authentic pluralism.* Despite mantras of "difference," I have been struck by a creeping hegemony in contemporary continental philosophy of religion. The field has developed an oddly monolithic flavor—one that tends to be dominated by a particular version of "religion" or spirituality that is allergic to the determinate religious institutions and traditions. In most cases this stems from a certain Derridean understanding of "religion without religion," but it can also be informed by the work of Vattimo or others.[18] Philosophies of religion that would be more properly Catholic are almost ruled out of court; indeed, they will be considered "unorthodox" vis-à-vis the regnant orthodoxy of "religion without religion" or "secular" theology.[19] But such a narrow and monolithic construal of the field is debilitating

---

18 Other streams are developing, including work in philosophy of religion in dialogue with non-phenomenological figures such as Deleuze, Žižek, and Badiou.
19 For instance, nothing raises the hackles of continental philosophers of religion more than Radical Orthodoxy. See, for instance, Clayton Crockett's "Introduction" to *Religion and Violence in a Secular World*, ed. Clayton Crockett (Charlottesville: University of Virginia Press, 2006), 10–13; John D. Caputo, "What Do I Love when I Love My God? Deconstruction and Radical Orthodoxy," in *Questioning God*, ed. John D. Caputo, Michael Scanlon, and Mark Dooley (Bloomington: Indiana University Press, 2001), 291–317, and the recent exchange between Elizabeth Castelli and Graham Ward in *Journal of the American Academy of Religion* 74 (2006): 179–93. The one thing that is heterodox for continental philosophy of religion is orthodoxy; see ch. 4 below.

for the conversation. Continental philosophers of religion should seek to encourage a bigger tent and foster a genuine pluralism within the field.

My sense and hope is that the field of continental philosophy of religion is healthy enough to both absorb critical discussion of our own habits and practices. This dialogue essay is offered as a means to get the conversation started, with the hope and desire of strengthening an important field within philosophy of religion.

4

A Logic of Incarnation

The Nicene Option in Continental Philosophy of Religion

Two Cheers for Postmodernism

Postmodernism, for me, is a shorthand reference to a constellation of philosophical sources and sensibilities emanating largely from France that, in the light of earlier German critiques (particularly in the work of Martin Heidegger), articulate various criticisms of "modern" frameworks that first emerged in the late Middle Ages and gained steam in the early modern period, up through the various Enlightenments (German, French, English, and Scottish). In other words, I take the "post" to be quite humble and responsible: this is not the announcement of a new era or of any radical rupture with the past, not the inbreaking of an unprecedented epoch nor the overturning of the entire philosophical tradition, and certainly not any kind of a messianic arrival of a god who will finally save us. But it does name a sense that "something's going on," both within philosophical discussions and on the ground in lived practice.

With respect to the latter, I think it is helpful to make a further heuristic distinction between postmodern*ism* as a constellation of philosophical and theoretical discourses and postmodern*ity* as another loose heuristic label for a plethora of cultural phenomena that are associated with late modernity: the globalization of markets and the homogenization of commercial cultures, the exponential development of technology (particularly communications technology), the ubiquity of new media, etc.[1] I take these phenomena to be the fruit and culmination of shifts effected in modernity. In the same way, while postmodern*ism* represents a critique *of* modernity, the philosophical voices of postmodernism certainly didn't accomplish any acrobatic rupture with respect to modernity; both Foucault and Derrida, for instance, would later identify their own work as extensions of modernity, situated within the Enlightenment project.[2] But one has to take such claims with a grain of salt since these "new" Enlightenments are also trenchant critiques of much of the founding *animus* of modernity. All this is just to say that things are messy: there is no neat-and-tidy school of "postmodernist" philosophers; there is no creed or manifesto of postmodernism and there are no party members required to heed a defined party line; postmodernism is not a radical, clean break from modernism, though it is a radical critique of modernity; and much that goes under the banner of "postmodern" is, in fact, the manifestation of the flowering of modernity (or its going to seed, depending on how you want to look at it).

My work has been concerned with discerning just what postmodernism means for theology, Christian philosophy, and the lived practice of the church's worship and discipleship. Undertaken in the spirit of "understanding the times" (1 Chr 12:32), I hope I have articulated a somewhat nuanced stance that boils down to something like this:

> *Insofar as* the church (and *mutatis mutandis*, Christian theology and philosophy) has bought into key assumptions of modernity;
>
> *And insofar as* these assumptions (for instance, regarding the nature of freedom, the model of the human person, the requirements for what counts as "rational" or "true," or what can be admitted to the "public" sphere of political or academic discourse) represent a rejection of biblical wisdom and the Christian theological heritage;
>
> *And insofar as* postmodernism articulates a critique of just these assumptions;

---

1 See James K. A. Smith, *Who's Afraid of Postmodernism? Taking Derrida, Lyotard, and Foucault to Church* (Grand Rapids: Baker Academic, 2006), 20n8.
2 See Smith, *Who's Afraid of Postmodernism?* 95–99; and James K. A. Smith, *Jacques Derrida: Live Theory* (London: Continuum, 2005), 88–91.

Then the postmodern critique of modernity is something to be affirmed by Christians, not *because* it is postmodern,[3] but because the postmodern critique of modernity can be a wakeup call for Christians to see their complicity with modernity, the inconsistency of this with a more integral understanding of discipleship, and thus actually be an occasion to creatively retrieve ancient and premodern theological sources and liturgical practices with new eyes, as it were.

This is a kind of "two cheers" approach to postmodernism, sometimes mistaken as a "three cheers"[4] stance by critics, as if I enthusiastically and wholeheartedly embrace all that is "postmodern," without critique and without reservation. But the key term in this formulation is *insofar as*: there are no blank checks in my approach, though I grant that it would require some reading across my corpus (meager as it is) to get this picture. In particular, in books like *Jacques Derrida: Live Theory* and *Who's Afraid of Postmodernism?* I sought to provide a charitable exposition of Derrida and deconstruction as a corrective to reactionary misrepresentations of his work by both friends and critics, particularly in the fields of literature and theology/religious studies. In addition, I believe that Derrida presents significant constructive resources for thinking through a variety of issues and problems from a distinctly Christian perspective. As a result, both of these works have a positive, even somewhat apologetic, flavor that tends to let criticism of Derrida recede into the background—to the point that some have suggested that my reading of Derrida represents a certain domestication of his thought,

---

3   I have perhaps underemphasized this point, but it is an important one. In *Who's Afraid of Postmodernism?* while I sometimes used the phrase "postmodern church," my argument emphasized postmodernism represented a catalyst and an opportunity for the church to remember who she is. So it is decidedly not a question of the church getting "with it," getting hip, or getting "relevant" and up-to-date. I emphasize this here only because I think that amongst some other theologians and church leaders who are enthusiastic about postmodernism there is a lingering sense that this comes down to a matter of relevance—as if the shape of faithful discipleship is somehow determined by the need to "be postmodern." This is characteristic not only of literature associated with the "emerging" church, but also of theologians who are otherwise more careful.

4   I'm not sure how far one could run with this metaphor, but it strikes me that Merold Westphal and James Olthuis also have a "two cheers" approach (maybe 2.5 cheers), whereas John Caputo and Pete Rollins represent a "three cheers" model.

reducing the monstrous threat of deconstruction into the sort of thing that you can comfortably take home to your parents. But within *WAP*, one will also find a fairly strident critique of the "Derridean" strain of "deconstructive" theology that has dominated continental philosophy of religion.[5] One will also already find a critique of Derrida in *The Fall of Interpretation* (2000), extended and re-articulated in *Speech and Theology* (2002), and then focused on the issue of how to read and receive Augustine in *Introducing Radical Orthodoxy* (2004). The critique is even more incisive in scholarly articles directed to more specialist audiences, though even here I continue to affirm much in Derrida's work as an important catalyst for Christian thought.[6] So my "two cheers" approach is meant to be a critical appropriation of postmodernism and deconstruction that walks a long way with Derrida, but parts ways at a critical juncture—not out of a timidity or an unwillingness to "go all the way," but because of a principled critique of what I think are problems internal to Derrida's thought.[7]

If there is a unique contribution to contemporary philosophy of religion and theology in this project, it could be organized under what I'm calling "the logic of incarnation." My goal in this chapter is to provide a summary account of what I mean by the logic of incarnation, and why it is perhaps a unique position vis-à-vis postmodernism, and more specifically, in contrast to "deconstructive" theology. I will do so by trying to show how it contrasts with a more dominant paradigm, what I'll call a "logic of determination" that characterizes the work of Jacques Derrida and John D. Caputo—two figures whose work looms over my own, and who cast very long shadows over discussions in continental philosophy of religion as well as more on-the-ground discussions of faith and postmodernism. My goal is to crystallize what I have elsewhere described as the logic of incarnation, contrast it with the

---

5   Smith, *Who's Afraid of Postmodernism?* 116–27.
6   See chs. 5–10 below.
7   More specifically, I would also emphasize that my critique of Derrida is not just a "transcendent" critique; that is, I do not think I (only) say that Derrida is wrong because he disagrees with orthodox Christian "positions"; rather, I hope my critique is also an "immanent" critique which—like any deconstruction—points out internal tensions that threaten to implode the project, but thereby open space for a new reading to emerge. I take it that there is no better way to be faithful to Derrida than to deconstruct him (cp. James K. A. Smith, *The Fall of Interpretation: Philosophical Foundations for a Creational Hermeneutic* [Downers Grove, Ill.: InterVarsity Press, 2000], 126–27).

logic of determination, and then suggest why the former represents a Catholic, and more persistent, postmodernism.

Competing Logics: Determination and Incarnation

"Haunted" and Unapologetic Postmodernisms

One of the central features of the postmodern critique of modernity is an appreciation of our *finitude*—our situatedness in time and space, in bodies, in histories, in communities, and in traditions. We can never get (and never really had) a "God's-eye view" of the world; rather, our perception and engagement with the world—how we "constitute" the world, phenomenologists would say—is shaped, informed, and conditioned by our situatedness: we come to our experience with particular expectations and habits of perception, particular ways of intending the world that have been handed down to us, constituting a sort of "tradition." Thus one might say that postmodernism, owning up to our finitude, entails an appreciation of particularity and the difficulty of achieving the sort of universality that was craved by Enlightenment dreams of a universal *polis*, a rational cosmopolis, populated by rational citizens who all shared the same vision of the Good dictated by "pure" Reason.[8]

Now, I want to suggest that while any postmodern critique worth its salt will be significantly committed to this emphasis on finitude and particularity, just how one *evaluates* and *responds to* this situation of finitude will be a point of demarcation between two different kinds of postmodernism. One strain—and it is a strain I find in Derrida and Caputo—rightly recognizes the inescapability of our finitude and particularity, but nonetheless seems to remain haunted by the Enlightenment dream of universality and purity. This strain, I have suggested, is a less persistent postmodernism (a "timid"[9] postmodernism?), because though it appreciates the ineluctable

---

8   Granted, such a vision was animated by the best of intentions, viz., overcoming the violent divisions of religious *particularity* that spawned the "wars of religion." For a particularly lucid rendition of this story, see Mark Lilla, *The Stillborn God* (New York: Knopf, 2008). For an account that calls this standard story into question, see William Cavanaugh, "A Fire Strong Enough to Consume the House: The Wars of Religion and the Rise of the State," *Modern Theology* 11 (1995): 397–420. For my own critique of Lilla, see James K. A. Smith, "The Last Prophet of Leviathan," in Smith, *The Devil Reads Derrida and Other Essays on the University, the Church, Politics, and the Arts* (Grand Rapids: Eerdmans, 2009), 113–18.

9   This label is a bit playful, since "timid" postmodernists such as Caputo and Rollins actually take themselves to be more radical precisely because they're willing to question and abandon "orthodoxy." I am suggesting that this is not radical at all—it's a repetition and

nature of our finitude and particularity, it still seems to *evaluate* this situation as if it is regrettable, lamentable, and problematic—variously associating the conditions of finitude with violence and injustice. For instance, with respect to knowledge, such haunted (or timid) postmodernism reasons as follows: given that universal, God's-eye-view knowledge is impossible for finite beings; given that the Cartesian and Kantian dreams of pure, rational, universal knowledge are impossible, we must conclude that we *cannot know*. "We can only believe," they'll add, in pious tones, with hand on their breast, looking up to heaven like Botticelli's *St. Augustine*. But wait a second: just because God's-eye-view knowledge is impossible, why should we conclude that knowledge per se is impossible? Doesn't such a concession actually leave the modern construal of knowledge in place, albeit it as an impossible ideal? Can you see why one might suggest that this strain of timid postmodernism seems to be persistently haunted by (modern) ghosts?[10] Thus this strain of postmodernism might just amount to modernism in despair[11]—and even reflect a kind of hyper-modernism, with a pedigree that is both Humean and Kantian.[12]

Another strain[13] of postmodernism that I have tried to sketch evaluates this situation very differently: it also recognizes the ubiquity and inescapability of our finitude and particularity. But rather than lamenting this situation, and refusing to be haunted by the ghosts of such dreams, this more "persistent" postmodernism relinquishes the very *requirements* of universality and purity as constitutive of knowledge, justice, etc. In other

---

completion of the project undertaken by Kant (see Smith, "Re-Kanting Postmodernism"). And thus, in a spirit equally playful and dead serious, I am suggesting that vis-à-vis such a modern deracination of religion, it is a creative retrieval of orthodoxy that is more radical.

10   This critique is articulated more fully in *Who's Afraid of Postmodernism?* 116–46.

11   This formulation was suggested to me from a different context, viz., Kei Yoshida's critique of Clifford Geertz as a "positivist in despair" in "Defending Scientific Study of the Social: Against Clifford Geertz (and His Critics)," *Philosophy of the Social Sciences* 37 (2007): 290–300.

12   This is why the fruit of "deconstructive" theology sometimes feel remarkably similar to a very "modern" theologian such as Gordon Kaufman.

13   This is not at all to suggest that there are only two possibilities; there are certainly still other "postmodernisms," including the post-postmodernism of, say, Badiou. We might also do well to go back and reconsider Rorty's pragmatism as a sort of postmodernism that is less haunted by these modern ghosts. For a relevant discussion, see Vaden House, *Without God or His Doubles: Realism, Relativism, and Rorty* (Leiden: Brill, 1994); Ronald Kuipers, *Richard Rorty*, Bloomsbury Contemporary American Thinkers (London: Bloomsbury, 2013); and James K. A. Smith, *Who's Afraid of Relativism? Community, Contingency, and Creaturehood* (Grand Rapids: Baker Academic, 2014).

words, the more persistent critique of modernity will not only point out that modernity cannot have what it wants; it will also point out that we should refuse to want what it wants. It is a critique not just of modernity's failures, but of modernity's desires.

What distinguishes "timid" and "persistent" postmodernisms, I suggest, are two very different "logics." By a "logic," here, I mean an implicit working assumption about how things relate to one another, what follows from what, how things hang together, and the rules that govern such relationships. And very importantly, the sorts of "logics" I am referring to here actually operate at the *pre*-theoretical level; they are akin to what Pierre Bourdieu describes as "pre-logical logic"[14] or what Thomas Kuhn describes as "paradigms." These "logics" are not so much conclusions to rational deduction, but the assumptions and presuppositions that precede, inform, and govern rational analysis. As such, they are contingent and contestable, and pretty much amount to something like "faith commitments"—even if they sometimes parade themselves as simply recognizing this is supposedly "the way things are." They amount to a *take* on the world. Or, to adopt the terminology employed by John Milbank, each constitutes a *mythos*.[15] In particular, I have suggested that "haunted" postmodernism amounts to a modernism in despair because it assumes a logic inherited from modernity, what I have called a "logic of determination." In contrast, what I'm calling "persistent" postmodernism works

---

14 I cannot do justice to Bourdieu's nuanced account here, which is also deployed for quite different reasons. But when he describes as "pre-logical logic of practice" that is distinct from "logical logic," he is hinting at the sort of "logics" I am naming as the logic of determination and the logic of incarnation. See Pierre Bourdieu, *The Logic of Practice*, trans. Richard Nice (Stanford: Stanford University Press, 1990), 19. Thus he emphasizes that "[p]ractice has a logic which is not that of the logician" (86). It seems that for Bourdieu, this is the difference between a *sens* and a *logique*. In that case, one might say I am describing a *sens* of determination and a *sens* of incarnation. I discuss this in much more detail in Smith, *Imagining the Kingdom: How Worship Works* (Grand Rapids: Baker Academic, 2013), 75–99.

15 Milbank does so in the context of emphasizing that there can be very different "takes" on difference: one he describes as a "differential ontology" which conceives all difference as ultimately oppositional, and a second he describes as an "ontology of peace" which conceives difference differently, as analogical relations of harmony (for discussion, see *Introducing Radical Orthodoxy*, 195–97). One cannot adjudicate between these by means of "logical logic" because they represent two different, competing "pre-logical" logics, two very different *mythoi*. Thus a critique must proceed by means of out-narrating the other. It is just this account of conceptions of difference as *mythoi* that, I think, makes my project analogous to Milbank's.

with a different logic, a logic of incarnation which represents a kind of "genius" given to thought by the Incarnation.[16] The genius of this logic is that it makes it possible to conceive difference differently, and thereby to understand finitude and particularity differently as well. Let me unpack each of these in a bit more detail.

The Logic of Determination: The Violence of Finitude

Like the religious wars that spawned Kant's vision of a peaceable kingdom, the resurgence of religious fundamentalisms—Christian, Islamic, Zionist—has given birth to a new critique of "religious violence." The contemporary critique, however, signals a new intensification of Enlightenment criticisms: whereas early modern philosophers tended to criticize violence as *inconsistent with* authentic religious faith, the contemporary (or "postmodern") critique suggests that determinate[17] religious faith *necessarily entails* violence. In other words, earlier critics of religious violence tended to view religious wars as an aberration and indication of the inauthenticity of a particular form of faith; but contemporary critics contend that the very particularity of religious confession is intrinsically violent and thus, not surprisingly, produces "real," political violence. However, the seeds for the postmodern critique were already planted by Kant during the Enlightenment. As I hope to demonstrate in chapter 6 below, Kant seeks to denude determinate religion of its historical particularity and thus disclose a "pure" religion of reason. In the contemporary context, such a project is taken up and intensified in the work of Jacques Derrida, whose account of "religious violence" has been influential for scholars in both philosophy and religious studies (for instance, in the work of Caputo and Hent de Vries[18]). For Derrida, religious violence stems from the *determination* or specification of religious belief by a particular content, linked to a particular historical tradition which appeals to a determinate revelation.

---

16 Here I just mean to invoke Kierkegaard's claim that the idea of the god condescending to leap over the abyss is not an idea that *we* could have come up with (*Philosophical Fragments*). I have discussed this in more detail in James K. A. Smith, *Speech and Theology: Language and the Logic of Incarnation* (London: Routledge, 2002), ch. 5. In an analogous fashion, Milbank argues that the ontology of peace is uniquely generated by biblical wisdom and the Christian doctrine of the Trinity.
17 That is, specified, particular religious confessions.
18 E.g., John D. Caputo, *On Religion* (New York: Routledge, 2001); Hent de Vries, *Religion and Violence: Philosophical Perspectives from Kant to Derrida* (Baltimore: Johns Hopkins University Press, 2002).

According to this account, the particularity of religious confession will lead only to tribalism, and ultimately violence.[19]

But what is the link between religion and violence? What is it about the nature of religion that would suggest this link to violence? For Derrida, unlike some "new atheist" screeds, it is not that religion is a unique poison; rather, religion's violence stems from its commitment to instantiating a *particular* vision of justice, the good life, etc. Thus Derrida's analysis would equally criticize "secular" visions like Marxism for exhibiting the same particularism. So what is it about particularity and determination, then, that is said to entail violence? In both his early and later work, Derrida persistently links the "determinate"—that is, particular or specified—nature of institutions to an inherent and inevitable violence. In his specific considerations of religion, Derrida argues that any and every particular, determinate, historical religion—i.e., any "institutional" religion—must be de facto violent and thus produce violence.[20] The same is true, he argues, of any particular determinate hope for political liberation or justice, criticizing Christian, Marxist and even liberal "hopes" as the basis for undertaking political violence. Because of their determination or specification of a particular vision of justice, Derrida argues that these social hopes would be (and have been) the basis for legitimating the worst injustices against those who would not submit to the vision. Because these social hopes are determinate, they must be exclusionary, and are thus necessarily implicated in violence. This necessitates Derrida's attempted disclosure of an *in*determinate, unspecified "messianic" religion (as opposed to concrete, determinate messian*isms*) which is the basis for hope for a justice which is always "to come."

At work in and behind this conflation of finitude with violence is a "logic of determination." According to this logic, determination itself is violent and leads to violence; therefore, in order to avoid violence we must have, for instance, a social hope which is *in*determinate and hopes for a justice which is unspecified. Derrida's premise, which equates determination with violence, can and must be called into question. However, a critique of the logic of determination cannot simply appeal to some sort

---

19 For further discussion, see Smith, "Determined Violence," ch. 5 below.
20 See Derrida, *Specters of Marx*, trans. Peggy Kamuf (New York: Routledge, 1994), esp. 49–75, and Jacques Derrida and Gianni Vattimo, eds., *Religion* (Stanford, Calif.: Stanford University Press, 1998), 1–78.

of neutral, universal criteria in order to demonstrate the problems with the logic of determination. Such "logics" are part of our most fundamental ways of seeing and understanding the world—they are just the sorts of assumptions that are prerational. As such, they constitute fundamental, albeit implicit, narrations of the world. In short, they have the same epistemic status as faith claims. One does not adopt the logic of determination because it is "rational," or because it is demonstrated by a syllogism; rather, such a logic is assumed as the very condition for our reasonings. At the level of such logics, we are beyond the ken of proofs—of tidy syllogisms that could point out the fallacious failures of such a logic. However, that does not mean that we are beyond critique, resigned to some sort of sophomoric relativism that resigns itself to "anything goes." The way to contest this logic is twofold: first, it needs to be unveiled as a contingent construal of the world; and as contingent, it could be otherwise. Second, it needs to be out-narrated; that is, one must offer an alternative description which can be "tried on" as an account of the world that pushes back on us through experience.

What, then, drives the logic of determination? What would make *that* logic plausible as a fundamental assumption? As I already suggested in *The Fall of Interpretation*, it seems to me that the determinate and finite would be construed as violent and exclusionary only if one assumes that finitude is somehow a "failure"—implying that we are somehow called to be Infinite. This is clearly seen in Derrida's work on ethics, where he argues that we are always already guilty because we—as finite creatures—cannot attend to the obligations of *all*.[21] As he quaintly puts it, when I feed my own cat, I am guilty for *not* feeding every other cat. But of course, as finite, it is simply impossible for me to feed every cat; therefore, I am guilty simply for being finite.

I would argue that not all finite decisions produce injustice. More specifically, it seems to me that one would conclude that finitude or particularity is inherently violent only if one operates with a notion of "infinite" responsibility which faults humanity for being finite. In short, I think in order to accept Derrida's premise that all determination or finitude

21 Jacques Derrida, "Force of Law: The 'Mystical Foundation of Authority,'" in *Deconstruction and the Possibility of Justice*, ed. Drucilla Cornell, Michel Rosenfeld, and David Gray Carlson (New York: Routledge, 1992), 3–67, and Derrida, *The Gift of Death*, trans. David Wills (Chicago: University of Chicago Press, 1995). For further discussion, see ch. 8 below.

constitutes violence, one would have to adopt some version of a gnostic ontology which construes finitude as a kind of "fall," an original violation. Across his corpus, Derrida links this critique of determinacy or particularity to a valorization of "purity" in the sense of a pure "regulative ideal"; that is, the erection of an ideal standard which is at the same time impossible to attain. Though he protests the label, it seems to me that Derrida constantly appeals to "regulative ideals" of purity in his later discussions of ethics, politics, and religion, such as a "pure hospitality" as the ideal for immigration, a "pure democracy" which is always future,[22] a "pure gift"[23] as an impossible but necessary structure of experience, or a "religion without religion" which is pure insofar as it has been purged of any determinant, historical content.

Indeed, it is interesting to track the logic of determination as a logic of *contamination*. In almost every case this is indicated by a thematics of "purity"—the "pure gift," "pure hospitality," or the other as "purely other"—which is both the criterion by which existing structures are judged unjust, but also a purity which can never be achieved. As such, we are always already unjust and implicated in an "essential violence." The result is that Derrida is, if we follow Moltmann's categories, a "utopian" thinker.[24] Let me try to unpack this claim a bit.

In matters of justice and emancipation, formulated in terms of a Levinasian ethic of "alterity," Derrida points to a number of quasi-absolutes which function as the criterion for justice. These are structures which point to a "pure" ideal—an ideal of which we always fall short (hence the inescapability of *in*justice). We can see this in several sites (I follow a regressive procedure and expand upon only a couple of examples here):

> (1) "Pure forgiveness": In a context which includes discussions of South Africa and Bosnia, Derrida argues that "forgiveness forgives only the unforgivable."[25] If forgiveness is undertaken for the achievement of some end or *telos* (redemption, reconciliation, reestablishment of an normality), "then the

---

22 Derrida, *The Politics of Friendship*, trans. George Collins (London: Verso, 1997).
23 Derrida, *Gift of Time*.
24 Jürgen Moltmann, *The Coming of God: Christian Eschatology*, trans. Margaret Kohl (Minneapolis: Fortress, 1996), 31–35, 194–95.
25 Derrida, *On Cosmopolitanism and Forgiveness* (London: Routledge, 2001), 32. Subsequent parenthetical references in this paragraph are to the same work.

'forgiveness' is *not pure*" (32, cp. 42, 44–45). Forgiveness, in order to be "pure," must be "*unconditional*, gracious, infinite, aneconomic, forgiveness granted *to the guilty as guilty*, without counterpart, even to those who do not repent or ask for forgiveness" (34, cp. 32, 36, 40, 45). And only this ideal of "absolute forgiveness" could be the "ground" for any ethics (35–36). We should keep in mind, however, that "pure forgiveness" is impossible, and so even our best shots at forgiveness remain unjust.

(2) "Pure hospitality": In a context which includes discussions of immigration and human rights, Derrida argues that justice demands an "absolute or unconditional hospitality" which is incommensurate with "hospitality in the ordinary sense."[26] "Just hospitality" breaks with ordinary hospitality because "absolute hospitality requires that I open up my home and that I give not only to the foreigner . . . but to the absolute, unknown, anonymous other, and that I *give place* to them" (25). Pure hospitality begins from an "unquestioning welcome" (29). However, the impossibility of this unconditional hospitality is tied to *finitude*: "since there is also no hospitality without finitude, sovereignty can only be exercised by filtering, choosing, and thus by excluding and *doing violence*. Injustice, a certain injustice . . . begins right away" (55, cp. 65).

One could repeat an exposition of a similar formula as it emerges in Derrida's consideration of the gift (in *Given Time*), friendship (in *The Politics of Friendship*), religion (particularly in GD and *Specters of Marx*), justice (in "Force of Law"), and the Other (in early work such as *Of Grammatology* and "Violence and Metaphysics"): a "pure" phenomenon is distilled as an ostensible motivator for undertaking strategies that will never reach it.[27] But this structure of an "impossible" or "pure" justice, I would

---

26   Derrida, *Of Hospitality*, trans. Rachel Bowlby (Stanford: Stanford University Press, 2000), 25. Subsequent parenthetical references in this paragraph are to the same work.
27   This "never" is different than Christian eschatology. In the Christian account, admittedly, there is a deep sense that "we" will never achieve a perfectly just society, etc.; but this is not the same as saying that such will never arrive. Rather, the claim is meant to signal the importance of grace. Derrida's account, however, seems to indicate a more abso-

contend, is the product of a repressed metaphysics rooted in what I have been describing as Derrida's logic of determination, which, rather than inspiring revolution, provides comfort to the status quo. Derrida's premise, which equates determination with violence, can and must be called into question. The determinate and finite would only be construed as violent and exclusionary if one assumes that finitude is somehow a "failure"—implying that we are somehow called to be infinite.

The Nature of the Gothic and the Logic of Incarnation

Despite suggestions that Derrida's account is "realistic," that it faces up to the "facts" of our finitude, in fact this is a *mythos*, a take on the world, a faith-informed construal of finitude that represents a prelogical commitment. But its epistemic status as a *mythos* means one could reject this premise that grounds Derrida's logic of determination and offer a counternarrative, an alternative *mythos* that would operate on the basis of a different logic. Thus, instead of adopting a logic of determination which construes finitude or particularity as a violence, I want to explore a logic of incarnation which honors finitude and particularity as a good. If one begins, instead, with an affirmation of embodiment as good, then the fact of finitude—e.g., that I can only feed so many cats—is not construed as injustice or violence, because with the rejection of Derrida's logic of determination one must also reject infinite responsibility as a regulative ideal.[28] Therefore, it would follow that the particularity of religious confession is not violent per se.[29]

So what would be different according to a logic of incarnation? First, it is informed by a narrative wherein the transcendent, infinite Other condescends to finite immanence *without loss* and *without remainder*. The logic

---

lutely impossibility. This is why I have always found myself puzzled that some folks find his account of justice somehow inspiring. While the Christian account is justly humble about what can be expected, work for just here and now (in our "not yet") will be taken up and fulfilled in the advent of justice and shalom in the new heavens and new earth. So there remains a continuity between little inbreakings of justice here and now and the justice that is to come and we hope ("expect") will arrive. But Derrida's anti-eschatology contends that day is never coming. Am I the only one who then thinks, "Then why bother?"

28 A similar point is articulated in Milbank's critique of Levinas and Derrida in "Can Morality Be Christian?" in *The Word Made Strange* (Oxford: Blackwell, 1997), 219–32, and "Grace: The Midwinter Sacrifice," in *Being Reconciled: Ontology and Pardon* (London: Routledge, 2003), 138–60.

29 Even here, it is not simply a matter of rejecting Derrida; in ch. 9 below I will suggest that there are hints of just such an incarnational logic in the early Derrida.

of incarnation is not just informed by a proto-Marxist Jesus of the sort one finds in Dominic Crossan or Caputo. In other words, this is not a logic that just draws upon a "prophetic" Jesus; it is a logic that is informed by the richness of Chalcedonian Christology which suggests that in Christ, we have *both* the fullness of God and humanity; not half-and-half; not one swapped for other; but rather the paradoxical[30] (yea, mad) affirmation that in the gritty, material person of Jesus we are also encountering the fullness of the Creator ("*pleased* as man with men to dwell," as the old Christmas hymn puts it).

Second, and crucial to this Chalcedonian logic, is its refusal of binary either/ors—the sort that both liberalism and fundamentalism are prone to fall into—and just the sort that I think the logic of determination replays. Notable here is the moment of evaluation that is implied in this: while the transcendent God condescends to inhabit immanence, this is not thereby a concession, and certainly not a lamentable or regrettable "necessary evil." It follows from a logic of creation which does not see the specification and particularity of finitude as an evil; rather the conditions of finitude (particularity, specification, this-ness, if you will) are affirmed as a good.[31] Indeed the Incarnation can only be properly understood in the light of the Ascension, which emphasizes that the Son's humanity is taken up and inhabited for eternity. This is why the logic of incarnation, which flows from and reaffirms the goodness of creation, finds its completion in the doctrine of the resurrection and an eschatology of the new heavens and the new earth—which is not any kind of escape from finitude as if finite particularity were inherently evil; rather, it is the hope of well-ordered particularity.

Third, as I tried to emphasize in the final chapter of *Who's Afraid of Postmodernism?* the logic of incarnation also entails an affirmation of the contingency of history. Rather than lamenting and criticizing the Christian community for drawing boundaries, demarcating doctrine (as the "grammar" of the community), and specifying its confession, the logic of incarnation sees such procedures as inherent to what it means to be a

---

30 Recall the central argument of Kierkegaard's *Philosophical Fragments*, which I draw upon in *Speech and Theology*, ch. 5.
31 This was the core argument of *The Fall of Interpretation*, though there I described it as a "creational hermeneutic"; now, in contrast to Derrida and Caputo, I tend to name the same construal of finitude as a "logic of incarnation."

finite community. And perhaps most scandalously, it is informed by a fundamental trust that the Spirit is at work in just such contingent, historical formulations (though this does not forestall internal critique). By affirming the contingencies of community development, the logic of incarnation rejects both the primitivism of Protestant fundamentalism (which wants to leap back over what it sees as the contaminating and regrettable influence of the church to the purity of Jesus and "New Testament Christianity") as well as the more sophisticated primitivism of the deconstructive Jesus (who, if you look closely, pretty much want to do the same thing—it is just that *their* Jesus and New Testament look quite different).

All this is just to say that the logic of incarnation is not haunted by "purity," which always comes off as a bit unworldly, even a bit gnostic. Indeed, if I could be permitted an analogy that stretches the conversation a bit, I would suggest that what John Ruskin describe as "the nature of the Gothic" is a pretty good translation of the logic of incarnation. Ruskin's widely influential essay of the same title, embedded in the second volume of *The Stones of Venice*, contrasts the Greek and classical aesthetic ideals of pristine perfection with the Gothic and Christian ideals, which celebrate a certain un-uniformity, even a kind of valued ugliness. In the Greek temple each column is perfect, symmetrical, and identical to the others—they look like they've been created by machines. In the Gothic cathedral, by contrast, one will find all sorts of differences and peculiarities, even blemishes and strange anomalies (think gargoyles). Behind this, Ruskin argues, is not just an "aesthetic," but an entire construal of human flourishing, including assumptions about the nature of human persons and the ideal human community. This is why, for Ruskin, the Gothic is not just a style—it is a vision of society, and of work in particular. For why was it that those Greek temples were characterized by machine-like precision, yea, "purity?" Because they were built by slaves. Ruskin emphasized that what distinguished Gothic architecture from earlier classical architecture, as well as later "industrial" building, was the *freedom of the craftsman*. Greek temples were built by slaves. The laborers were not properly craftsmen but rather human tools and machines. Thus classical architecture has a kind of pristine perfection about it that is artificial and mechanistic; it shows no stamp of individual artists, no mark of their particularity or specificity. And this desire for a pristine perfection and uniformity is, in fact, a suppression of nature and individuality.

For Ruskin, the "modern" laborer was not qualitatively different. While not a "slave" in the traditional sense, he was still reduced to an unthinking machine. He put it this way:

> It is verily this degradation of the operative into a machine, which, more than any other evil of the times, is leading the mass of the national everywhere into vain, incoherent, destructive struggling for a freedom of which they cannot explain the nature themselves. Their universal outcry against wealth, against nobility, is not forced from them either by the pressure of famine, or the sting of mortified pride. These do much, and have done much in all ages; but the foundations of society were never yet shaken as they are at this day. It is not that men are ill fed, but that they have no pleasure in the work by which they make their bread, and therefore look to wealth as the only means of pleasure. It is not that men are pained by the scorn of the upper classes, but they cannot endure their own; for they feel that the kind of labour to which they are condemned is verily a degrading one, and makes them less than men. Never had the upper classes so much sympathy with the lower, or charity for them, as they have at this day, and yet never were they so much hated by them: for, of old, the separation between the noble and the poor was merely a wall built by law; now it is a veritable difference in level of standing, a precipice between upper and lower grounds in the field of humanity, and there is pestilential air at the bottom of it.[32]

So the "modern" preoccupation with pristine perfection and exquisite finish is bought with a price: viz., the effective enslavement of the "divided" laborer. But the Gothic—which is a distinctly Christian architectural grammar—rejects such slavery:

> But in the mediaeval, or especially Christian, system of ornament, this slavery is done away with altogether; Christianity

---

32 Ruskin, "The Nature of the Gothic," in *The Stones of Venice*, vol. 2, *The Sea-Stories* (London: George Allen, 1898), 116.

> having recognized, in small things as well as great, the individual value of every soul. But it not only recognizes its value; it confesses its imperfection, in only bestowing dignity upon the acknowledgment of unworthiness. . . . Therefore, to every spirit which Christianity summons to her serve, her exhortation is: Do what you can, and confess frankly what you are unable to do; neither let your effort be shortened for fear of failure, nor your confession silenced for fear of shame. And it is, perhaps, the principal admirableness of the Gothic schools or architecture, that they thus receive the results of the labour of inferior minds; and out of fragments full of imperfection, and betraying that imperfection in every touch, indulgently raise up a stately and unaccusable whole.[33]

So to the so-called perfection of classical and modern architecture, Ruskin contrasts the beautiful *im*perfection of the Gothic:

> And on the other hand, go forth again to gaze upon the old cathedral front, where you have smiled so often at the fantastic ignorance of the old sculptors: examine once more those ugly goblins, and formless monsters, and stern statues, anatomiless and rigid; but do not mock at them, for they are signs of the life and liberty of every workman who struck the stone; a freedom of thought, and rank in the scale of being, such as no laws, no charters, no charities can secure; but which it must be first aim of all Europe at this day to regain for her children.[34]

The logic of incarnation, I want to suggest, is characterized by this Gothic affirmation of imperfection as nonetheless good, even beautiful, whereas the logic of determination is haunted by notions of (impossible) perfection and (impossible) purity, ends up constructing such gritty particularity as a contamination and a fall. This is just to say that when we begin from a logic of incarnation, we refuse to be haunted by modern ghosts. In this respect, an incarnational philosophy of religion must begin with an exorcism.

---

33   Ruskin, "Nature of the Gothic," 157–58.
34   Ruskin, "Nature of the Gothic," 160–61.

Nietzsche's Faith: Or, Why We Need an Even More Radical Hermeneutics

It is important to emphasize that the logic of determination and the logic of incarnation are two different stories about difference and particularity, two different construals of finitude, both of which have the epistemic status of faith commitments. On the one hand, then, I am trying to point out that the construal of particularity and finitude as violent is just that: a construal, a "take" on things, a story that can be out-narrated. On the other hand, and this has been the burden of my work, I hope to make some start at "out-narrating" this story by articulating the logic of incarnation.

To clarify this point, it might be helpful to return to some key issues of hermeneutics, and to return to the figure of Nietzsche, who had somewhat fallen off the radar of continental philosophy of religion (after an enthusiastic phase following the work of Mark C. Taylor, but that is changing).[35] More specifically, revisiting Nietzsche allows me to revisit an older version of the debate between Caputo's "religion without religion" and what I am now calling a "Catholic postmodernism."

In a way, my work from the beginning to the present is very much concerned with hermeneutics. This is why Caputo's *Radical Hermeneutics*[36] was for me—like so many others—a revolutionary entrée into the field of contemporary Continental philosophy. To draw a Heideggerian analogy, Caputo was my Husserl: he "opened my eyes."[37] Here I want to pursue a theme in Caputo's work to which I have been drawn from the very beginning: the thematics of *undecidability* and its correlation with the place of Nietzsche in Caputo's thought, considering in particular how Caputo construes the undecidability which inhabits the space between what he earlier described as "the religious" in Kierkegaard and "the tragic"

---

35 See Merold Westphal, *Suspicion and Faith: The Religious Uses of Modern Atheism* (Grand Rapids: Eerdmans, 1993), 219–82; Bruce Ellis Benson, *Graven Ideologies: Nietzsche, Derrida, and Marion on Modern Idolatry* (Downers Grove, Ill.: InterVarsity Press, 2002), and *Pious Nietzsche: Decadence and Dionysian Faith* (Bloomington: Indiana University Press, 2007); Stephen N. Williams, *The Shadow of the Antichrist: Nietzsche's Critique of Christianity* (Grand Rapids: Baker Academic, 2006); and Craig Hovey, *Nietzsche and Theology* (London: T&T Clark, 2008). Also relevant in this context is the work of David Goicoechea, such as *Zarathustra's Love Beyond Wisdom* (Binghamton, N.Y.: Global Academic Publishing, 2002).
36 John D. Caputo, *Radical Hermeneutics* (Bloomington: Indiana University Press, 1987) (henceforth abbreviated as RH).
37 Martin Heidegger, *Ontologie (Hermeneutik der Faktizität)*, GA 63, ed. Käte Bröcker-Oltmanns (Frankfurt am Main: Klostermann, 1988), 5.

in Nietzsche (RH 272). By tracing this theme from RH, through *Against Ethics* and *The Prayers and Tears of Jacques Derrida*, up to *More Radical Hermeneutics* and *On Religion*, I will suggest that an interesting shift has taken place between RH and OR regarding the place and status accorded to "the tragic" in general, and Nietzsche in particular, in the project of Caputo's "radical hermeneutics."[38] My conclusion will include a brief recommendation for how this shift might be continued, or how a Catholic postmodernism represents an even more radical hermeneutics.

Undecidability, Faith, and the Limits of Knowledge

Undecidability, Caputo has repeatedly protested, is not a matter of *indecision*, but rather the condition of possibility of any decision which demands that one decide.[39] As he later summarizes, "[u]ndecidability does not mean the apathy of indecision but the passion of faith, the urgency of forging ahead where one does not see, where in principle one cannot see" (PT 338). This Derridean theme has been central and persistent throughout Caputo's corpus.

The first crystallization of undecidability—the first advent of its acute challenge—is located in the final chapter of RH (prototypical of the works to follow), where Caputo unfolds two ways of understanding suffering, two different takes on the face of the suffering other which are, strictly speaking, undecidable: the "religious" embodied in Kierkegaard (RH 278–82) and the "tragic" response of Nietzsche (RH 282–88). It is at this juncture that the haunting specter of Nietzsche makes its entrance onto the stage of radical hermeneutics, playing a major role from RH to AE.

What I have always found curious about this role for Nietzsche, however, is the way in which he in fact plays a privileged part which seems to escape undecidability. In RH, the truth is cold (RH 273), which is to say,

---

38   John D. Caputo, *Against Ethics* (Bloomington: Indiana University Press, 1993); *The Prayers and Tears of Jacques Derrida* (Bloomington: Indiana University Press, 1997); *More Radical Hermeneutics* (Bloomington: Indiana University Press, 2000); *On Religion* (New York: Routledge, 2001) (henceforth abbreviated as AE, PT, MRH, and OR).
39   This was first helpfully clarified in the early exchange between Caputo and Olthuis. See James H. Olthuis, "A Cold and Comfortless Hermeneutic or a Warm and Trembling Hermeneutic? A Conversation with John D. Caputo," *Christian Scholars' Review* 19 (1990): 345-62; John D. Caputo, "Hermeneutics and Faith: A Response to Professor Olthuis," *Christian Scholars' Review* 20 (1991): 164–70; and James H. Olthuis, "Undecidability and the Impossibility of Faith: Continuing the Conversation with Professor Caputo," *Christian Scholars' Review* 20 (1991): 171–73.

the truth is Nietzschean. It is almost as if Nietzsche has some kind of privileged "realistic" access to the way things "really are"—they are not good!—while Kierkegaard can just offer us a "construal," a therapeutic take on things which helps us "cope" with this cold reality via an "accommodation" with the chill of the "flux" (RH 271, 281).[40] The religious response of faith is simply "a certain facility to construe the darkness, to grope in the dark" (RH 279). "Faith makes its way in the dark," he concludes, "seeing through a glass darkly, and it is genuine only to the extent that it acknowledges the abyss in which we are all situated" (RH 281).

Hence early Caputo (is it late enough to say that now?) is "transfixed by Nietzsche's tragic vision, kept up at night by his account of the disaster" (AE 54). This Nietzschean movement of radical hermeneutics seems to reach its crescendo in AE, where Caputo is also most concerned with Deleuze. What in RH was the undecidability of the "tragic" and the "religious" is now the undecidable distinction between Dionysius and the Rabbi, between "heteromorphism" and "heteronomism," between the configurations of Nietzsche/Deleuze and Levinas/Derrida (AE 42–68). In AE, it is still Nietzsche who delivers "the cold truth" and has the courage to tell us "the cold fact that becoming makes no dialectical progress, that it does not recoup its losses, that the flux is the endless destruction of whatever it produces" (AE 51). This is why, in AE, the religious remains a mere coping mechanism, a way of construing the way things "really" are.

> Faith is a matter of a radical hermeneutic, an art of construing shadows, in the midst of what is happening. Faith is neither magic nor an infused knowledge that lifts one above the flux or the limits of our mortality. Faith, on my view, is above all the *hermeneia* that Someone looks back at us from the abyss, that the spell of anonymity is broken by a Someone who stands with those who suffer, which is why the Exodus and the Crucifixion are central religious symbols. *Faith does not, however, extinguish the abyss but constitutes a certain reading of the abyss, a hermeneutics of the abyss.* (AE 245, emphasis added)

---

40 Indeed, it seems that the difference between a "radical hermeneutics" which keeps things difficult and a "hermeneutics of ease" is not qualitative, but quantitative: a hermeneutics of ease is a little too accommodating, or not accommodating enough, since it is "especially adept at repressing and excluding the flux and trying to arrest its play" (RH 271).

In this sense, faith sounds like deluding ourselves, acting "as if" the abyss were something else. This, of course, is a definition of faith that plays right into the hands of the masters of suspicion such as Freud or Marx. While in AE Caputo seems to waver with some just plain indecision,[41] there is at the same time this nagging sense that things have been decided with respect to the abyss (what are we naming here?); so the question is whether we'll be able to develop a coping mechanism that prevents us from going mad with the supposed "reality" of the abyss. In a very Freudian way, Caputo suggests that it is precisely the mad who see the abyss for what it is: "I do not think people who are driven to the edge are getting things all wrong," he argues, "so much as that they are unreasonably right, right to an excess. . . . They pay too close attention to life. They are scrupulously, infinitely attentive to life and—to their misfortune—*see through* its masks, the very structures that have been put in place for our own protection. They do not know how to ignore, forget, forgive, *repress*, move on" (AE 239–40, emphasis added). So it seems those gone mad are precisely those ones who do *not* see through a glass darkly, but just plain see through things to the way the abyss "really" is. The result of forcing "the abyss out of hiding" is too often self-destruction, "a function of overexposing oneself to something from which most of us have the prudence to take shelter" (AE 240). The rest of us—especially the religious—are more mature egos who have developed coping mechanisms which help us repress the "cold reality" of the abyss. This is why faith cannot "extinguish" the abyss, only construe it "differently," "as if" Someone were looking back (AE 245).[42] But in the end, "[w]e can never build a shelter against the winds of the flux" (RH 282).

Despite Caputo's claim that he rejects "all forms of privileged positions above the flux and binary oppositional schemes" (RH 279), it seems to me that the very categories of the "flux" and the "abyss" are themselves accorded just that: a privileged, quite decidable status (which is quite clear if you are mad). We are told that the flux is "cold" and "dark," and hence

---

41   So, too, in RH: "I do not think that anyone ever really succeeds in getting to one side or the other of this undecidable rift, that one really 'is' or 'is not' religious, wholly Augustinian or wholly Nietzschean. . . . I do not think that we know whether we believe in God or not, not if we face the cold truth" (RH 287–88).

42   In ch. 10 below I will analyze these themes with respect to Caputo's understanding of the relationship between "faith" and "philosophy," arguing that throughout his corpus—perhaps with the exception of *On Religion*—Caputo maintains a certain quasi-Kantian affirmation of the autonomy of philosophical reason vis-à-vis faith, even when, with Derrida, he insists on a formal *credo ut intelligam* structure.

the religious "construal" of the flux otherwise always comes second. This means that somehow Nietzsche is always on the scene first; the flux seems to be always already inscribed by a Nietzschean stylus, as though things were "really" that bad. The flux is always already an "abyss." In what seems a curious revival of Heideggerian *a-letheia*, Caputo concludes that "[f]rom time to time the abyss shows through, the anonymous void by which we are inhabited breaks out and we are swallowed up, or very nearly.... The abyss bleeds through the cracks and crevices of ordinary existence; the void peers out from behind the minimalia of everyday life" (AE 239). So "[t]he abyss is just another name for what happens" (AE 239); but that name, of course, is not neutral, but already an evaluation, a perspective, a construal, a "take" on things which is loaded with value. The project of a radical hermeneutics is to point out the radical contingency of our perspectives (a Nietzschean "truth," to be sure), but despite thematizing the distinction between the "religious" and the "tragic" responses to the abyss, it seems to me that Caputo fails to recognize that they very description of this "reality" as a cold, dark abyss is itself just another perspective, another "take" on things, itself a "construal." Because this undecidability does not go all the way down, in these early works I do not think radical hermeneutics is radical enough.

Contra Nietzschean Positivism

In light of its haunting dominance in the earlier works, it is interesting to note how few lines this specter of Nietzsche has in the later works such as PT and OR. Or to put it otherwise: in the later works, Jack seems to be getting more sleep. Not that the difficulty of life does not keep him up late, but Zarathustra's laughter seems to have abated. Why is that? Why the diminished role for this Nietzschean specter in the later work?

I would suggest that this is due to the further radicalization of radical hermeneutics.[43] By this I mean that the vestiges of a kind of "Nietzschean positivism" in RH and AE (in the description of the "abyss" and "flux") tend to drop out due to a more radical understanding of the relationship between faith and reason. In other words, it seems to me that RH and AE operated with a more classically Kantian understanding of the relationship between faith and reason, whereas the later works operate with

---

43 Which, ironically, one might also understand as a further Nietzscheanization of radical hermeneutics, if, at the "heart" of Nietzsche (if he has one) is located his *perspectivalism*.

a more Augustinian understanding of this relationship. This is due in no small part, of course, to the unveiling of such Augustinian structures in Derrida's own work, particularly *Of Spirit* and *Memoirs of the Blind*. So unlike in RH, where deconstruction seemed to inhabit a space between faith and "reason" (in Nietzschean guise), in PT Caputo opens by arguing that "[d]econstruction proceeds not by knowledge but by faith" (xxvi). This, of course, does not mark the elimination of undecidability, or a way of averting undecidability, but precisely the radicalization of undecidability that was missing from RH and AE—an omission that prevented undecidability from going "all the way down." With this more radical conception of the relationship between faith and reason, undecidability is inscribed at the origin, so to speak. This would mean that even the descriptions of the "abyss" as "cold" and "dark"—indeed, the very *naming* of the abyss—is always already called into question, thus displacing the priority of Nietzschean construals. So the religious is not simply a construal which papers over the way things "really" are—as though we were always warding off Nietzsche; instead, one can begin with a radically different construal of that "space."[44] To put this in terms of a different context, I think RH and AE accorded a primordiality to what John Milbank describes as an "ontology of violence," whereas the later works recognize the contingency of such, opening the space for a construal of original peace.[45]

While this shift begins in PT (I don't think Zarathustra ever gets to laugh at Abraham there), we see this shift culminate in OR, where it is equally emphasized that Nietzsche's "terrifying vision of the world" is also a construal, a myth, a "fiction" (OR 54). What this points to is "the *pre-*metaphysical situation of faith. That puts Nietzsche and St. Paul on the same page, at least on this point. . . . Nietzsche had argued for the historical contingency of our constructions, the revisability and reformability of our beliefs and practices, all of which, as he said, are 'perspectives' that we take on the world and that have emerged in order to meet the needs of life" (OR 58). In RH and AE, Nietzsche was not exposed to his own perspectivalism;[46] but in OR it is finally admitted that what went under the

---

44 As suggested, for instance, in James Olthuis' understanding of this space as a "womb," or the "wild-spaces of love." John Milbank's project regarding an "ontology of peace" would be another example.
45 See John Milbank, *Theology and Social Theory* (Oxford: Blackwell, 1990), 278ff.
46 Perhaps we could say that RH and AE remain "secular" in this regard, while PT and OR are "post-secular" (see OR 56–59).

supposedly neutral rubric of the "flux" and "abyss" is always already a perspective: "Nietzsche's argument boomeranged in a way that nobody saw coming," Caputo observes. "What the contemporary post-Nietzschean lovers of God, religion and religious faith took away from Nietzsche was that psychoanalysis (Freud), the unyielding laws of dialectical materialism (Marx), and the will to power itself (Nietzsche) are *also* perspectives, *also* constructions, or fictions of grammar" (OR 59). The result is a redefinition of "reason" itself "as a historically contingent 'take' we have on things—which makes it look a lot more like 'faith'" (OR 64).

A Final Frontier for Catholic Postmodernism: Revelation

This radicalization of perspectivalism means a more radical hermeneutics must call into question the vestiges of realism at work in RH and AE. But I would like to suggest that in Caputo's more radical hermeneutics there remain two other, yet related, vestiges of a kind of Enlightenment realism, one last pocket of "secularity" which prevents perspectivalism from going "all the way down." The first I have address in chapters 5 and 6 below—viz., the notion of a formal or structural "religion without religion"—so I won't tackle that here. Instead, I will briefly consider a closely related topic: Caputo's dismissal of *revelation*.

Despite his powerful *apologia* for faith and religion (even, at times, institutional religion—even, God forbid, Pentecostalism![47]), Caputo repeatedly refuses any notion of "revelation": "We have not, to my knowledge, been visited by some Super-revelation, some Apocalyptic Unveiling, that settles all our questions" (OR 20). "The skies do not open up and drop The Truth into our laps," he continues (OR 21). Instead, "we find ourselves forced constantly to traffic in 'interpretations,' the inescapability of which is a good way to define 'hermeneutics'" (OR 21). Thus Caputo constructs a dichotomous opposition between the inescapability of interpretation on the one hand, and any notion of "revelation" on the other.[48] For Caputo,

---

47 OR 94–95.
48 It also seems that Caputo confines "revelation" to the "Word of God" understood *textually*, distinguishing between the Incarnation and revelation (MRH 286n28). Such a distinction stands in need of a Barthian—or better, biblical—understanding of the Incarnation itself as the primary site of God's revelation, the Word become flesh (John 1:14). Though God has spoken at various times and in various ways, he has now spoken *in Son* (Heb 1:1-2). The text of the Scriptures is a (second-order) testimony to this primordial revelation of God in Christ.

any notion of revelation must entail a rejection of the ubiquity of interpretation; a notion of revelation must be linked to claims of immediacy which bypass the structure of interpretation or, in other words, claims to "bail us out and lift us above the flux of undecidability" (MRH 193). "What else does 'revelation' mean if not that The Secret has been 'revealed' to us, has been handed over to us courtesy of a 'Special Delivery'" (MRH 193)? Hence Caputo's critique: "A revelation is an interpretation that the believers believe is a revelation, which means it is one more competing entry in the conflict of interpretations" (OR 22).

In an attempt to further radicalize radical hermeneutics, I would offer two criticisms at this juncture: First, I think Caputo has been reading too much Jean-Luc Marion (MRH 201-7),[49] or has at least fallen prey to an overgeneralization which assumes that any claims regarding revelation must also be claims to immediacy and hence denials of the ubiquity of hermeneutics.[50] But not everyone operates with such theories of revelation; my alternative exemplar of choice would be Kierkegaard's incarnational understanding of revelation, which begins from an affirmation of the inescapability of finitude (entertained by Caputo himself, it seems [MRH 201-2; 209]).[51] So it is *not* self-evident that "[t]he Divine Word is a word *outside* the text, if ever there was one!" (MRH 197). A faith-affirmation of the reality of revelation does not necessarily entail either an anti-hermeneutic claim to immediacy nor triumphalism since it remains, on this radical hermeneutic, a claim rooted in faith, which is always a claim made only through and in the face of undecidability.[52] Thus I think Caputo's critique of claims to revelation only holds for those who think they *know* they have a revelation in a positivist sort of way: those whose faith is not faith at all, but a kind of apodictic certainty constituted by full presence and characterized by the Husserlian dream of apodicticity (which is just plain impossible). For those who understand

---

49 See Jean-Luc Marion, *God without Being*, trans. Thomas A. Carlson (Chicago: University of Chicago Press, 1991), 139-58.
50 For my criticism of just such notions of revelation, see *The Fall of Interpretation*, 17-60 and ch. 12 below.
51 For further articulation of this critique of Marion, see *Speech and Theology*, 157-63 and chs. 11 and 12 below.
52 Any believer worth her salt would be happy to concede with Caputo that "[u]ndecidability is the condition, the quasi-transcendental condition, of faith, the thing that makes faith (im)possible, *the* impossible" (MRH 220-21).

faith as a decision made on the basis of undecidability, and who appreciate the epistemic humility that must attend creaturely finitude, trust in revelation is not attended by such (dangerous) "knowledge."

Second, Caputo seeks to critique the believer's claim to revelation by unveiling the fact that such is only an *interpretation*. For example, the believer's confession that God was in Christ—that in Jesus of Nazareth the "Word became flesh" (John 1:14)—is only one interpretation of such an event. But the believer—unless he or she is a rationalist (i.e., a fundamentalist)—would happily concede such a point: yes, the claim that God was in Christ is an interpretation made within a horizon of faith. *But*—and here's the rub—so too is the claim that Jesus is *not* God incarnate, or the interpretation of revelation which says there is no revelation. Every rejection of the possibility of revelation would also operate on the basis of a particular faith, a particular interpretation—which means that not only should believers be less triumphalistic, but that those who reject the possibility of revelation should also pull back the troops. In other words, if undecidability really goes all the way down—if we really mean to have a more radical hermeneutics—it seems to me that the question of revelation should remain more open than Caputo treats it. Such an opening would produce an even more radical hermeneutics.

As I've emphasized above, a Catholic postmodernism embraces the scandalous contingency and particularity of God's revelation in Christ, without apology, but also without Inquisitions. It's not so much a matter of staking a claim to "a revelation" as being claimed by a Revelation which then calls us to be a peculiar people marked by our suffering *for* the world, not our triumph over it.[53]

Who's Afraid of Orthodoxy? The Incarnation as a More Radical Hermeneutics

I've been spending time unpacking the logic of incarnation by demarcating it from what I take to be one of its most winsome and influential competitors—the logic of determination articulated by John Caputo (and indebted to Jacques Derrida). It is the latter's "religion without religion"

---

53 While I am critical of Jean-Luc Marion's account of revelation as overwhelming the conditions of interpretation, I am here nonetheless drawing on his phenomenology of revelation in *Being Given: Toward a Phenomenology of Givenness*, trans. Jeffrey L. Kosky (Stanford: Stanford University Press, 2002), 234–45.

which has most captivated not only academic discussions in continental philosophy of religion but also reflections on the church, particularly in "post-evangelical" circles. These two worlds come together in Caputo's most recent book, *What Would Jesus Deconstruct?* Since I am already clearly on record[54] as a friend and fan of John Caputo's winsome twenty-first-century rendition of Sheldon's *In His Steps*, in closing I would like to take an opportunity to push the conversation further, taking the spirit of Caputo's book seriously enough to disagree with it. I will do so by taking a position that is not only unpopular but will seem downright counterintuitive to many. My claim is relatively simple: that despite all the bad press and caricatures from supposedly enlightened liberals, it is in fact *orthodoxy* that constitutes the most radical appreciation of "deconstructibility." To put it a little more stridently and provocatively, I would suggest that the Jesus of Pope Benedict XVI represents a more radical hermeneutic than the Jesus we get from Schillebeeckx.

It seems to me that Caputo's project—which in an important sense stands within a prophetic tradition of critique—operates on the basis of a distinction taken up from Derrida: a careful (though admittedly hard-to-draw) distinction between what is "deconstructible" and what is not, between what can be deconstructed and what is "undeconstructible." And it is the undeconstructible which calls out for a critique of the deconstructible. This is not simply a demolition project, but a de-*con*-struction—a dismantling of harmful, oppressive, and unjust structures with a view to building more peaceful, just structures that are more conducive to human flourishing. For instance, for Derrida this distinction between the deconstructible and the undeconstructible maps onto the distinction between "law" and "justice": as a contingent and historical institution of human making (that is, the fruit of *culture*), law is by its very (human) nature subject to deconstruction. Its particularity and finitude can't help but be violent, exclusionary, and unjust. As something that has been constructed, it is also thereby subject to de-construction (with a view to *re*building). Thus law is distinguished from *justice*, which is undeconstructible precisely because it has not been constructed: it remains *to come*. It's what law and legal institutions should be

---

54 See my "Series Editor's Foreword" to John D. Caputo, *What Would Jesus Deconstruct?* Church and Postmodern Culture Series (Grand Rapids: Baker Academic), 15–17.

after. So when we deconstruct the law and its institutions, we do so with a view to justice, haunted by justice, *called* by justice.

In *What Would Jesus Deconstruct?* Caputo puts this distinction to work on different quarry, drawing an analogous distinction between "the church"—which is very much deconstructible and well *deserves* deconstruction—and "the kingdom"—which is undeconstructible and which calls us to the deconstruction of the church for the sake of the kingdom.[55] The church's "man-made" traditions, laws, and rules are so much deconstructible chaff that needs to be winnowed in order to preserve the kernel of Jesus' undeconstructible kingdom message of faith, hope, love, and peace. With Nietzschean echoes (and very much in the spirit of Nietzsche's friend, the theologian Franz Overbeck), Caputo proposes that such a deconstruction of the church for the sake of the kingdom comes down to the task of sorting out the "human all too human" from the "divine": later (Pauline) accretions regarding sexual ethics or the institution of an episcopacy are "human" elements that deserve deconstruction, while Jesus' calls to nonviolence and to tend to the poor are taken to be "divine" undeconstructibles. Deconstruction is "good news" for the church insofar as it helps us sort out the two.

I would like to push back on this thesis a bit. First, very briefly, this is a particularly odd sort of distinction to invoke in the name of deconstruction, which, from its earliest days, campaigned against unstable binaries.[56] To what extent does such a vision of the kingdom function as an "original supplement?" How or why is this kingdom not akin to Rousseau's dream of an original speech (so roundly criticized by Derrida in *Of Grammatology*)? What are the prospects for articulating the supposedly impossible and undeconstructible Gospel without immediately falling back into the mire of deconstructibility? And if such a Gospel eludes articulation, then are we not back to a transcendental signified (again, the subject of sustained critique in *Of Grammatology*)? While I do not have space to do so here, it

---

55   At times the distinction also feels like it plays out as a distinction between Jesus (undeconstructible) and Paul (very much deconstructible), echoing folks like John Dominic Crossan. Or a distinction between "the Gospel" and "the Bible."

56   Granted, I think this is a problem internal to the Derridean corpus. While on the one hand I have argued for a fundamental continuity between the "early" and "later" Derrida, against claims of some sort of Heidegger-like *Kehre* in his thought (see Smith, *Jacques Derrida*), I have also argued that there are important ways that the early Derrida deconstructs just these sorts of distinctions evoked by Derrida in the 1990s. See ch. 9 below.

would be interesting to take Caputo's *What Would Jesus Deconstruct?* and drop it in as a replacement to Rousseau's *Origin of Language*, and then undertake the same sort of deconstructive critique to which Rousseau's *Essay* was subject in *Of Grammatology*. Indeed, it would be interesting to take Derrida's own "Force of Law" (clearly a key text for Caputo's project) and subject it to the same kind of careful critique to which Derrida subjected Rousseau in 1967. Reading early Derrida against later Derrida, noting the instabilities and internal dissension within his corpus, is a way of being faithful to Derrida's deconstruction. Subjecting Caputo's church/kingdom distinction to the same deconstructive critique might also be more faithful to *l'esprit de deconstruction* than maintaining it.

Finally, and more importantly, I want to suggest that Catholic orthodoxy actually makes a more radical affirmation of deconstructibility than Caputo's Derridean Jesus. Let me put it this way: Catholic orthodoxy affirms not only the desconstructibility of the church, it even affirms the deconstructibility of *the kingdom*! According to orthodox eschatology not only is the church contingent, particular, and constructed, so too is the coming kingdom.[57] "Kingdom come" is characterized by the same contingency, particularity, and finitude. The deconstruction of injustice, including the reform of the church, is not driven by some dream of an impossible, undeconstructible kingdom, but in the light of a particular and still-deconstructible vision of justice.

And here's the crucial difference: the Trinitarian God of Catholic faith is not scared off by contingency, particularity, or deconstructibility. Unlike the Wholly Other of the Derridean gospel, the Incarnate God exhibits no allergy to the deconstructible. Indeed, this is the very distinctive logic of incarnation: God does not call for the deconstruction and dismantling of the deconstructible on the basis of or with a view to some undeconstructible and impossible kingdom; rather, God condescends *to inhabit the deconstructible*. If we want to ask ourselves what Jesus would do, we might consider what Jesus *did*. The Incarnation is the mad story of the undeconstructible God who did not consider undeconstructibility as something to be grasped, nor did he despise deconstructibility, but rather, taking the

---

[57] The other crucial difference between a Derridean gospel and the Catholic tradition is precisely the Catholic affirmation of eschatology as such (viz., that a particular instantiation of the kingdom is coming *and will arrive*) whereas the Derridean kingdom is always and only *to come* and will never arrive. Indeed, for Derrida, any arrival would only be the arrival of a new regime of injustice, but I cannot address this difference here.

"human, all too human form" of a servant, he humbled himself to the point of inhabiting the very deconstructible structures of human law and culture—even to the point of suffering death at the hands of these institutions. But he did so *not* with a view to eviscerating the deconstructible, but rather to rightly ordering[58] it such that the contingent particularity of this deconstructible creation might reach its proper *telos* (a loose paraphrase of Phil 2:5-11). It is not "deconstructibility" that's the problem; it is the particular, wrongly ordered configurations of the deconstructible that are at issue.

The scandal of Catholic ecclesiology is that this logic of incarnation then extends to an *institution*, the church Catholic, which is now configured as the body of which Christ is the head. The same Spirit that inhabited and empowered the incarnate Jesus (e.g., Luke 4:1, 14, 18) is given to the ecclesial community (Acts 1:8). This continues the logic of incarnation: the undeconstructible God continues to condescend and inhabit the very deconstructible institution that is the church. Far from being infallible or perfect, nonetheless the institution is an extension of this logic and bears within it all the resources it needs to make sense of its own failures. Indeed, two of its most significant seasons (Advent and Lent) are seasons of penitence; it gathers as a community weekly to confess its failures. But in contrast to the logic of purity that seems to motivate the Derridean critique of deconstructibility as itself a problem, the logic of incarnation testifies to a God who inhabits, affirms, and takes up all the messiness of a deconstructible institution. The Catholic affirmation of the institutional church is rooted in this logic of incarnation, which is a continuing testimony of what Jesus *did*. This logic—that embraces the scandal of particularity and contingency—is, I am suggesting, a more persistent postmodernism, indeed a *Catholic* postmodernism.

---

58 I mean to allude here to Augustine's notion of the "right order of love," particularly as articulated in *City of God*, where the discussion is most germane to our context here.

II
Derrida, Marion, and the Possibility of a Christian Phenomenology

5

Determined Violence

Derrida's Structural Religion

Meditating on and grappling with the "return of religion" in the contemporary world on the isle of Capri in 1995, Jacques Derrida offered a political (and psychoanalytic) investigation of violence, undertaking "a program of analysis for the forms of evil perpetrated in the four corners of the world 'in the name of religion.'"[1] Politics and religion: two things of which we have been instructed to never speak, to avoid speaking (*Comment ne pas parler?*)—things concerning which it is better not to speak (just ask Salman Rushdie).[2] A consideration of "religious wars" locates this intersection of religion and politics—the site, then, of religio-political violence. And for Derrida, it is the inevitable political consequences of religion (viz., war), which implicate religions in a legacy of the most unjust violence. In response, Derrida evokes what would seem to be an old and very *modern* political gesture, seeking to instantiate "a certain *epoché*" which consists in thinking religion "within the limits of reason alone"—a fundamentally *political* gesture of the most Kantian sort which does not seek to eliminate religion but rather to reinscribe it, to give it a different place, to keep it within its bounds (*limites*) of a certain

---

1   Jacques Derrida, "Foi et savoir: Les deux sources de la 'religion' aux limites de la simple raison," in *La Religion*, ed. Thierry Marchaisse (Paris: Éditions du Seuil, 1996), 22 (henceforth abbreviated as FS).
2   At the end of the lecture (presented in 1995 on the isle of Capri), Derrida appends just such a prohibition as it appears in Genet: "One of the questions I will not avoid is that of religion" (FS 86). Derrida also mentions the Rushdie affair (14).

abstraction (FS 16–17). So in the face of the violence of religion, Jacques becomes the most enlightened of *Aufklärers*, sketching and outlining what he calls, in the tradition of Kant's "reflective faith," a "religion without religion," a "structural messianism," a "messianism without content," or simply "the messianic." And all of this religion—without religion—is offered in the name of justice and democracy in the face of the unbridled violence which has accompanied the "return of religion" in the strictest sense.[3]

However, Derrida is very much aware of the difficulties associated with such a proposal, which has the audacity, in the face of deconstruction, to suggest a pure, transcendent, contentless, universal structure of religion—a messianic structure "without content and without identifiable messiah."[4] When later confronted in a discussion at Villanova University, led by Catholics and watched over by Augustine (and not a few Augustinians), he confessed to his weakness: "this is really a problem for me, an enigma,"[5] echoing his acknowledgment elsewhere that "the possibility of religion without religion" is an "immense and thorny question" to which he must return elsewhere.[6] But is there perhaps another question to be answered, a question which Derrida has not asked himself, let alone promised to return to? Has not the purveyor of *différance* been forced to defer a thorny problem which he has created for himself? And if so, how was he lead into this temptation which seems to be a "falling back" into what has been deconstructed?[7] Thus, in addition to and before (*avant*)[8]

---

3   "This justice alone, which I distinguish from law, permits the hope, beyond the 'messianisms', of a universalizable culture of singularities" (FS 28).
4   Derrida, *Specters of Marx*, trans. Peggy Kamuf (New York: Routledge, 1994), 28 (henceforth abbreviated as SM).
5   "Deconstruction and Tradition: The Villanova Roundtable with Jacques Derrida," in *Deconstruction in a Nutshell*, ed. John D. Caputo, Perspectives in Continental Philosophy (New York: Fordham University Press, 1997).
6   Derrida, *The Gift of Death*, trans. David Wills (Chicago: University of Chicago Press, 1995), 49 (henceforth abbreviated as GD).
7   That is, a pure, transcendent, universal structure would seem to be everything deconstruction has set out to dismantle. Thus, if Derrida's movements have brought him to a site where he must posit just such a structure, it would seem helpful to recall that in one of his earliest texts, Derrida warned of the perils of deconstruction, "constantly risking falling back within what is being deconstructed." See Derrida, *Of Grammatology*, trans. Gayatri Chakravorty (Baltimore: Johns Hopkins University Press, 1976), 14.
8   The site of the *avant*, the "before," plays an important role in Derrida's discussion of religion inasmuch as it points to that which is "'before' every question, thus 'before' all knowledge, every philosophy, etc." (FS 79). Before the questioning of philosophy there is a fundamental trust in the promise (*Of Spirit: Heidegger and the Question*, trans. Geoffrey Bennington and

the question of its production, it seems necessary to consider what motivates the distinction between determinate messianisms, which produce war, and a transcendent religion without religion, which is the condition for justice. This chapter follows three movements: first, an engagement and exposition of Derrida's messianic/messianism distinction, followed by a discussion of its means of production as suggested by Derrida as well as indicated by historical analogues. The third operation, however, is the most critical: having considered the nature of Derrida's structural messianism, I will return to the question of its origin or motivation, suggesting that the dilemma which Derrida has created for himself can be avoided if we were to begin with another reading of religion—a reading, moreover, with which it is necessary (*il faut*) to begin.

The Logic of Messianicity

While Derrida has made several confessions regarding *his* religion, "my religion about which nobody understands anything,"[9] in this context I am concerned with proposals he makes not for a private religion but in fact a universal religion, albeit a religion without dogma or content (FS 28)—a religion of pure form, a formal religion. It is a religion of "formalization" whereby the "logic" of certain structures, which appear in the texts of determinate religions, are distilled or disclosed by a process that Derrida describes as "desertification." By this process of desertification, structures are emptied of their content; that is, the structures are made "arid" by means of a "desert abstraction."[10] After this "complete formalization" which exhausts and impoverishes the determinate religious structures, "nothing remains."[11] Thus Derrida makes his exodus into the desert in order to "inhabit the desert," for one "deals in the desert with radical atheism" (ON 53, 80). The structures disclosed by this operation are then

---

Rachel Bowlby [Chicago: University of Chicago Press, 1989], 129–34); and before the "seeing" of "knowledge" (*voir/savoir*) there is the faith of blindness (*Memoirs of the Blind: The Self-Portrait and Other Ruins*, trans. Pascale-Anne Brault and Michael Naas [Chicago: University of Chicago Press, 1993]). I have analyzed these themes much more extensively in "The Art of Christian Atheism: Faith and Philosophy in the Early Heidegger," *Faith and Philosophy* 13 (1996).
9 Derrida, *Circumfessions*, trans. Geoffrey Bennington in Bennington and Derrida, *Jacques Derrida* (Chicago: University of Chicago Press, 1993), 154.
10 Derrida, *Circumfessions*, 27.
11 Derrida, *Sauf le nom*, translation of *On the Name*, ed. Thomas Dutoit, trans. David Wood, John P. Leavey, Jr., and Ian McLeod (Stanford: Stanford University Press, 1995), 49–51 (henceforth abbreviated as ON).

devoid of any determinate content and thus mark, he claims, a certain universal "logic." The different logics, which are many names for the same structure, would then include the logic of the gift, the logic of the promise, the logic of sacrifice, the logic of invention, and the logic of coming or the "come" (*Viens!*).[12] Further, echoing Levinas, Derrida argues that the structure is fundamentally that of *justice* inasmuch as it is a structure which indicates an absolute alterity, a wholly other (*tout autre*) who calls us to do justice to her alterity, irrespective of any religious or metaphysical backup system of justification; it is a justice, to be distinguished from law, which alone "permits hope, beyond the 'messianisms,' of a universalizable culture of singularities" (FS 28). That, for Derrida (*per* Levinas), is religion or the messianic: the call of absolute alterity and an impossible future which makes us responsible. For what is religion, Derrida asks? "Religion—that is to respond" (*La religion, c'est* **la réponse**) (FS 39). Religion is responsibility to the Other.[13]

The procedure, then, that produces this universal structure of justice, consists of "a *thinking* that 'repeats' the possibility of religion without religion" in order to arrive at "a logic that at bottom (that is why it can still, up to a certain point, be called a 'logic') has no need of *the event of revelation or the revelation of an event*" (GD 49). The religious event, then, can be formalized or desertified in order to distill a universal logic. In *The Gift of Death*, for instance, Derrida takes up Kierkegaard's reading of Abraham's sacrifice of Isaac and, by means of abstraction (and a healthy dose of Levinas), arrives at a universal structure which has no need of either Abraham, Isaac, or Yahweh but rather revolves around the responsible self, the Wholly Other to whom I am responsible (justice), and the third who also beckons (ethics). As such, the story is translated and thus

---

12   Derrida links all of these motifs as ways of asking the "question of the gift" (*Given Time: I. Counterfeit Money*, trans. Peggy Kamuf [Chicago: University of Chicago Press, 1992], x). Each of these logics is explored in different texts: on the gift, see *Given Time*; on the promise, see *Of Spirit*; on sacrifice, see *Gift of Death*; concerning the logic of invention, see "Psyche: Inventions of the Other," trans. Catharine Porter in *Reading de Man Reading*, ed. Lindsay Waters and Wlad Godzich (Minneapolis: University of Minnesota Press, 1989), 25–65; and on the logic of *Viens!* see "Of an Apocalyptic Tone Newly Adopted in Philosophy," trans. John P. Leavey, Jr. in *Derrida and Negative Theology*, ed. Harold Coward and Toby Foshay (Albany: SUNY Press, 1992), 25–71. For further discussion, see ch. 8 below.
13   Cp. Emmanuel Levinas, *Totality and Infinity*, trans. Alphonso Lingis (Pittsburgh: Duquesne University Press, 1969), 40, 80.

thinks the condition of possibility without thinking the event itself. Once the story of Abraham's decision is formalized as such,

> [i]t implies that God, as the wholly other, is to be found everywhere there is something wholly other. And since each of us, everyone else, each other is infinitely other in its absolute singularity, inaccessible, solitary, transcendent, nonmanifest, originally nonpresent to my *ego* . . . , then what can be said about Abraham's relation to God can be said about my relation to *every other (one) as every (bit) other* (*tout autre est tout autre*), in particular my relation to my neighbor or my loved ones who are as inaccessible to me, as secret and transcendent as Jahweh. (GD 78)

While the structure remains religious, inasmuch as it is a structure of transcendence (and one which requires faith), it is nevertheless disburdened of any connection to a particular, determinate ("positive") religion and thus not implicated in the religio-politics—i.e., war—of the "Abrahamic religions" or the "religions of the Book."

The same operation is at work in *Specters of Marx*, where Derrida formalizes the structure of determinate messianisms (including Marxism) that seek a justice "to come"—which inevitably means the justice of a particular ideology and hence means violence for those excluded. The result of the desertification is the production of the "messianic in general" which consists of an "*epokhé* of the content . . . as thinking of the other and of the event to come" which is simply the "formal structure of the promise." In the end (*eschatos*),

> what remains irreducible to any deconstruction, what remains as undeconstructible as the possibility itself of deconstruction is, perhaps, a certain experience of the emancipatory promise; it is perhaps even the formality of a structural messianism, a messianism without religion, even a messianic without messianism, an idea of justice—which we distinguish from law or right and even from human rights—and an idea of democracy—which we distinguish from its current concept and from its determined predicates today. (SM 59)

He goes on to describe this messianic justice as "a spirit of Marxism which I will never be ready to renounce . . . a certain emancipatory and *messianic* affirmation, a certain experience of the promise that one can try to liberate from any dogmatics and even from any metaphysico-religious determination, from any *messianism*," including Marxism (SM 89). The product of this desertification is a "universal structure" of messianic justice, a justice which is absolutely future and thus always "to come" (SM 167).

We could also refer to *Sauf le nom*, where the operation is applied to the desire of the *via negativa*, which seeks and gropes for that which it cannot reach, in a sense wills its demise inasmuch as it desires that which is wholly other than thought. Negative theology seeks to experience *the* impossible and thus marks an "absolute interruption of the regime of the possible" by absolute heterogeneity (ON 43). In its desire to make a passage to the limit, "the apophatic design is also anxious to render itself independent of revelation." In its desire for universalization ("in a way, a kind of spirit of the Enlightenment"), "this mysticism remains, after the fact, independent of all history of Christianity, *absolutely* independent, detached even, perhaps absolved, from the idea of sin, freed even, perhaps redeemed, from the idea of redemption" (ON 71). Pushing this discourse to its limit by means of "a process of absolute formalization," Derrida "withdraws it, like negative theology itself, from all its dominant determinations in the Greek or Christian world" (ON 47) and discloses a logic of desire for the other divorced from any determinate religious affiliation: "The other is God or no matter whom, more precisely, no matter what singularity, as soon as any other is totally other (*tout autre est tout autre*)," for that is the structure of the impossible (ON 74). He is even able to produce a formula: "Each thing, each being, you, me, the other, each X, each name, and each name of God can become the example of other substitutable X's" (ON 76). And again, this logic of absolute alterity is the structure of justice.

The examples could be multiplied for most of Derrida's work in the 1990s and 2000s, all reproducing this logic which consists in the repetition of certain religious structures "without putting forth theses or *theologems* that would by their very structure teach something corresponding to the dogmas of a given religion" (GD 49).[14] As such, the logic or structure is

---

14   Here he is specifically describing the work of Jan Patoka, suggesting that the same operation is at work in Marion, Levinas, Ricoeur, Kant, Hegel, Kierkegaard, and Heidegger. He deals more extensively with Heidegger's "repetition" in GD 23 and FS 77–82 (§48).

not tied to any determinate claims or place, to any revelation or promised land:[15] "this messianic dimension does not depend on any messianism, does not follow any determinate revelation, does not properly belong to any abrahamic religion" (FS 28).

The Production of the Logic of Messianicity

The means of producing this structure or logic of the messianic is variously described as a process of abstraction (FS 9–10, 28–29), desertification (FS 27), formalization (ON 76), repetition (GD 23, 49), or a suspension by means of a certain *epoché* (SM 59; ON 67; FS 16). By freely associating the operation with a kind of *epoché*, this movement of deconstruction exhibits its debts to the phenomenological reduction, inasmuch as it signals a "suspension of all *doxa*, of every positing existence, of every thesis" (ON 67). It would even bear similarities to a certain Kantian modality of critique, "a certain *epoché* which consists . . . of thinking religion 'within the limits of reason alone'"—an *epoché* which also opens the space for a political event (FS 16–17). Thus, the messianic is the product of an operation of suspension, whereby the content of a certain determinate religious structure or event is "bracketed" (in Husserl's language) in order to distill a *formal* logic devoid of determinate content.

However, as one of the interlocutors in *Sauf le nom* observes, such a distinction between the messianic and messianisms

> would remain prisoner of a problematic opposition between form and content. But this so traditional disjunction between concept and metaphor, between logic, rhetoric, and poetics, between sense and language, isn't it a philosophical prejudgement not only that one can and must deconstruct, but that, in its very possibility, the event named "negative theology" will have powerfully contributed to calling into question? (ON 49)

That is to say, in Derrida's opposition between the messianic and the messianisms, or between religion without religion and determinate, historical religions, have we not arrived at the oldest of structures and one of the first to be dismantled by deconstruction, viz., the classical distinction between

---

15   "The Promised Land, is this not also the essential bond joining the promise of place and historicity?" (FS 17) In contrast, he elsewhere suggests that the desert is "a figure of the pure place" (SN 57).

the medium and the message, between form and content, between writing and speech? How can the progenitor of deconstruction and purveyor of poststructuralism offer a pure, transcendent, universal structure of religion? Is this not a little *incroyable*, maybe even a little sacrilegious?

Derrida is very much aware of what is at stake here, viz., a very old metaphysics of the universal and the particular. As he asks, himself, at the conclusion of *Specters*,

> If the messianic appeal belongs properly to a universal structure, to that irreducible movement of the historical opening to the future, therefore to experience itself and to its language ..., how is one to *think* it *with* the figures of Abrahamic messianism? Does it figure abstract desertification or originary condition? (SM 167)

Left with only questions in that text, the question was later put to Derrida by another, where again the discussion ends with questions: "The problem remains for me," he continues, "—and this is really a problem for me, an enigma—whether the religions, say, for instance, the religions of the Book, are but specific examples of this general structure, of messianicity" or whether "the events of revelation, the biblical traditions, the Jewish, Christian and Islamic traditions, have been absolute events, irreducible events which have unveiled this messianicity."[16] Thus he again offers two possible relations which correspond to those suggested in *Specters*: either the universal messianic structure is the condition of possibility for the determinate messianisms ("originary condition"), or the messianic structure is only produced because of the irreducible events of revelation which have preceded it ("abstract desertification").[17]

The first gesture would be, as Derrida suggests, a Heideggerian maneuver which seeks to locate "the fundamental ontological conditions of possibilities of religions, to describe the structure of messianicity on the ground of the groundless ground on which religions have been made

---

16 Derrida, "Deconstruction and Tradition," 23.
17 "Between the two possibilities," he continues, "I must confess I oscillate and I think some other scheme has to be constructed to understand the two at the same time, to do justice to the two possibilities. That is why—and perhaps this is not a good reason, perhaps one day I will give up this—for the time being I keep the word 'messianic.' Even if it is different from messianism, messianic refers to the word Messiah; it does not simply belong to a certain culture, a Jewish or Christian culture" ("Deconstruction and Tradition," 23).

possible."[18] The second option would be a Levinasian operation of "translation" in which the religious (here, Judaic) tradition is the site of a shocking impetus which indicates a thought other-than-philosophical, an idea which philosophy per se cannot think, which is then translated into the idiom of philosophical discourse—that is, into Greek. Thus an irreducible event or revelation—by means of translation, abstraction, formalization, etc.—is introduced into philosophy or a certain kind of phenomenology, such that the structure then bears a universal weight as the description of a universal structure which has no need of the religious event that occasioned its identification. As such, it bears a universal validity and marks a universal responsibility.[19]

If the second model of abstraction or translation is that which produces Derrida's messianic, then it is impossible for him to maintain, as he does incessantly, that the universal messianic structure "does not depend on any messianism, does not follow any determinate revelation" (FS 28), for it would be precisely the determinate, irreducible, historical event which is the occasion for the messianic structure. And that, as will discussed below, would then implicate the messianic in precisely the religio-politics that Derrida seeks to avoid (viz., war). But on the other hand, the first model which purports to locate the transcendental condition for religion would situate the messianic as a pure transcendental (and not just a quasi-transcendental), which is precisely what deconstruction has opposed religiously since its inception. Further, if that is indeed the case, then why keep the name (*sauf le nom*) "messianic," which inevitably links the supposed universal structure to several very particular religions? Does this perhaps betray that the supposed universal religious structure is quite Bookish, tied to Abrahamic traditions, inasmuch as the messianic structure seems quite foreign to Eastern religion? Would this not indicate that the transcendent structure is not quite so pure, but remains tainted by one

---

18 "Deconstruction and Tradition," 23. Thus Heidegger's early corpus is filled with disclaimers that his analyses of "religious" structures are in fact investigating the pre-religious, ontological structures which make the religious possible. See, for example, his analyses of fallenness and their accompanying disclaimers in *History of the Concept of Time: Prolegomena*, trans. Theodore Kisiel (Bloomington: Indiana University Press, 1985), 283, and *Being and Time*, trans. John Macquarrie and Edward Robinson (New York: Harper & Row, 1962), 220, 224.
19 For a helpful discussion of Levinas' project of "translation" and the relationship between the Judaic and philosophy in his thought, see Jill Robbins, *Prodigal Son / Elder Brother: Interpretation and Alterity in Augustine, Petrarch, Kafka, Levinas* (Chicago: University of Chicago Press, 1991): 100–132.

or several particular messianisms? And would this not indicate that the messianic itself remains a messian*ism*?

As an alternative to these two options, John Caputo suggests a third way of thinking through this dilemma which he locates in the young Heidegger's notion of "formal indication" (*formale Anzeige*), which is a new conceptuality, another way of thinking the relationship between the universal and the particular. Heidegger proposes to engage pre- and other-than-philosophical sources (the facticity of the New Testament, the Greek ethical experience) in order to retrieve and then sketch a kind of phenomenology of revolutionary experiences, whereby philosophy is shocked by that which is other than philosophy, by its pre-philosophical other. However, the project is not one of "translation" (as in Levinas) which gives the upper hand to academic philosophy; rather, Heidegger forges a new way of conceptualizing with a different arsenal of quasi-concepts which do not purport to distill essences or grasp factical life conceptually, but rather honor the excessiveness and irreducibility of experience by merely "pointing" to structures of existence. "In a formal indication," Caputo summarizes, "the individual, the singularity, is not taken as an *instance* or example of the universal, does not become a subsumable case or a *causus* that falls off the pedestal of Greek universality, a temporal specimen of an unchanging species. Rather, the singular is affirmed in all of its singularity, respected in all of the richness of its idiosyncratic *haecceitas*, this-ness."[20] Seizing on this structure as a way of thinking Derrida's messianic, Caputo goes on to suggest that,

> [o]n such a reading, the messianic in general would be a formal indication of the concrete messianisms that are to be found in the religions of the Book. But a formal indication, on Heidegger's accounting, has the status of an empty schema which lacks existential *engagement* whereas Derrida's "messianic" is the very structure of urgency and engagement. The messianic goes to the heart of deconstruction and of deconstruction's passion and deconstruction's religion, its affirmation of and engagement in the world, in events, in what is happening, in traditions and what is to come.[21]

---

20 John D. Caputo, *The Prayers and Tears of Jacques Derrida: Religion without Religion* (Bloomington: Indiana University Press, 1997), § 10.
21 Caputo, *Prayers and Tears of Jacques Derrida*, § 10.

The messianic, then, would be a "kind" of universal, a rather modest universal rather than a thoroughly Greek universal or modern transcendental, which would then allow Derrida to escape from falling back into a very old metaphysics which deconstruction long ago dismantled.

However, as Caputo rightly perceives, if Derrida were to take this path out of the difficulty, it must also be concluded that the messianic remains somewhat determinate and historically conditioned. Thus Caputo suggests that "rather than taking Derrida's messianic as in any way overarching the three historical messianisms of the religions of the book, or the three plus one, if you include Marx's messianism, I would say that Derrida's is a fifth . . . , that is to say, *one more* messianism." Despite the fact that Derrida insists that it is a faith without dogma or content, "the Derridean messianic does have *certain* determinable features," such as an affinity for democracy (FS 29) and the prophetic tradition of justice;[22] that is, "Derrida's messianic has emerged under determinate historical conditions and takes a determinate form."[23] There is, then, a certain amount and kind of content to Derrida's structural messianism.

But if any content is admitted into the "messianic dimension," or if the transcendent structure of "religion without religion" is determined in any way by particular messianisms, then would it not be something which one would fight for, perhaps even religiously, provoking yet another religious war?

The Motivation of the Production of the Messianic

Why the messianic? Why does Derrida think it necessary to locate a religion without religion, a contentless religion, a formal structure of religion divorced from any determinate instantiation? What *motivates* the distinction between the universal messianic and the determinate messianisms? Apart from and before its possibility or impossibility (as discussed above), it is necessary to question the reason for positing such a transcendental structure, particularly given the difficulties that it produces. At this juncture, it must be recalled that it is the *political* consequences of determinate religions which spur the production of a religion without religion, which is supposed to be a little safer, a saving name (*sauf, le nom*) more apt to lead to salvation by at least saving lives—the (transcendent) name

---

22 Derrida, "Deconstruction and Tradition."
23 Caputo, *Prayers and Tears of Jacques Derrida*, 135–36.

"above" all (particular) names by which men (and women and children) must be saved from the violence of religion (in the strict sense of the term). For inevitably, on Derrida's accounting, determinate, content-ful religion always ends up in war, precisely because of its determination to guard the contents of its positive revelation. As he observes, this plays itself out in the theater of the Middle East on a regular basis: "three other messianic eschatologies mobilize there all the forces of the world and the whole 'world order' in the ruthless war they are raging against each other." And any *political* analysis of this situation "can no longer avoid granting a determining role to this war of messianic eschatologies in what we will sum up with an ellipsis in the expression 'appropriation of Jerusalem.' The war for the 'appropriation of Jerusalem' is today the world war." Further, he characterizes "Middle-Eastern violence as an unleashing of messianic eschatologies" and "holy alliances." Thus, Derrida is moved to propose the production of "a structural messianism, a messianism without religion."[24]

Religions, such as the religions of the Book, have a disturbing legacy of violence which is linked to claims of uniqueness with universal pretension, claims to possession of *the* Law, *the* definitive revelation, *the* Truth, *the* one and only Way, *the* Messiah, even. "As soon as you reduce the messianic structure to messianism," Derrida argues, "then you are reducing the universality and this has important political consequences. Then you are accrediting one tradition among others and a notion of an elected people, of a given literal language, a given fundamentalism."[25] Thus, historically determined religions, inasmuch as they are particular, will *necessarily* produce violence because of competing claims—a competition of historical religions which sees its ghastly consequences in the war over Jerusalem. And so it is necessary, in the name of justice, to produce a structure which is divorced from the content of any particular, historical, determinate, positive religion—in short, a (transcendent) religion without (any content from a particular) religion.

Different texts undertake this operation from different sites. In *The Gift of Death*, Derrida on the one hand appropriates the universal structure of responsibility as located in the story of Abraham (as read by Kierkegaard) and indicated in the texts of Patočka. However, this structure must be formalized and divorced from Patočka's (and Kierkegaard's implicit)

---

24 All quotes in this paragraph are from SM 59.
25 Derrida, "Deconstruction and Tradition."

"Christian politics" and "Christian Europe" inasmuch as such a determinate political structure inevitably leads to violence, particularly if you are not a Christian; after all, "no Christian politics ever advised the West to love the Muslims who invaded Christian Europe" (GD 103). Kierkegaard's reading would remain confined within a certain New Testament economy of exchange, an economy of "ethnicity" which cannot prevent the production of violence in its name. However, once the content of this structure is desertified and one can distill a universal logic (A gives X to B), then the determinations which produce violence are eliminated and a structure of justice produced.

Despite its silence, even negative theology remains plagued by this violence inasmuch as it claims to have a "secret" which is accessible only to those on the "inside." The outsider, then, must be initiated by one who has the secret, instituting a *Ecclesiastical Hierarchy* (and patriarchy) of "master and disciples" which revolves around a violent political economy.[26] Further, negative theology faces a double paradox: it both wants to be universalized but at the same time remains the son of a determinate father, "an idiom of Greco-Latin filiation" which it affirms and reaffirms along with its movement of negation (ON 71, 48).

> I am thinking of what is happening in Europe itself, in which the Pope appeals to the constitution or to the restoration of a Europe united in Christianity—which would be its very essence, and its destination. He tries to demonstrate, in the course of his voyages, that the victory over the totalitarianisms of the East has been carried off thanks to and in the name of Christianity. In the so-called Gulf War, the allied western democracies often kept up a Christian discourse while speaking of international law. (ON 78)

Thus, while deconstruction shares with negative theology the desire to delineate "the very experience of the (impossible) possibility of the impossible" (ON 43), it must nevertheless desertify these structures in order to avoid the "political and pedagogical consequence" of negative theology's determination.[27]

---

26 Derrida, "How to Avoid Speaking: Denials," trans. John P. Leavey, Jr. in *Derrida and Negative Theology*, 88–94.
27 Derrida, "How to Avoid Speaking," 94.

Thus the "return of the religious," as analyzed in "Foi et savoir," is accompanied by the most radical evil and violence, a violence which even accompanies "ecumenical" proposals inasmuch as they mark a world-Latinization (*mondialatinisation*) and colonization which violates difference in the name of hegemony—a way of "pursuing war by other means" (FS 57–58). Even an ecumenical religion, which does not claim to be a fundamentalism, remains implicated in war, albeit a war under another name, viz., "peace" (*pacification*). In short, as a determinate religion its political consequences do not differ from that of fundamentalisms; determinate religion (*la doxa déterminé*) is always already a fundamentalism because as particular—tied to a particular history and particular place—their myths exclude the possibility of justice for all, and hence will mean violence for those outside of the tradition or story, or those who get in the way of the story as its eschatology unfolds (e.g., the Canaanites or the Palestinians). And it is precisely this determinate content "that is always deconstructible" and must be deconstructed in the name of justice. Religion, understood in the traditional sense as a set of dogmas or institutions such as the church, "can be deconstructed, and not only can but should be deconstructed, sometimes in the name of faith."[28]

But what now of Derrida's religion, or deconstruction's religion without religion, this messianic, transcendent, structural religion? (And here we return to the discussion above.) What about its history? Would it not also admit of genealogical analysis, even geographical analysis which would suggest some links to a certain time and place? Does not this messianic "logic" constitute a spatial and temporal topo-logic which would determine its *place* in time and history? Does it not, as Caputo suggests, have a certain amount or kind of *content*?

(1) If, in order to avoid any implication of the messianic in the wars of the determinate messianisms, we evacuate the messianic structure of any content, then we must conclude, as Caputo rightly observed, that the messianic is not a quasi-transcendental but a pure transcendental *stricto sensu*—a pure, Greco-modern universal of the most classical species which remains immune to history and space; and that, as far

---

28 Derrida, "Deconstruction and Tradition."

as deconstruction is concerned, is heresy, along with being a little *incroyable*. Further, beyond the question of its possibility (which it is not), is it not precisely the history of transcendentals and universals which has bequeathed to us the most disturbing history of violence? Has not history demonstrated that transcendentals divorced from place and history have been the justification for the most horrifying crimes against those confined to the wrong place and time, those from a different place? Have not transcendentals also been the condition for a number of fundamentalisms, such as a Platonic fundamentalism of the Good? And if so, how is it that Derrida assumes that the desertification of determinate structures will somehow prevent violence or signal justice?

(2) If, in the face of an impossible and dangerous "universal," we admit *content* into Derrida's messianic structure, as Caputo suggests, and at the same time assert that such a logic of the messianic sketches the fundamental structure of *justice*, then either (a) this content must be deconstructed in the name of justice, for it is "content that is always deconstructible" (SM 90); or, (b) it must be concluded that content does not *necessarily* produce violence or end in war. That is, Caputo wants to suggest that Derrida's messianic is another, albeit open-ended, messian*ism*. But if this is the case, it allows content to "reenter," and if content can be admitted, then the other messianisms, *as determinate and content-ful,* cannot be excluded *a priori* but rather only on the basis of performative criteria. While I would agree with Caputo that the most helpful avenue is for Derrida to admit or recognize that his is another messian*ism*, I want to further suggest that Derrida must then concede that the content of other determinate messianisms are not necessarily violent, though they may at times produce violence, even in the name of that content (event, revelation, Book). However, the historical production of violence must be distinguished from the necessary production of violence, opening a political space which can grapple with both the

possibility of peace and violence—that is, a political structure which confronts violence *as violence* precisely against a horizon of possible peace and justice.

What if, *perhaps*, instead of construing every determinate religion as a violent fundamentalism—which would have to include Derrida's messianic religion inasmuch as it is conditioned by a determinate place and history—we were to understand religion, in a fundamentally deconstructive gesture, as pharmacological, site of both poison and cure, violence and peace, exclusion and healing. Would not a more consistent and persistent deconstructive indication of the *pharmakon* be forced to admit (I ask for forgiveness) the healing possibilities of fundamentalism (though not ignoring its other poisonous form)? *Must* we not do so, insofar as a religion apart from historical determination is inaccessible and, given the danger, undesirable? In other words, if it is impossible to have a purely structural religion, but discourse nevertheless remains grounded in some faith[29] and the structure of justice remains a religious structure of alterity and transcendence, then we must address how particular, determinate, religious faith plays a role in the call for justice, and how it can be kept from violence. By recognizing the pharmacologicality of determinate religion, a way is opened for maintaining Derrida's concern regarding the violence and exclusionary impulse of particular religious expressions and yet at the same time recognizing the role played by the determinate content of religion in Derrida's discourse on justice. The means, then, of avoiding violence would not be a suspension of religious content or the production of a "religion without religion," but rather an ethical vigilance accompanied by a recognition of the integral role of determinate religions in the production and determination of justice. The determination of religion need not necessarily or structurally end in violence; rather, as we see in Derrida's messianism, religion determines justice. *La doxa détermine, c'est la réponse.*

29   See n8 above.

6

Re-Kanting Postmodernism?

Derrida's Religion within the Limits of Reason Alone

C ould it be that deconstruction is in fact simply a new attempt to liberate humanity from its self-incurred tutelage? In other words, is deconstruction simply a new Enlightenment, a project we can trace to Kant? And conversely, could it be that Kant was (unwittingly) engaged in deconstruction? Derrida himself seems to hint at just such a genealogy, suggesting something of a German origin of this French movement: "I am resolutely in favor," he proclaims, "of a new university Enlightenment (*Aufklärung*)."[1] And more recently, expressly evoking the Kantian tradition of critique, he has undertaken the task of considering religion "within the limits of reason alone"—a "religion without religion"[2] which, in the spirit of Kant's "reflective faith,"[3] would constitute a "universal" religion.[4] For Derrida, like Kant, such a religion is ulti-

---

1 Jacques Derrida, "The Principle of Reason: The University in the Eyes of Its Pupils," trans. Catherine Porter and Edward P. Morris, *Diacritics* 13 (1983): 5. This essay might be read as Derrida's "What Is Enlightenment?" or in the spirit of Kant's *The Conflict of the Faculties*. Derrida engages the latter at 19–20. Cp. also Michel Foucault's engagement with Kant in "What Is Enlightenment?" in *The Politics of Truth*, 2nd ed. (Los Angeles: Semiotext[e], 2007), 97–119.
2 Jacques Derrida, *The Gift of Death*, trans. David Wills (Chicago: University of Chicago Press, 1995), 49.
3 Kant, *Religion within the Limits of Reason Alone*, trans. Theodore M. Greene and Hoyt H. Hudson (New York: Harper & Row, 1960), 48 (henceforth abbreviated as RWLRA).
4 Jacques Derrida, "Foi et savoir: Les deux sources de la 'religion' aux limits de la simple raison," in *La religion*, ed. Thierry Marchaisse (Paris: Éditions du Seuil, 1996), 23 / "Faith

mately a matter of ethics or justice, such that the "religion" which Derrida discloses is remarkably similar to Kant's "moral religion," including the tie which binds it to democracy.[5] Further, this plays itself out within a framework that understands the relationship between faith and knowledge in a manner we might describe as "hyper-Kantian," faulting even Kant for failing to radically think religion within the limits of reason alone—for not being enlightened enough (FS 19/11). Thus Derrida, the consummate "postmodernist," lays claim to a filiation which is distinctly modern, making deconstruction a child of the Enlightenment.

Derrida's appropriation of Kant when reflecting on religion, along with his affirmation of a new *Aufklärung*, raises the question of the (dis)continuity between modernity (and Kant, in particular) and what has been commonly described as "postmodernity." Is postmodernity a "new Enlightenment?" If so, in what sense is it "new?" Derrida's philosophy of religion and his account of the relationship between faith and reason seem to be little more than a repetition of Kant's own account, and thus subject to the same critique as other Enlightenment accounts of the "essence" of religion (FS 34/23), of which Kant's *Religion within the Limits of Reason Alone* is a celebrated example.[6] Further, this specter of Kant (evoked by Derrida himself) problematizes accounts of postmodernism which posit a

---

and Knowledge: The Two Sources of 'Religion' at the Limits of Reason Alone," trans. Samuel Weber, in *Religion*, ed. Jacques Derrida and Gianni Vattimo (Stanford: Stanford University Press, 1998), 14 (henceforth abbreviated as FS, followed by French and English pagination). In addition, Derrida suggests in *Sauf le nom* that this project is moved "in a way" by "a kind of spirit of the Enlightenment." See Derrida, *On the Name*, ed. Thomas Dutoit, trans. David Wood, John P. Leavey, Jr., and Ian McLeod (Stanford: Stanford University Press, 1995), 71.

5   Here Derrida also follows the lead of Emmanuel Levinas, for whom "religion" *is* ethical responsibility (see, e.g., Levinas, *Totality and Infinity*, trans. Alphonso Lingis [Pittsburgh: Duquesne University Press, 1969], 40, 80). Thus Derrida will ultimately conclude that religion is *responsibility*: "*La religion, c'est* **la réponse**" (FS 39/26, emphasis original). On Levinas' relation to Kant, see John Llewelyn, *Hypocritical Imagination: Kant and Levinas* (New York: Routledge, 1999). It is precisely the commitment to democracy which leads Derrida to a Kantian *epoché* or liberating "abstraction" (FS 16/8): "this abstraction, without denying faith, liberates a universal rationality and the political democracy that cannot be dissociated from it" (FS 29/19). The democratic element of this project will be further discussed below.

6   The other quintessentially modern account, though operating from a standpoint very critical of Kant, would have to be Schleiermacher's *On Religion: Speeches to Its Cultured Despisers*, trans. Richard Crouter (Cambridge: Cambridge University Press, 1996), especially the Second Speech, "On the Essence of Religion" (18–54).

radical discontinuity with the modern, Enlightenment project.[7] Instead, it seems that these purported "postmodern" accounts of religion differ little from Enlightenment criticisms. For some, this would be a redeeming trait of postmodernism. But what if that Enlightenment critique of religion was itself subjected to criticism? In that case, Derrida would here simply be repeating one of the most problematic Enlightenment prejudices against determinate or "dogmatic" religion—a prejudice that should be unveiled as such (*per* Gadamer[8]) and subject to (postmodern) critique.

Building on the analyses of chapter 5, the goal of this chapter is to provide an exposition of the way in which Derrida repeats Kant's project of thinking religion within the limits of reason alone (concurrently pursuing questions about the relationship between modernity and postmodernity) and its disclosure of a purportedly "pure" moral religion, and then subject such a project to a more persistently postmodern (and perhaps Augustinian) critique, developing an alternative understanding of the relationship between faith and reason.

As noted in chapter 5, the occasion for Derrida's reflection on religion is the surprising "return of religion" (FS 13/5); or better, the so-called "return" of religion, which surprised only a post-Marxist or post-Feuerbachian academic community—which is to say, a post-Kantian, post-Enlightenment community.[9] But why is this so surprising? Does it not only surprise those who naïvely opposed religion and science (Enlightenment, Reason, Criticism)—"as though the one could not but put an end to the other" (FS 13/5). Instead, Derrida argues, a different "schema" will be required to think the relationship between faith and knowledge, suggesting that Derrida will provide an alternative to the Enlightenment notion of an "autonomous" reason which is untainted by faith (found in Kant, Hegel, Marx, and Feuerbach). Here several problems arise which need to

---

7   I have addressed these questions further in my "A Little Story about Metanarratives: Lyotard, Religion, and Postmodernism Revisited," *Faith and Philosophy* 18 (2001): 261–76.
8   For the Enlightenment, religion itself constitutes a prejudice from which we need to be liberated. Here I would follow Gadamer's unveiling of the Enlightenment *prejudice* against prejudice: "The fundamental prejudice of the Enlightenment is the prejudice against prejudice itself." See Hans-Georg Gadamer, *Truth and Method*, 2nd ed., trans. Joel Weinsheimer and Donald G. Marshall (New York: Continuum, 1989), 273. It is not a matter of escaping or eliminating prejudice (which would be impossible), but of becoming aware of prejudice and subjecting it to critique.
9   Later Derrida suggests that Marx's critique of religion itself depends upon the "appeal to a heterogeneity between faith and knowledge" (FS 23/14).

114   The Nicene Option

be explored. First, does Derrida really provide an alternative schema for the relationship between faith and knowledge, or is it in fact a hyper-modern notion of "autonomous" reason—a repetition of Kant? Second, is this critique of religion—whether found in Kant or Derrida, whether modern or postmodern—a philosophically viable project, or is it itself subject to critique? Third, are there other elements of Derrida's analysis of religion which undermine his attempt to think religion within the limits of reason alone, resulting in the deconstruction of Derrida's critique?[10]

Thinking Religion within the Limits of Reason Alone: Derrida's Repetition of Kant

For Derrida, in a gesture he describes as Kantian (FS 16/8), the question of religion opens as a question of *abstraction*:

> How "to talk religion?" Of religion? Singularly of religion, today? How dare we speak of it in the singular without fear and trembling, this very day? And so briefly and so quickly? . . . To give oneself the necessary courage, arrogance or serenity, perhaps one must pretend for an instant to abstract, to abstract from everything or almost everything, in a certain way. Perhaps one must take one's chance in resorting to the most concrete and most accessible, but also the most barren and desert-like, of all abstractions. (FS 9/1)

Thus abstraction becomes linked to a discussion of "salvation" and liberation; but here a question arises: "Should one save oneself *by* abstraction or *from* abstraction" (FS 9/1, emphasis added)? Derrida seems to opt for the former: in order to speak of religion, one must ("perhaps") engage in abstraction from the concrete and determinate religions ("almost")—a kind of flight to the desert, separated from the particularity of historical, determinate religions in order to discover, in this desert of abstraction, a "universal" religion whose structure is a relation of justice. By this process

---

10   It should be emphasized here that for Derrida, "deconstruction" is something that happens in the middle voice, something which texts do to themselves, not something a reader or interpreter does to a text. So it is not a matter of *my* deconstructing Derrida, but rather of locating these opposing trajectories within the text and allowing it to deconstruct itself.

of "desertification" (FS 27/17), Derrida proposes to disclose a structure of ethical obligation which precedes the structures of determinate religion and morality: "Even if it is called the social nexus, link to the other in general, this fiduciary 'link' would precede all determinate community, all positive religion, every onto-anthropo-theological horizon" (FS 26/16). In other words, this process of abstraction exhibits a basis of ethical responsibility which does not depend upon any conditions of experience.[11]

Abstraction, then, is the movement by which Derrida seeks to disclose the religious structure of responsibility, or the outline of a "pure moral religion" lifted out of the determinate and concrete historical religions. Throughout "Foi et savoir," Derrida takes up this question of the relationship between the universal and the particular (or better, the universal and the *singular*[12])—so central to Kant's ethical framework as outlined in both the *Groundwork* and RWLRA—through the metaphor of *topos*: of place (*lieu*), location. Could there be a religion which is not tied to a particular place—a "Promised Land"[13]—and so a particular *history* of revelation (FS 17/8)? If the foundation for ethical obligation were to be located in a particular religion, with ties to a particular revelation and place, we would compromise its universality. But it is precisely this penchant for universality which pushes Derrida to the "desert" of abstraction. As he reflects on the Isle of Capri, these particular individuals who have gathered to "talk religion" share "an unreserved taste, if not an unconditional preference, for what, in politics, is called republican democracy as a universalizable model" (FS 16/8)—an ideal which can be traced to the lights of the Enlightenment and the project which sought liberation from all external authority and power, *especially* religious dogmatism.[14] And thus our predilection for republican democracy as a *universal* ideal would seem to commit us to a certain *epoché*—thinking religion "within the limits of reason alone" (FS 16/8), which for Derrida is to think religion "in the desert." The "desert," for him, is a kind of metaphor for a level of

---

11   Kant, *Religion within the Limits of Reason Alone*, 94–96.
12   The notion of "singularity" in Derrida is appropriated from Kierkegaard. To my knowledge, the earliest discussion of singularity, with reference to Kierkegaard, is in Derrida's first essay on Levinas, "Violence and Metaphysics: An Essay on the Thought of Emmanuel Levinas," in *Writing and Difference*, trans. Alan Bass (Chicago: University of Chicago Press, 1978), 110–11, and more recently and extensively in *Gift of Death*.
13   Or Rome: "We are not far from Rome, but are no longer in Rome" (FS 12/4).
14   Which, however, "does not mean from all faith" (FS 16/8)—only from a *certain* doxa.

abstraction or universality which is disconnected from all particularities of place and history, such that this "desert" of abstraction would represent a "*place* that could well have been *more than* archi-originary, the most anarchic and anarchivable place possible" (FS 26/16). Elsewhere, this desert of abstraction is described as a place that is not a place, a place which "comes under no geography, geometry, or geophysics."[15] Once this *epoché* is effected, the ethical structures of democracy that remain are understood as a priori[16]—divorced from any particular historical or geographical heritage, even if they maintain a certain affinity with particular determinate religious traditions.

It is Kant's notion of a "reflective (*reflektierende*) faith" which Derrida describes as "a concept whose possibility might well open the space for our discussion" (FS 19/10, trans. modified). This is a faith which "does not depend essentially upon any historical revelation and thus agrees with the rationality of purely practical reason" (FS 19/10), which is why it is opposed to "dogmatic faith," which "claims to *know* and thereby ignores the difference between faith and knowledge" (FS 19/10). There is an important difference, he notes, between "believing one knows and knowing one believes" (FS 54/40). Reflective faith has been purged of its particularity, immune to any contamination of time or place. Thus, while Kant remained indebted to his Pietist heritage,[17] the impetus for his reflections on religion were philosophical, and more specifically, the telos of his own critical project, such that *Religion within the Limits of Reason Alone* has been described as a kind of "fourth critique."

At the heart of this Kantian project is a distinct concept of the relationship between faith and reason, presaged in the famous dictum from the Second Preface to the *Critique of Pure Reason*: "I have therefore found it necessary to deny *knowledge*, in order to make room for *faith*."[18] The

---

15 Derrida, *On the Name*, 57.
16 Derrida would resist such a description, perhaps opting to say that these structures are "quasi-*a priori*." But it seems hard not to conclude that a structure which is divorced from and precedes all particular conditions of experience must be *a priori* in a Kantian sense.
17 On Kant's (and Derrida's) terms, the nature of this "debt" would be problematic. It could not be that Kant's disclosure of the Categorical Imperative, for instance, was a thinly disguised "Pietist" imperative, since this would undo its universality. While below we will see that Derrida seems to make just such a charge against Kant, I will argue below that Derrida is subject to the same critique.
18 Kant, *Critique of Pure Reason*, trans. Norman Kemp Smith (London: Macmillan, 1933), Bxxx (henceforth abbreviated as CPR).

relationship between faith and knowledge is precisely one of *heterogeneity*: arriving at the limits of scientific knowledge, it is necessary to displace a dogmatic metaphysics in order to make room for faith and a concept of God—one of the positive implications of laying out the principles of pure reason. In other words, the procedures of reason which issue in knowledge are autonomous vis-à-vis faith: knowledge is the product of operations which do not in any way involve faith, whereas our consciousness (not "knowledge") of freedom and moral obligation is characterized by a faith that displaces any priority speculative reason might seek for itself.[19]

This question of the relationship—or rather, heterogeneity—between faith and knowledge is taken up more systematically after the ethical works, which further clear the space and mark the necessity for thinking religion within the limits of reason alone. Thus RWLRA operates with an understanding of the relationship between faith and reason laid down much earlier. While space was cleared for religious faith through a critique of reason, faith itself is subject to critique; that is, the boundaries or limits must be established lest faith, as reason is wont to do, seeks to claim more than it can deliver. This concern is already seen in the *Critique of Pure Reason*, where Kant remarks: "No one, indeed, will be able to boast that he *knows* that there is a God, and a future life; if he knows this, he is the very man for whom I have long [and vainly] sought" (A828–29/B856–57). Faith needs to be reminded that it is just that—faith, and *not* knowledge. It is in the first of four *parerga* in RWLRA that this same concern is expressed by the distinction between "reflective" and "dogmatic" faith. Broaching the matter of grace, Kant suggests that "[r]eason believes this with a faith which (with respect to the possibility of this supernatural complement) might be called *reflective*; for *dogmatic* faith, which proclaims itself as a form of *knowledge*, appears to her dishonest or presumptuous" (RWLRA 48). "In making such assertions and pretensions to

---

19   Gilles Deleuze makes a case for the role of the imagination in moral understanding, arguing that "the consciousness of morality, that is to say the moral common sense, not only includes beliefs, but the acts of imagination through which sensible Nature appears as fit to receive the effect of the suprasensible. Imagination itself is thus really part of common sense." Deleuze, *Kant's Critical Philosophy: The Doctrine of the Faculties*, trans. Hugh Tomlinson and Barbara Habberjam (Minneapolis: University of Minnesota Press, 1984), 43. "Thus faith," he continues, "is not related to a particular faculty, but expresses the synthesis of the speculative interest and the practical interest at the same time as the subordination of the former to the latter" (44). On this subordination, see *Critique of Practical Reason*, 1.2.2.3.

knowledge," he later remarks, "reason simply passes beyond the limits of its own insight" (RWLRA 63–64), claiming to know where it cannot see. In other words, dogmatic faith fails to recognize itself *as* faith, and thus fails to recognize the heterogeneity between faith and knowledge.

In his lectures, Kant not only lays out this distinction but demonstrates why it is beneficial: faith in these matters is, in a sense, more virtuous. For instance, our moral belief in the existence of God is not a mere "hypothesis" or "opinion" (arguing from the contingency of the world to a supreme author), but rather demands "firm belief" because it follows from "some absolutely necessary datum."[20] "Hence our faith," Kant concludes,

> is not scientific knowledge, and thank heaven it is not! For God's wisdom is apparent in the very fact that we do not *know* that God exists, but that we should *believe* that God exists. For suppose we could attain to scientific knowledge of God's existence, through our experience or in some other way (even if the possibility of this knowledge cannot be immediately thought). And suppose further that we could really reach as much certainty through this knowledge as we do through intuition. Then in this case, all morality would breakdown.[21]

Morality would break down because it would no longer be voluntary, and the moral agent would act out of fear of punishment rather than virtue. Thus, "as regards our morality, it is very good that our knowledge is not scientific knowledge but faith. For in this way the fulfillment of my duty will be far purer and more unselfish."[22] Hence we can see why the confusion of faith and knowledge—as in "dogmatic faith"—would in fact be detrimental to morality. For the sake of morality, it is imperative that we recognize and maintain the heterogeneity between faith and knowledge.

The result will be a "pure religious faith" (RWLRA 94)—"rational" or "reflective" faith—which has both purged itself of dogmatism (RWLRA 48, 63–64) and extirpated any vestige of elements which derive from particular, determinate, historical faiths (RWLRA 94–115). The latter "kenotic" movement is necessary in order to achieve the universality

---

20   Kant, *Lectures on Philosophical Theology*, trans. Allen W. Wood and Gertrude M. Clark (Ithaca: Cornell University Press, 1978), 123.
21   Kant, *Lectures on Philosophical Theology*, 123.
22   Kant, *Lectures on Philosophical Theology*, 163.

which is required of a moral religion—the only "true" religion (RWLRA 95, 98). Indeed, "a church dispenses with the most important mark of truth, namely, a rightful claim to universality" (RWLRA 100; cp. 105). Thus "pure moral religion" stands not only in contrast to "dogmatic faith" (which fails to recognize the heterogeneity of faith and knowledge), but also "ecclesiastical faith," which is dependent upon a particular, historical revelation (RWLRA 96). Kant in fact argues that the term "religion" ought to be used more prudently, advocating that what we describe as "religions" ought to be termed "faiths," since "[o]ne does too great honor to most people by saying of them: They profess this or that religion. For they know none and desire none—statutory ecclesiastical faith is all that they understand" (RWLRA 98–99). In a manner very similar to Derrida's concern regarding "wars of religion" in the Middle East and Eastern Europe,[23] Kant argues that "so-called religious wars" were in fact devoid of religion and are only "wrangles over ecclesiastical faith" (RWLRA 99).

This distinction between "faiths" which are particular, historical, and determinate and a "religion" which is universal is reproduced in Derrida's own distinction between particular "messian*isms*" and the "messianic" as a universal structure. Motivated by a similar concern regarding the contingency of the historical and determinate, the *messianic*, or "messianicity without messianism," is defined as "the opening to the future or to the coming of the other as the advent of justice but without horizon of expectation and without prefiguration" (FS 27/17). But why this latter requirement? Why must it be a justice which cannot be predetermined or "prefigured?" Because any predetermination would be precisely a *determination*, and for Derrida, it is precisely determination itself which is unjust. In other words, any "horizon of expectation" (*horizon d'attente*) or predelineated anticipation would undo the universality of such justice, representing an *in*justice. Thus the "messianic exposes itself to absolute surprise" (FS 28/17); it is a "general structure of experience" which denotes a responsibility to the other as justice (FS 28/18). This responsibility must be determined *by the other* and therefore cannot be prefigured or determined by the subject of responsibility. As such, to delineate this general

---

23 One of the tasks of FS is "a programme of analysis of the forms of evil perpetrated at the four corners of the world 'in the name of religion'" (FS 22/13). Elsewhere, Derrida considers the "war of the messianisms" in the Middle East. See Derrida, *Specters of Marx*, trans. Peggy Kamuf (New York: Routledge, 1994), 58.

"messianic" structure, one must engage in *abstraction*, such that abstraction becomes a kind of liberation, an "abstract messianicity" (FS 28/18). This "general structure of experience," which is the structure of justice,

> does not depend upon any messianism [i.e., determinate religion], it follows no determinate revelation, it belongs properly to no Abrahamic religion (even if I am obliged here, "among ourselves," for essential reasons of language and of place, of culture, of a provisional rhetoric and a historical strategy of which I will speak later, to continue giving it named marked by the Abrahamic religions) [FS 28/18].

Thus, like a Kantian moral religion, Derrida's "messianic" is not dependent upon any historical, determinate "revelation" (cp. RWLRA 94–95).

However, while both Kant's "pure moral religion" and Derrida's "messianic" (or "religion without religion") eschew any dependence upon particular, determinate faiths, they both still affirm the priority of faith in matters practical. Thus both are characterized by a dual movement: on the one hand, discharging determinate religion in the name of universal rationality; on the other hand, displacing knowledge in order to make room for the faith of practical reason—justice, responsibility, *la religion* which is *la réponse*. The tie that binds me to the other in responsibility is, at root, a bond of faith—a "fiduciary 'link'" (FS 26/16). "This abstract messianicity," Derrida argues, "belongs from the very beginning to the experience of faith, of believing, of a credit that is irreducible to knowledge and of a trust that 'founds' all relation to the other in testimony" (FS 28/18). This would be a "universal" faith before every determinate faith, akin to Kant's "pure religious faith" which would be the condition of possibility for any "ecclesiastical faith" (RWLRA 95). So "religion"—a universal religion—whose structure is unveiled as the messianic (not a messian*ism*), is in its very structure a relation of justice: my responsibility to the other. But it is not a responsibility that I know; rather, one that I believe. So it is necessary to deny knowledge in order to make room for this responsibility. And it is "[t]his justice, which I distinguish from law[24] (*droit*), [that] alone allows the hope, beyond all 'messianisms,' of a universalizable culture of singularities" (FS 28/18)—a kind of "kingdom of ends" where the singularities are

---

24 I have modified Weber's translation here; he translates as "right," but it is *du droit*, with the article.

precisely *others* (echoing both Kierkegaard and Levinas). This is because "the other makes the law, the law is other: to give ourselves back, and up, to the other. To every other and to the utterly other (*A tout autre et au tout autre*)" (FS 47/34). This faith inscribes itself at the very origin of language and thus is characterized by universality.[25] And it is "the universalizable culture of this faith" which "alone permits a 'rational' and universal discourse on the subject of 'religion'" (28/18). It is a messianicity which is "stripped of everything, as it should, this faith without dogma" which marks the possibility of a universal justice (FS 28/18) which leads Derrida to associate this founding faith with what Montaigne and Pascal describe as "the mystical foundation of authority" (29/18).[26]

Thus the universal structure of ethical obligation, on the one hand clearly disengaged from any particular faith or religion, is nevertheless itself "known" only by a kind of practical faith or trust. Here we see the clear repetition of the Kantian dual movement noted above. Further, such abstraction has, according to Derrida, liberating implications: "this abstraction, without denying faith, liberates a universal rationality and the political democracy that cannot be dissociated from it" (FS 29/19).

Kant, however, has not made it to the "desert." In fact, Derrida criticizes Kant for not properly carrying out a radical abstraction or "desertification" of moral obligation. While repeating Kant's demand that a pure moral religion be decontaminated of any particular, determinate, historical faith, Derrida concludes that such a process of decontamination was not properly completed by Kant. This in two ways: first, Kant continues to privilege the Christian religion, such that "the Christian religion would be the only truly 'moral' religion" (FS 19/10). Second, "pure morality and Christianity are indissociable in their essence and in their concept" (FS 19/10). In other words, it would be a contradiction for moral obligation to be purely "rational" and non-Christian and so must remain, in a veiled sense, linked to the particularity and historicity of a Christian revelation. "The unconditionality of the categorical imperative," Derrida concludes, "is evangelical. The moral law inscribes itself at the bottom of our hearts

---

25   This is also analyzed in Derrida, *Of Spirit: Heidegger and the Question*, trans. Geoffrey Bennington and Rachel Bowlby (Chicago: University of Chicago Press, 1989), 93–94, 129–36. I have considered this in more detail in ch. 10, "Deconstruction—an Augustinian Science?"
26   See also Derrida, "Force of Law: The 'Mystical Foundation of Authority,'" in *Deconstruction and the Possibility of Justice*, ed. Drucilla Cornell, Michel Rosenfeld, and David Gray Carlson (New York: Routledge, 1992), 3–67.

like a memory of the Passion. When it addresses us, it either speaks the idiom of the Christian—or is silent" (FS 19/11). This is why Derrida considers his disclosure of the "messianic" a completion of the process of decontamination. The messianic, he claims, even if it remains linked "in name" to the Abrahamic religions, remains a completely universal structure of responsibility which in no way depends upon any particular religion or messian*ism*. This, of course, does not call into question Kant's project, but rather completes it: an unveiling of the structure of moral obligation which is decontaminated of any dependence upon a particular, determinate, historical religion—and yet which is "known" only by faith.

The Very Idea of Religion within the Limits of Reason Alone: A Postmodern Critique

So Derrida (the postmodern) does not question the Kantian (modern) project of thinking religion within the limits of reason alone; indeed, he takes it up in order to complete it. The problem which arises, for Derrida, is just *how* such a project would be possible: "How then to think—within the limits of reason alone—a religion which, without again becoming 'natural religion,' would today be effectively universal" (FS 23/14)? But this is a question that Kant also tackles when he considers the relationship between "historical" or "ecclesiastical faith" and "pure religious faith." What is the relationship between these two? While the latter is superior to the former, is ecclesiastical faith nevertheless the necessary condition for the idea of morality which characterizes pure religious faith? Kant is somewhat ambiguous on this point, though I think we can infer his answer. He simply states that, "[i]n men's striving towards an ethical commonwealth, ecclesiastical faith thus naturally precedes pure religious faith" (RWLRA 97). But what does Kant mean by saying the one "naturally precedes" the other? This is somewhat clarified by a brief note which asserts that "morally, this order ought to be reversed" (RWLRA 97n). In other words, it seems that Kant argues that "morally"—which must also mean "rationally"—pure religious faith is prior to any ecclesiastical faith, but historically speaking, ecclesiastical faiths are the means by which we come to reflect on and understand the "one true religion." In the order of knowing, ecclesiastical faith is prior, but in the order of being, pure religious (i.e., moral) faith comes first. Thus Kant routinely refers to historical or ecclesiastical faiths as "vehicles" for the propagation of pure religious faith: "it remains true once for all that a statutory *ecclesiastical faith* is associated with pure religious faith as its vehicle and as the means of public union of men for its promotion" (RWLRA 98).[27] And eventually, one would hope pure religious faith could makes its way around on its own, no longer needing a ride from ecclesiastical faith. As Kant projects:

> When . . . an historical faith attaches itself to pure religion, as its vehicle, but with the consciousness that it is only a vehicle, and when this faith, having become ecclesiastical, embraces the principle of a continual approach to pure religious faith, in order to finally dispense with the historical vehicle, a church thus characterized can at any time be called the *true* church. (RWLRA 106)

The job of the church, then, as a still particular historical faith, is to work itself out of a job, to no longer be needed as a promoter for pure religion. As a kind of "tutor" to the moral law, ecclesiastical faith plays only a propaedeutic role. Derrida, as we have noted above, questions this genealogy, suggesting that the roles of father and son have been reversed—that, in fact, the Categorical Imperative remains, by filiation, Christian and hence both dependent upon and product of a particular, determinate "ecclesiastical" faith (FS 19/10–11).

This question of precedence or conditions also arises, not surprisingly, in Derrida's very Kantian approach to the issue. For Derrida, the question is: does the messianic or "religion" here outlined *precede* determinate messianisms, as their condition of possibility? Or is it possible to sketch this universal messianic structure only on the basis of particular, determinate revelations?

The question remains open, and with it that of knowing whether this desert can be thought and left to announce itself "before" the desert that we know (that of the revelations and retreats, of the lives and deaths of God, of all the figures of kenosis or of transcendence, of *religio* or of historical "religions"); or whether, "on the contrary," it is "from" this last desert [historical religions] that we can glimpse that which precedes the first, which I call the desert in the desert (FS 31–32/21).

---

27   For a discussion of particular faiths as "vehicles," see also Kant, *Perpetual Peace*, trans. Lewis White Beck in *On History* (London: Macmillan, 1963), 113n7.

While here Derrida seems content to remain undecided, even advocating "tolerance" (FS 32–33/21–22), this response to the question is disappointing and, in truth, a punt on Derrida's part. This is not a question of ethical "undecidability" (which is a condition of all decisions which demands precisely that one decide) but simple indecision on his part, since *either* possibility (and I cannot see other options) would be problematic for him on his own grounds. He would either end up siding with a particular determinate religion (and here it is precisely his Enlightenment penchant for universality which prevents him from doing so), or for a purely transcendental structure—also a deconstructive heresy (as we discussed in chapter 5). Further, he has earlier already answered the question, opting for the latter stance: the "messianic," he has told us, "does not depend upon any messianism, it follows no determinate revelation, it belongs properly to no Abrahamic religion" (FS 28/18). The messianic, then, as *a priori*, is a transcendental condition for all particular, determinate religions and is itself immune from any particular faith.

Here I would unpack two criticisms of Derrida, which also constitute criticisms of Kant and the general modern project of thinking religion within the limits of reason alone. First, affirming Derrida's unveiling of the determinate "evangelical" heritage of the Categorical Imperative, we must subject Derrida's claims to the same criticism he leveled against Kant, viz., that the ethical structure disclosed by this process of desert abstraction retains very distinct geo-political ties: to Abrahamic understandings of ethical obligation and to political democracy. In other words, the elements of this "general structure" remain determined by a particular time, history, and place; indeed, one of deconstruction's articles of faith is that it could not be otherwise. As a result, both Kant's and Derrida's own project of a "purely rational religion" must falter on this inescapable particularity. It is true that Derrida claims that the messianic is "Abrahamic" only in name (FS 28/18). But if so, then why that name? Why not another?[28] Could this ethical structure be described as "karmic" or "Taoist?" Why not? Because in the end—or rather, in the beginning—it remains an understanding of ethical obligation which owes its disclosure to a determinate prophetic tradition, the same tradition which gave birth to Kant's

---

28 Derrida does also consider this under the name *chora* (drawing on Plato's *Timaeus*), but this would only offer an alternative, Western naming and would not signal a rupture with time and place altogether.

Categorical Imperative. Further, it remains committed to a very determinate political ideal: republican democracy.[29] While Derrida does concede that our understanding of this moral obligation is a matter of faith, he fails to recognize that it is also particular and determinate. However, it should be noted that the particular or determinate genealogy of this ethical structure does not disqualify it from moral import; that would only be the case if we continued to operate with the hope of being able to step outside history, which is precisely what is challenged by Derrida. Instead, I would argue that we ought to: (1) recognize that every ethical and political framework must necessarily have a determinate and historical origin, even a "religious" origin, broadly understood;[30] and (2) recognize that the ethico-political ideal outlined by both Kant and Derrida finds its determinate heritage in the prophetic and Christian tradition.

This points to the second criticism. The notion of an autonomous or "pure" reason—untainted by either history or faith (or prejudice) is an Enlightenment myth. Derrida's project of thinking religion within the limits of reason alone depends upon a heterogeneity between faith and knowledge which presupposes that reason conducts itself within a pure, autonomous arena. Such a pure reason in Kant has been the subject of criticism since Hegel. As Merold Westphal observes, "For Kant, the forms and categories that constitute the phenomenal world are at work in all human cognition, at all times, and in all places. But almost immediately people began to notice the operation of historically specific

---

29   Derrida seems to think that this notion of "democracy" is somehow a pure transcendental structure which is completely undetermined, such that he will speak of the "messianic" as a "democracy to come." If I were to ask Derrida whether this call for a "democracy to come" was assuming anything determinate, he would say, "No." Well, then, can I speak of "the theocracy to come?" Certainly not, he would reply. Then it must be the case that he has some idea of what this "democracy to come" must look like; in other words, the notion of democracy entails some content, in which case it is not a pure or merely formal idea but, in fact, another messian*ism*.

30   Within this broader understanding of "religion," even a traditionally "secular" worldview such as Marxism would be religious insofar as it is grounded in fundamental commitments. Derrida suggests the same by describing Marxism as yet another "messian*ism*" (*Specters of Marx*, 58–59). This accords with a Reformational (in the tradition of Kuyper and Dooyeweerd) understanding of "religion." For a helpful unpacking of this concept in an ethical and political context, see Richard J. Mouw and Sander Griffioen, *Pluralisms and Horizons: An Essay in Christian Public Philosophy* (Grand Rapids: Eerdmans, 1993). See also Roy A. Clouser, *The Myth of Religious Neutrality: An Essay on the Hidden Role of Religious Belief in Theories*, rev. ed. (South Bend: University of Notre Dame Press, 2005).

a prioris constituting a variety of human worlds."[31] In other words, reason itself is not free and cannot be free of all prejudice, but rather begins from certain cultural assumptions or, at the very least—as Derrida notes—an implicit *trust* in language. More specifically, as I will argue in chapter 10 below, reason is always already grounded in a worldview which constitutes a fundamental trust or commitment.[32] As a result, faith and knowledge are not as heterogeneous as Kant and Derrida would have us believe. It is here that I would locate the Augustinian moment of this critique of Kant and Derrida: I do not believe only where I cannot know; rather, I believe in order to know. Faith—whatever that faith might be—is the condition for knowledge. So their relation is not one of heterogeneity but rather dependence. Thus the attempt to think religion within the limits of reason alone would not be a project of formalization or secularization (attempting to distill a "purified" or "uncontaminated" rational religion), but more a kind of comparative theology: the attempt to think one faith within the limits of another faith.

As such, the project itself becomes questionable, or at least the assumptions which motivate it would be dismantled. At that point it would seem fair to ask why the project should be carried out at all. That is not to say, of course, that one is opposed to enlightenment, or even critique; but it would open the space for a new appreciation of enlightenment as "illumination"—which is just to say a retrieval of an Augustinian account of knowledge.

---

31   Merold Westphal, "Christian Philosophers and the Copernican Revolution," in *Christian Perspectives on Religious Knowledge*, ed. C. Stephen Evans and Merold Westphal (Grand Rapids: Eerdmans, 1993), 172.
32   See also James K. A. Smith, "The Art of Christian Atheism: Faith and Philosophy in Early Heidegger," *Faith and Philosophy* 14 (1997): 76–79.

7

Determined Hope

A Phenomenology of Christian Expectation

We have every reason to hope...[1]

In chapters 5 and 6, I called into question Derrida's (modern and Kantian) logic of "purity" which undergirds his critique of "determination" as inherently violent—a critique that is haunted by the specter of "indeterminacy" or "purity." My goal here in chapter 7 is to consider a specific instance of this tension: Derrida's account of "hope" and eschatology. Within the larger constructive project of thematizing the contours of Christian hope and eschatological expectation, I will take up a critical analysis of Derrida's quasi-eschatology, his "hope without hope," as a construct demanded only by a logic already put into question. Alongside this, we will also consider something of a sibling rival to deconstruction's hope without hope: Rorty's liberal hope for a social utopia.

What to Expect when You're Expecting

Whether culled from jeremiads on the right or hymns of (to?) despair on the left, one is impressed by what seems a pervasive hopelessness or melancholy which characterizes late modernity.[2] Our (modern) gods have

---

1   Richard Rorty, "I Hear America Sighing," *New York Times Book Review*, November 7, 1999, 16. See also his discussion of hope in "The End of Leninism, Havel, and Social Hope," in *Truth and Progress*, Philosophical Papers, vol. 3 (Cambridge: Cambridge University Press, 1998), esp. 242–43 (where he, consistently, rejects the notion of radical evil).
2   For versions of this story and diagnosis from different perspectives, see Andrew Delbanco, *The Real American Dream: A Meditation on Hope* (Cambridge: Harvard University

failed us and in this twilight we are left without a sun and no prospects for new illumination. Having been confidently marching toward the Garden to recapture paradise, we found the gates barred by flaming swords—World Wars, genocide, apartheid . . . (so many swords). And yet the disappointment seems to have caught us by surprise, for as Auden observed, our confidence had blinded us:

> Till lately we knew of no other, and between us we seemed
> To have what it took—the adrenal courage of the tiger,
> The chameleon's discretion, the modesty of the doe,
> Or the fern's devotion to spatial necessity:
> To practise one's peculiar civic virtue was not
> So impossible after all; to cut our losses
> And bury our dead was really quite easy: That was why
> We were always able to say: "We are children of God,
> And our Father has never forsaken His people."[3]

But "then we were children," he continues, suggesting another loss of innocence. "That was a moment ago / Before an outrageous novelty had been introduced into our lives. / Why were we never warned? Perhaps we were." Now everything has changed,[4] our confidence and hope has been shattered, and we late moderns find ourselves slipping under the surface, being pulled down by the eddy of despair.[5] Even (only?) the intellectuals are getting sucked in, Rorty suggests: "Whereas intellectuals of the nineteenth century undertook to replace metaphysical comfort with historical hope, intellectuals at the end of this century, feeling let down by history,

---

Press, 1999), and Richard Bauckham and Trevor Hart, *Hope Against Hope: Christian Eschatology at the Turn of the Millennium* (Grand Rapids: Eerdmans, 1999), 1–43.

3   W. H. Auden, "Advent," from *For the Time Being: A Christmas Oratorio*, ed. Alan Jacobs (Princeton: Princeton University Press, 2013), 6.

4   "It's as if we had left our house for five minutes to mail a letter, and during that time the living room had changed places with the room behind the mirror over the fireplace" (Auden, "Advent," 6).

5   Rorty sees symptoms of this in political philosophy, which no longer constructs narratives which engender hope but rather begin from abstract principles. "This seems to me," he concludes, "the result of a loss of hope—or, more specifically—of an inability to construct a plausible narrative of progress. A turn away from narration and utopian dreams toward philosophy seems to me a gesture of despair." Rorty, "Globalization, the Politics of Identity and Social Hope," in *Philosophy and Social Hope* (New York: Penguin, 1999), 232.

are experiencing self-indulgent, pathetic hopelessness."[6] We have lost our faith, and so our hope.[7]

Given this apparent consensus regarding postmodern hopelessness, we might be somewhat surprised to find expressions of hope articulated by two supposedly quintessential "postmoderns":[8] Richard Rorty and Jacques Derrida. With almost evangelical fervor, both hope against hope, proclaiming hope for a justice to come in the face of the grossest injustices. "In the place of knowledge,"[9] Rorty maintains a pragmatist hope "that full social justice can be attained"[10]—perhaps even in the next hundred years.[11] Derrida's hope—different from Rorty's in important ways (but perhaps not *so* different)—is no less utopian in its expectation.[12] His too is a hope for justice which is Marxist "in spirit":[13] a "justice, which I distinguish from law, [which] alone allows the hope, beyond all 'messianisms,'

---

6 Rorty, "Afterword: Pragmatism, Pluralism, and Postmodernism," in *Philosophy and Social Hope*, 263.

7 That is to say that hopelessness or despair (or melancholy) is the result or symptom of the failure of a basic trust or commitment. It seems to me that this is thematized in Giddens' analysis of basic trust, where he argues that it is precisely this trust which produces hope: it is "sentiments of love which, combined with trust, generate hope and courage" [faith, hope, and love!] (*Modernity and Self-Identity*, 46; see also 38–40). Thus, we can conclude that a loss of hope implies a crisis of trust. This will be confirmed by Rorty, who traces the loss of hope to a failure to *believe* in the stories of progress.

8 On my hesitations with the term "postmodernism," see James K. A. Smith and Shane R. Cudney, "Postmodern Freedom and the Growth of Fundamentalism," *Studies in Religion/Sciences Religieuses* 25 (1996): 25–46. However, the term perhaps still carries some heuristic value; in this chapter I have used it interchangeably with "late modernity" as analyzed by Anthony Giddens, *Modernity and Self-Identity: Self and Society in the Late Modern Age* (Stanford: Stanford University Press, 1991). In general, I think we might distinguish between "postmodernity" as a social and cultural phenomenon and "postmodernism" as an intellectual or philosophical "movement" (but if pressed, I would concede the distinction is a slippery one). In any event, I would only resist analyses which posit some radical discontinuity between modernity and postmodernity, or between the "Enlightenment project" and postmodernism (on the continuities, see ch. 6 above)

9 This raises questions about the epistemology of hope, to which we will return below.

10 Rorty, "Failed Prophecies, Glorious Hopes," in *Philosophy and Social Hope*, 203.

11 As envisioned (backwards) in his "Looking Backwards from the Year 2096," in *Philosophy and Social Hope*, 243–51, where Rorty suggests a revival of Walter Rauschenbusch's "social gospel" in the latter half of the twenty-first century (249).

12 I use "utopian" here in the sense explicated by Moltman in *Theology of Hope*, trans. James W. Leitch (Minneapolis: Fortress, 1993), 25: "Hope and the kind of thinking that goes with it . . . cannot submit to the reproach of being utopian, for they do not strive after things that have 'no place,' but after things that have 'no place *as yet*' but can acquire one."

13 This is a central claim in Derrida, *Specters of Marx*, trans. Peggy Kamuf (New York: Routledge, 1994), 92–93. For Rorty's suspicion regarding just which "spirit" deconstruction

130   The Nicene Option

of a universalizable culture of singularities"[14]—which is to say, hope for a "democracy to come."[15] Indeed, as John Caputo comments, "deconstruction comes down to an affirmation, an invocation, a *hope in the future*, and what is that if not a certain *faith*, indeed the passion of an extreme faith in the unbelievable, in *the* impossible."[16] And developing this further, in his own voice, Caputo concludes: "The name of God is the name of a chance for something absolutely new, for a new birth, for the expectation, the hope, the hope against hope in a transforming future. Without it we are left without hope and are absorbed by rational management techniques."[17]

Both Rorty and Derrida, however, are critical of particularly Christian hopes. Like Greek philosophy, Rorty argues, the New Testament accepts the premise "that the social conditions of human life will never change in any important respect," and it is this conviction which "leads the writers of the New Testament to turn their attention from the possibility of a better human future to the hope of pie in the sky when we die."[18] While Rorty faults the Christian vision for an "otherworldliness"[19] which is morally and politically debilitating, Derrida criticizes Christian hope for its political violence. Because of its determination of a particular vision of justice, Derrida argues that Christian hope would be the basis for legitimating the worst injustices against those who would not submit to the vision. Alluding to what Derrida describes as the "war of messianic eschatologies"[20] and his concern regarding "the forms of evil perpetrated in the four corners of the world 'in the name of religion,'"[21] Caputo concludes that "the *determinable* messianisms, the specific biblical and philosophical

---

has asked into its heart, and whether we really need Marx for hope, see "A Spectre is Haunting the Intellectuals: Derrida on Marx," in *Philosophy and Social Hope*, 210–22.

14   Jacques Derrida, "Foi et savoir: Les deux sources de la 'religion' aux limites de la simple raison," in *La religion*, ed. Thierry Marchaisse (Paris: Éditions du Seuil, 1996), 28; trans. Samuel Weber as "Faith and Knowledge: The Two Sources of 'Religion' at the Limits of Reason Alone," in *Religion*, ed. Jacques Derrida and Gianni Vattimo (Stanford: Stanford University Press, 1998), 17. On the distinction between "messianisms" (concrete, particular religions) and the "messianic" (as a universal, formal structure of obligation), see my "Determined Violence," 199–207.

15   Derrida, *Specters of Marx*, 59, 64–65.

16   John D. Caputo, *The Prayers and Tears of Jacques Derrida: Religion without Religion* (Bloomington: Indiana University Press, 1997), 133 (first italics added).

17   John D. Caputo, *On Religion* (New York: Routledge, 2001), 11.

18   Rorty, "Failed Prophecies, Glorious Hopes," 208.

19   Rorty, "Failed Prophecies, Glorious Hopes," 207.

20   Derrida, *Specters of Marx*, 58.

21   Derrida, "Foi et savoir," 22; "Faith and Knowledge," 13.

messianic eschatologies, are consummately dangerous. They describe a scene of violence and war, among which is to be included not only the wars that are raged over the holy city of Jerusalem but Marxism itself."[22] So it is precisely the determination of Christian (and Marxist) hope which implicates it in violence, necessitating Derrida's disclosure of an indeterminate "messianic" religion which is the basis for hope for a justice which is, always, "to come."

While these discourses of hope offer "good news," the task of this chapter is to question these hopes in two fundamental ways: first, and here I am engaging Rorty primarily, what (if anything) *grounds* such hopes, thereby distinguishing them from mere wishful thinking? What *reason* do they give us to be hopeful?[23] Second, and here I am thinking of Derrida, what are they hoping *for*? What is the object or content of their hope? Can hope be hopeful without content? Can we hope for nothing? Here it is not a question of ground but rather *determination* of the object-hoped-for and the *horizons* within which hope is expressed.

I will argue that Rorty's hope lacks ground (or at least based on a questionable, insufficient ground) and Derrida's hope lacks determination, and that as a result both are disqualified, in a sense, from functioning as genuine hopes. More specifically, my goal is to critique Derrida's position in order to show that determinacy per se cannot disqualify particular hopes; indeed, hope must be determinate and cannot be otherwise. Therefore, Christian hope cannot be excluded simply by virtue of its determinacy. But in order to articulate this critique, I will first provide a phenomenological analysis of the formal structure of hoping as a mode of intentional consciousness, in order to discern the features which are common to all hopes and acts of hoping. This will provide the basis for a critique of Rorty and Derrida which in turn will open the space for a (post-critical) proclamation of a distinctly Christian hope and sense of expectation as viable in late modern society—and perhaps even our only hope.

22 Caputo, *Prayers and Tears*, 128.
23 Let me here note, to head off initial reactions from post-foundationalists, that below I will argue this matter of "reasons" or "ground" is not unjustified even in a post-foundationalist climate, since hoping without reason would be simply *illusion*, of which both Rorty and Derrida are critical. So any knee-jerk reply about the notion of "ground" as (God forbid) "foundationalist" will first have to work through the phenomenology of hope sketched below, where I will contend that the very structure of hope demands a ground but that the nature of that grounding is not foundational in the rationalist sense.

132 The Nicene Option

Structures of Hope: A Phenomenology of Expectation

Hoping, like loving and believing (to invoke both a Pauline and Husserlian relation), is a mode of consciousness and a particular way of "intending" the future. As such, and like other acts of consciousness such as perceiving and willing, hoping should be amenable to phenomenological analysis.[24] In order to carry this out, we will need to briefly outline three key elements of phenomenology. First, as Husserl observes (in contrast to Descartes), consciousness is *intentional*; that is, consciousness is never without an object or a world; rather, I always have before me—whether I am perceiving, judging, feeling, or remembering—an object of consciousness. I cannot think without thinking *of* something. Thus, the first fundamental insight of phenomenology, known as the doctrine of *intentionality*,[25] observes that consciousness is always consciousness *of*. . . . Second, the object intended is *constituted* by the ego. This simply means that the ego "makes sense" or, literally, "gives sense" (*Sinngebung* [*Sinn*, meaning; *-gebung*, given]) to experience by "putting together" or constituting the data of experience into an identifiable object.[26] The wave of data coming at my senses right now is put together and "made sense of" by consciousness so that rather than waves of color and light, I perceive before me a screen, books, a watch, etc. Anything that would be completely undetermined could not be constituted into an object, and thus could not be "intended" in any way. It would have no "significance" (recalling the connection between something having *meaning* and being *significant*) and could not, in the technical sense, be "experienced." Third, this process of constitution can only happen within *horizons* of constitution which provide the context within which I "make sense" of what is before me. In other words, constitution happens within horizons of meaning which enable me to see the object before me *as* a lamp or *as*

---

24 For fuller elucidation, see Edmund Husserl, *Cartesian Meditations*, trans. Dorion Cairns (Dordrecht: Kluwer, 1993). To the best of my knowledge, Husserl never undertook a specific analysis of hope as a mode of intentional consciousness.
25 Consciousness is described as "intentional" because it always "aims" at objects; the Latin term for this kind of aiming (found in Aquinas' epistemology, for instance) is *intentio*. In Husserl's terminology, to intend an object is also to "mean" an object, to intend it *as* something; this relates to the principles of constitution and horizonality below.
26 This is a largely passive process according to Husserl, and is governed by processes of habituation and the historical formation of the ego (at least in later works such as *Cartesian Meditations*).

Determined Hope 133

a cup.[27] Thus these "horizons of expectation," we might say, while functioning as conditions, are also precisely what enable me to make sense of my experience; indeed, these horizons of expectation enable me to *have* an experience, to be conscious of something.

With these three elements of phenomenology in hand—intentionality, constitution, and horizonality—we can now turn to the specific mode of intentional consciousness we find in *hope*. First, as a mode of consciousness, it must be intentional, to hope is to always hope for . . . something, hope for . . . x.[28] That would mean that hope can never be without an object—*some* intention—even though this object can admit of *degrees* of determination. For instance, I can hope to win my golf game tomorrow, or I can hope to win by five strokes. The former is intentional, but less determinate than the latter. However, as intentional, hope cannot be completely *un*determined. This is because, on a phenomenological register, in order for me to "know" or relate to any object, it must be constituted or determined to some degree. The completely indeterminate is also nonsensical—literally, *Unsinnig*. Second, the intending of the object of hope and its correlate constitution happens within particular horizons of constitution. Without the horizons, there is no constitution;

---

27 This is analogous to the role of *as*-structures in Heidegger's *Sein und Zeit*. (It is precisely when these horizons are "out of joint"—as in cross-cultural situations—that I constitute objects differently. I might, for instance, like Ariel the Little Mermaid, find myself in a foreign environment where I have difficulty constituting the objects before me because I lack horizons, or I constitute them differently, as when Ariel spots the fork and constitutes it as a "dinglehopper," an object for combing her hair.)
28 It seems to me that it is impossible to think of hope as lacking an object, for a couple of reasons: first, if this were possible, it would not be a mode of consciousness, since consciousness is necessarily intentional. And if hope is not an act of consciousness, what else could it be? Who else can hope but subjects? Second, while one might simply *say* "I hope," the verbal claim seems to necessitate an implicit object of hope on the level of consciousness, even if not verbally articulated. Can I, for instance, simply "love?" If I say "I love," the first question someone will put to me is: "Love what?" Can I love without some object of my affection? Or consider whether it would be possible to simply say, "I will." Can one will without some determinate end? Perhaps what might help is a distinction between "epistemological" or "linguistic" indeterminacy and, for lack of a better word, "ontological" indeterminacy. One might not verbally be able to articulate the object of one's hope, as when I say, perhaps with tears, "I hope . . ." But that is different than saying that, ontologically or phenomenologically speaking, hope has no object (which, we will see below, is very close to Derrida's claim). This phenomenological analysis would admit the possibility of the former but deny the possibility of the latter.

without constitution, there is no object of hope; without an object of hope, there is no hope.

It seems then that a phenomenological description of hope would distinguish four or five key elements of any hope; that is, this would be a general structure or form which could have different contents, but the structure would be the same for all:[29]

> (1) There must be a hop*er*, a subject who hopes; thus, without a person who hopes, there is no hope. While my analysis will not focus on this aspect, one could here focus on the psychological state of the hoper, and perhaps what we might describe as the "virtue" of hope which disposes an agent to be hopeful.
>
> (2) There must be an object that is hop*ed for*. As a way of intending the future, hope is expectant and thus is "waiting" for something to come, which is the object-hoped-for. We must also note that this expectant intending of the future is only hope if that which is expected is *good* (where "good" is understood in the very broad sense of that which is desired).[30] We can expect other things about the future, including both future *adiaphora*, we might say, to which we are indifferent (such as the expectation of the phone bill arriving or the sun rising) as well as future threats. Fear and anxiety are also modes of futural consciousness. What distinguishes them from hope is the perceived good or ill of the object.
>
> (3) There must be the *act* of hope, which is to say an act of consciousness. Two things should be noted in this regard: (a) an "act of consciousness" (what Husserl describes as a *cogitation*) is not an "act" in the mundane sense of jumping or running; it is a mental act. Thus, (b) this act of hope or hoping must be distinguished from acts which are done "from" hope, "out of" hope, or "in" hope—for instance, feeding the

---

29 And this would hold even for Pieper's distinction between fundamental, genuine, or ultimate "Hope" and penultimate or mundane "hopes." See Josef Pieper, *Hope and History*, trans. Richard Winston and Clara Winston (New York: Herder & Herder, 1969). The difference, we will see, would be in the nature of the object-hoped-for.
30 On this point see Pieper, *Hope and History*, 19.

poor, building low-rent housing, amending constitutions, etc. The latter are qualitatively different acts which are nevertheless grounded in hope. We might describe them as "hopeful actions," but they are not "acts of hope" or hoping itself in the sense of conscious acts.[31]

(4) There is the *ground* of hope. Here we are trying to attend to the evidence, as Husserl would say, by simply observing hope in itself. This ground or basis for hope might reside in the subject who hopes or may lie outside the hoper. I think it important to introduce this concept of ground in order to be able to distinguish hope from either "illusion" or "wishful thinking," both of which are modes of intending the future, but flawed precisely because they either lack ground or because of a flawed character of their ground.[32] It is precisely the ground of hope which contributes to the confidence of hope, so that my hope is only "confident" relative to the ground for my hope. Further, an epistemology of hope (which I will sketch below) will need to consider just how one "relates" to this ground of hope.

(5) We need to consider *fulfillment* as an integral part of hope. In a sense, this might be an aspect of the object hoped for, or a characteristic of how we intend objects of hope; nevertheless, it seems important to note that we are not content to simply have objects for our hopes; part of the very way in which we intend objects-hoped-for means that we want our hopes fulfilled. We want our hopes to, one day, no longer be hopes, but realities. And while hope does not guarantee or necessarily entail fulfillment,[33] it certainly seems to imply a *desire* for fulfillment. "Dashed hopes" or "shattered hopes"— hopes that are *not* fulfilled—do not indicate that our hopes

---

31 Perhaps we should note, since someone might protest that this is an overly conscious or intentional model, that even "attitudes" are acts of consciousness insofar as they are "ways of thinking."
32 We will have to return to the question of what would constitute "legitimate" ground below in the context of a critique of Rorty.
33 Indeed, as Pieper observes, that which is guaranteed can*not* be hoped for (Pieper, *Hope and History*, 20).

were not genuine hopes, but rather remind us of the element of contingency that characterizes hope. Hope differs from a guarantee, even though it is also characterized by a certain confidence without guarantee.[34]

We could then diagram the formal structure of hope as follows:

A Phenomenology of Hope

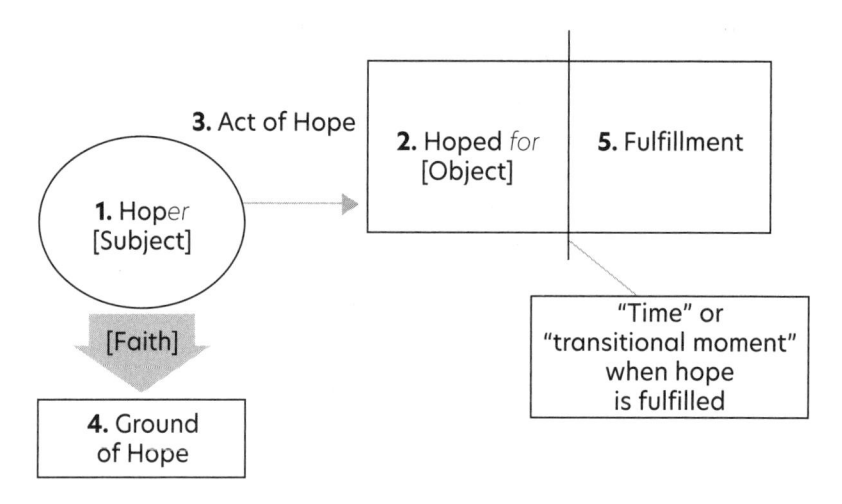

- **1.** Hop*er* [Subject]
- **2.** Hoped *for* [Object]
- **3.** Act of Hope
- **4.** Ground of Hope
- [Faith]
- **5.** Fulfillment
- "Time" or "transitional moment" when hope is fulfilled

Hope without Hope? A Critique of Postmodern Expectations

If the analysis above is correct, then all hopes—whether ultimate or penultimate, whether regarding eschatological futures or tomorrow's weather—are characterized by this formal structure of a hoper who intends something in the future as that which is hoped *for* on the basis of a particular ground of hope. If any element is missing, we are without hope.[35]

With this structure in place, I think we are provided with a grid which might help us to both recognize and interpret historical shifts which have taken place with respect to hope. For instance, in modernity—where there

---

34 On these themes, see the seminal analyses of Pieper, *Hope and History*, 19–22.
35 Though we might still have some mode of intending the future: "wishful thinking," for instance, is a way of intending the future, but without ground; or fear and anxiety are also ways of intending the future, but in expectation of something evil or detrimental. Both modes of intending the future, however, are not hopeful in the sense I have specified.

is no lack of eschatologies[36]—we still find a structure of hope and expectation about the future. In fact, one might suggest that in important ways, it is not so much the *object* which changes in modernity (we will qualify this) but rather the *ground* of hope which is transformed. For instance, both Kant's vision of "perpetual peace" and Marx's vision of justice as embodied in a classless society are consistent with the Christian hope for a peaceable kingdom and the advent of justice. Even Rorty, commenting on the New Testament and the *Communist Manifesto*, concludes that "both documents are the expressions of the *same* hope: that some day we shall be willing and able to treat the needs of all human beings with the respect and consideration with which we treat the needs of those closest to us, those whom we love."[37] So *what* we're hoping *for* is not so radically different, except in this important respect: in modern narratives of hope, the hoped for "kingdom" and justice is *immanentized*, so that the object-hoped-for lacks any transcendence. It is a kingdom which is completely continuous with history and the immanent structures of the world as a closed system. As Rorty indicates, the object-hoped-for has not really changed, just the engine and locus of its arrival:

> We moderns are superior to the ancients—both pagan and Christian—in our ability to imagine a utopia here on earth. The eighteenth and nineteenth centuries witnessed, in Europe and North America, a massive shift in the locus of human hope: a shift from eternity to future time, from speculation about how to win divine favour to planning for the happiness of future generations. This sense that the human future can be made different from the past, unaided by non-human powers, is magnificently expressed in the Manifesto.[38]

36 In this regard, Karl Löwith offers something of a "secularization" thesis with respect to eschatology in his *Meaning in History: The Theological Implications of the Philosophy of History* (Chicago: University of Chicago Press, 1949), where he argues that modern philosophy of history is dominated by a secularization of Christian eschatology. As Jürgen Moltmann notes, however, Löwith "meant this in anything but a positive sense." See Moltmann, *The Coming of God: Christian Eschatology*, trans. Margaret Kohl (Minneapolis: Fortress, 1996), 133.
37 Rorty, "Failed Prophecies, Glorious Hopes," 202–3, emphasis added. While he has concerns about the New Testament (see below), he nevertheless recommends that "[p]arents and teachers should encourage young people to read both books. The young will be morally better for having done so" (203).
38 Rorty, "Failed Prophecies, Glorious Hopes," 208. It is not within the scope of my chapter here, but I should indicate that I think Rorty's notion of a future advent of justice without

What modernity hopes for carries on the tradition of Christian expectation, but it diverges from that tradition with respect to *where* those hopes will be realized or fulfilled.[39]

Corresponding to this immanentization of the locus/*object* of hope to a "this-worldly utopia"[40] is an immanentization of the *ground* of hope, which is the most marked distinction between modern, secular eschatologies and Christian hope. Note, however, that as hope, modern intendings of the future still have a ground, but that ground is no longer transcendent. Thus the confidence of modern expectation does not derive from anything like Providence or faithfulness of God, but rather the self-sufficiency of human abilities to realize their own hopes. As Rorty noted above, modernity places its hope in humanity, without the need of aid from transcendent powers—indicating a fundamental rejection of grace.[41] Thus whether it is confidence in human rationality (Kant), belief in the engine of dialectical materialism (Marx), or faith in the powers of technology and the market (Fukuyama?), the ground of modern hope is always immanent to humanity and history. The problem is, once these foundations crumble beneath us, we lose our ground and so lose our hope.[42] That, we might suggest, is a diagnosis of the postmodern condition.

And yet, in the midst of this late modern crisis of hope, we have two prophets crying out in this wilderness: Rorty's proclamation of hope for a liberal utopia and Derrida's hope for a justice "to come." In light of our analysis of the phenomenological structure of hope above, how should we evaluate these postmodern pieces of "good news?" Do they give us reason to hope? And hope for what?

---

any historical discontinuity fails to do justice to the structural depth of injustice, which can only be eradicated by revolutionary (though not necessarily "human") change. His hope is, as he confesses, "reformist" (208).

39   It seems to be the burden of Pieper's *Hope and History* to challenge this proposition. Thus he asks, "Is man's hope at all of such nature that it can be satisfied within the area of history" (28)? The answer, for Pieper, is a resounding "Nein!"

40   Pieper, *Hope and History*, 28. One sees that it is really only on the basis of a very facile reading of Christian faith as "otherworldly" that Rorty criticizes the New Testament (207–8). Somebody should introduce him to Gutiérrez.

41   A certain tale could be woven, here, regarding the Thomistic valorization of "natural, unaided reason," through Scotus' radical disjunction between nature and grace, to the modern rejection of grace. But I'll not tell the story here.

42   For a consideration of this "despair," see Jürgen Moltmann, *Theology of Hope: On the Ground and the Implications of a Christian Eschatology*, trans. James W. Leitch (New York: Harper & Row, 1967), 22–26.

Rorty and Reasons to Hope

Considered against the structure of hope above, Rorty's pragmatic hope is not lacking in the determinacy of its object. Indeed, his vision for a liberal, democratic utopia is stated in the most concrete terms, particularly the features of *equity* and *fraternity*. On the first score, Rorty envisions a world where economic injustices are finally rectified: where teachers make as much as lawyers[43] and where minimum wage is actually a living wage. Thus it is in light of this hope for equity that

> [w]e should raise our children to find it intolerable that we who sit behind desks and punch keyboards are paid ten times as much as people who get their hands dirty cleaning our toilets, and a hundred times as much as those who fabricate our keyboards in the Third World. . . . Our children need to learn, early on, to see the inequalities between their own fortunes and those of other children as neither the Will of God nor the necessary price for economic efficiency, but as an inevitable tragedy. They should start thinking, as early as possible, about how the world might be changed so as to ensure that no one goes hungry while others have a surfeit.[44]

The concrete hope for economic and material equity is made possible by the expectation of a coming, fundamental "fraternity" which overcomes current selfishness and prioritizes "love of neighbor" and encourages the virtue of self-sacrifice.[45] Writing from an imagined 2096, Rorty envisions the greatest transformation to be from a selfish, rights-based political discourse to a sacrificial, fraternal understanding of responsibility; from a focus on "I" to a sense of "we"; from considering myself first to first considering the neighbor. "Perhaps no difference between present-day [2096] American political discourse and that of 100 years ago is greater than our assumption that the first duty of the state is to prevent gross economic and social inequality."[46] One might say, then, that it is precisely fraternity

---

43   Rorty, "Education as Socialization and as Individualization," in *Philosophy and Social Hope*, 121.
44   Rorty, "Failed Prophecies, Glorious Hopes," 203–4.
45   Rorty, "Failed Prophecies, Glorious Hopes," 206–7.
46   Rorty, "Looking Backwards from the Year 2096," 246 and passim. This article, when originally published, was entitled "Fraternity Reigns."

which is the condition of possibility for equity. In any case, this is the future Rorty confidently expects and for which he hopes.

Indeed, "[w]e have every reason to hope," Rorty declares, "that once today's economic bubble bursts, once we start reinventing the interventionist state, Americans will relearn what Delbanco calls 'the lesson of Lincoln's life' . . . that the quest for prosperity is no remedy for melancholy, but that a passion to secure justice by erasing the line that divides those with hope from those without hope can be."[47] We have every reason—we do not lack reasons—to hope for the realization of justice in America. But unfortunately, Rorty fails to give an account of the reason for his hope that lies within.[48] It is here that Rorty's hope, in light of our phenomenological analysis, must be called into question. In order for hope to be hope, as opposed to mere illusion or wishful thinking, there must be (a) some ground or basis for that hope, and (b) some proportionality between the ground of hope and the object-hoped-for. For instance, to choose a mundane example, if I hope to slam dunk a basketball (despite the fact that I am 5′6″) on the basis of the fact that my mother told me that I can do anything I put my mind to, then it seems to me that I am being deluded. There is some basis or ground for my hope, but that ground is not proportionate or relevant to my hope.[49] It does not constitute a "good reason" to hope for such a telos. Such expectations of the future we often describe as "wishful thinking" or as "*false* hopes" and are to be distinguished from (genuine) hope. And the distinction is not a merely theoretical one: when people operate on the basis of false hopes, the most disastrous consequences can often follow.[50]

---

47   Rorty, "I Hear America Sighing," 16, referring to Delbanco, *The Real American Dream*, 74.

48   I am alluding, of course, to 1 Pet 3:15 and will return to consider this more carefully below.

49   And to assert this is not to require that there be a one-to-one correspondence between the ground and my hope, since hope is precisely that which is not guaranteed (Pieper, *Hope and History*, 20). In other words, the ground of my hope does not need to yield "certainty" in order to qualify my expectation of the future as *hope*; in fact, such certainty or guarantee would disqualify it from being hope, since I do not hope for that which is inevitable. Nevertheless, in order to distinguish hope from false hopes or wishful thinking, there must be what I am calling here a *proportionality* of the ground to the hope. What needs to be worked out, then (if possible), would be the criteria which would determine whether a ground is proportional or not.

50   For a relevant discussion of the detrimental effects of false hopes in medicine, see Bert Musschenga, "Is There a Problem with False Hope?" *The Journal of Medicine and Philosophy*

Determined Hope   141

What is the ground of Rorty's hope for a liberal, democratic utopia? *Is* there a ground for this expectation, or is it merely a false hope, perhaps a delusion? Rorty is not entirely forthcoming in this regard—he offers no *apologia*—but if we look carefully, it seems that he thinks the narrative of history itself is the reason for such hope. Criticizing contemporary political philosophy for abandoning historical narration (in particular, a narrative of progress[51]), he argues that "it is the kind of historical narrative which segues into a utopian scenario about how we can get from the present to a better future. Social and political philosophy usually has been, and always ought to be, parasitic on such narratives."[52] Thus elsewhere he emphasizes that it is precisely reflection on this historical narrative of progress which keeps our hopes for a liberal utopia buoyant:

> If human hope can survive the anthrax-laden warheads, the suitcase-sized nuclear devices, the overpopulation, the globalized labour market, and the environmental disasters of the coming century[can it?], if we have descendants who, a century from now, *still have a historical record to consult and are still able to seek inspiration from the past*, perhaps they will think of Saint Agnes and Rosa Luxemburg, Saint Francis and Eugene Debs, Father Damien and Jean Jaurès, as members of a single movement.[53]

Can history really function as the ground for Rorty's hope? Will our consulting of the historical record give us good reason to believe that his vision for justice will be realized? Would not a look at the history of the past century—of regress rather than progress, of increased violence rather than peace—lead only to despair and hopelessness? The problem here, it seems to me, is a *dis*proportionality between Rorty's hope and that which seems to ground it. The ground simply cannot yield the hope he has described; in fact, this history would seem to lead us to expect just the opposite and intend the future in the mode of fear and anxiety rather than hopeful expectation.

---

44 (2019): 423–41 and Marleen Eijkholt, "Medicine's Collision with False Hope: The False Hope Harms (FHH) Argument," *Bioethics* (2020): 1–9, https://doi.org/10.1111/bioe.12731.
51 Rorty, "Globalization, the Politics of Identity and Social Hopes," 232.
52 Rorty, "Globalization, the Politics of Identity and Social Hopes," 231.
53 Rorty, "Failed Prophecies, Glorious Hopes," 203. He is here making the connection between Christian and Marxist hope in the pairing of these figures.

Thus, at times, Rorty himself seems to suggest that this hope is *without ground*. Considering some of the "reasons why it seems absurdly improbable that we shall ever have a global liberal utopia,"[54] he basically concedes these as valid reasons for "historical pessimism." As he admits, "[t]his shift leaves us nothing with which to boost our social hopes." With nothing to boost our hopes, we would seem to be without ground—without good reason to hope. "*But*," Rorty continues, "that does not mean there is anything wrong with these hopes. The utopian social hope which sprang up in nineteenth-century Europe is still the noblest imaginative creation of which we have record."[55] Though we have no reason to do so, we continue to hope. But without ground, can this really be hope? Given our analysis above, an expectation for good in the future which lacks ground is not hope. If Rorty counters that we have fallen prey to a "foundationalist" understanding of hope—that we just need to get over this need for grounding—then he seems also to concede that we cannot make any distinction between hope and false hope, illusion, or mere wishful thinking. I do not think this is a concession that he would want to make, since it would undercut his own criticisms regarding alternative expectations for the future (e.g., expecting the consummation of history on the grounds of belief in Providence, which he would describe as deluded, would not be any qualitatively different than Rorty's expectation for a liberal utopia). Further, as mentioned above, undercutting the distinction between hope and wishful thinking or false hope would have important negative consequences in the practical and political spheres. Thus, in order to maintain the distinction, we need to understand hope as grounded in some sense; and as such, Rorty's hope for a liberal utopia—which lacks ground—is disqualified, so to speak. When we have no "good reasons" to do so, we ought not hope.

54   Rorty, "Afterword: Pragmatism, Pluralism, and Postmodernism," 273. The reasons for lack of hope are: (1) a global democracy would require a global standard of living equivalent to that in European nations, but there are too few natural resources to sustain this globally; (2) "greedy and selfish kleptocrats" and military leadership always find new ways to subvert democracy and adapt well to changes; and (3) "achieving a liberal utopia on a global scale would require the establishment of a world federation" which seems increasingly impossible to achieve (273–74).

55   Rorty, "Afterword: Pragmatism, Pluralism, and Postmodernism," 277, emphasis added.

Derrida and the (In)Determination of Hope

While we might also question the ground for Derrida's hope, I want to focus on problems around the object-hoped-for and the act of hoping. So first, what does Derrida expect when he is expecting? For what does Derrida hope and pray? Or, to put it otherwise, does deconstruction have an eschatology?[56]

While deconstruction is concerned to call into question any notion of a programmable future,[57] Derrida does nevertheless sketch what he describes as a "messianic eschatology."[58] As such, it is a structure of radical expectation, of waiting for the future; but as "messianic" it is divorced from any particular, determinate messian*ism* (i.e., any determinate religion or tradition) and thus is without any determinate expectation for what is "to come." Thus,

> We will not claim that this messianic eschatology common both to the religions it criticizes and to the Marxist critique must be simply deconstructed. While it is common to both of them, with the exception of content,[59] it is also the case that its formal structure of promise exceeds them or precedes

---

56   Derrida, unlike Caputo (*Prayers and Tears*, 96), is not spooked by the notion of an "eschatology." In fact, Derrida says that his project is in contrast to French Marxists such as Althusser who attempt to "dissociate Marxism from any teleology or from any messianic eschatology" (*Specters of Marx*, 90), whereas his concern "is precisely to distinguish the latter from the former"; that is, to distill a "messianic eschatology" dissociated from the determinate content of Marxism (which is, on Derrida's accounting, a messian*ism*).

57   Derrida reminds us that one of the first jobs of deconstruction was to call into question "the onto-theo- but also archeo-teleological concept of history—in Hegel, Marx, or even in the epochal thinking of Heidegger" (*Specters of Marx*, 74). This was to "open up access to an affirmative thinking of the messianic and emancipatory promise as promise: as *promise* and not as onto-theological or teleo-eschatological program or design" (75). While I cannot do so here, I would argue that Christian eschatology—when it retains its integrity and resists the lures of modernity—is *not* onto-theological but rather closer to the structure of "promise" Derrida describes. Perhaps this is the flip side of my argument that Christian faith is not grounded in a metanarrative in the technical sense. (For this argument, see my essay "A Little Story about Metanarratives: Lyotard, Religion, and Postmodernism Revisited," *Faith and Philosophy* 18 [2001]: 261–76.)

58   Derrida, "A Little Story about Metanarratives," 59, 90.

59   It is interesting to note that Derrida sees a disjunction between Christian hope and Marxist hope, whereas Rorty emphasizes their continuity and similarity (in "Failed Prophecies, Glorious Hopes").

them. Well, what remains irreducible to any deconstruction, what remains as undeconstructible as the possibility itself of deconstruction is, perhaps, a certain experience of the emancipatory promise; it is perhaps even the formality of a structural messianism, a messianism without religion, even a messianic without messianism, an idea of justice . . . and an idea of democracy.[60]

This messianic—which elsewhere he argues is a "general structure of experience"[61]—would be "the opening to the future or to the coming of the other as the advent of justice, but without horizon of expectation and without prophetic prefiguration."[62] So this messianic eschatology awaits and expects justice "to come" (*à venir*) as a democracy "to come."[63] But at the same time this messianic hope must remain completely indeterminate, otherwise we might begin to confuse democracy "here and now" (which is fraught with injustice) with the democracy which is (always) "to come." Thus Derrida asserts that this "idea"[64] of justice and democracy signals

> the opening of this gap between an infinite promise . . . and the determined, necessary, but also necessarily inadequate forms of what has to be measured against this promise. To this extent, the effectivity or actuality of the democratic promise, like that of the communist promise, will always keep within it, and it must do so, this *absolutely undetermined messianic hope* at its heart, this eschatological relation to the to-come of an event *and* of a singularity, of an alterity that cannot be anticipated.[65]

---

60 Derrida, *Specters of Marx*, 59.
61 Derrida, "Foi et savoir," 28; "Faith and Knowledge," 18.
62 Derrida, "Faith and Knowledge," 27; 17.
63 *Specters of Marx*, 64–65.
64 Because of his employment of this Kantian language of the "idea" of justice, one finds him constantly protesting that his notion of justice is *not* a regulative ideal (e.g., *Specters of Marx*, 64–65; see also Caputo, *Prayers and Tears*, 129). While methinks they do protest too much (and unsuccessfully), Derrida's claim is that this cannot be a regulative ideal because it is indeterminate, and therefore there is no way to gauge our "progress" towards it. But if the claim to absolute indeterminacy is impossible (see below), then Derrida is left with no way to distinguish his democracy "to come" from a simple regulative ideal.
65 Derrida, *Specters of Marx*, 65, emphasis added.

Determined Hope   145

To wait for the messianic is to be expectant for—*who knows what?* Literally. "For it belongs to the very essence of *venir* and *à venir*," Caputo comments, "that what is coming be unknown, not merely factually unknown but structurally unknowable. . . . Otherwise nothing is really coming, nothing *tout autre*."[66] As such, "[t]he messianic exposes itself to absolute surprise and, even if it always takes the phenomenal form of peace or of justice, it ought, exposing itself so abstractly, be prepared (waiting without awaiting *itself*) for the best as for the worst, the one never coming without opening the possibility of the other."[67] It is the "absolutely undetermined" character of this "messianic hope" which exposes us to this danger, all the while expecting the advent of justice.

Given this "object" of Derrida's hope, we must also consider *how* one can hope for such, or what we might describe as the correlate mode of expectation. Recalling the structure of hope above, we here consider the *act* of hope: How can one hope for the indeterminate? How does one wait for who-knows-what? As Derrida recognizes, the (conscious, intentional) act of hope must be a waiting "without horizon of expectation" (*sans horizon d'attente*).[68] Why? Because any horizon of expectation would predetermine—which is to say, *determine*—what is expected and that for which we hope. But Derrida has contended that we must be open to the absolutely indeterminate. Therefore, our expectation must be without horizon, without predetermination, because any predelineated anticipation would undo the universality of such justice, representing an *in*justice.

This brings us to one final, and perhaps most important, component of Derrida's messianic hope. He has argued that our hope for the future, though a hope for justice, must be "absolutely undetermined"; and in order to await such an indeterminate "object," we must be waiting without horizons of expectation, since these horizons would always already condition the wholly other of the future, would cram the democracy "to come" into our current understandings, converting it into some kind of "law." Why must we be so vigilant about preventing the determination

---

66   Caputo, *Prayers and Tears*, 101–2. Aside from a curious resurrection of "essences," I would question by which logic this is necessary (see below).
67   Derrida, "Foi et savoir," 28; "Faith and Knowledge," 18. On the dangers of this openness, see Richard Kearney, "Desire of God," in *God, the Gift, and Postmodernism*, ed. John D. Caputo and Michael J. Scanlon (Bloomington: Indiana University Press, 1999), 112–45, esp. 122–28.
68   Derrida, "Foi et savoir," 27; "Faith and Knowledge," 17; *Specters of Marx*, 168.

146   The Nicene Option

of justice? Because determination itself is unjust insofar as it *limits* possibilities and necessarily entails *exclusion*. Every decision is an incision,[69] and every determinate erection of justice is attended by injustice. And not only does determination itself constitution a kind of violence, the determination of justice by particular religions or regimes often leads to real violence and injustice, all "in the name" of religion or communism or—if you can believe it—democracy. Thus Caputo suggests that "[i]f the *tout autre* ever won the revolution, if the Messiah ever actually showed up, if you ever thought that justice has come—that would ruin everything."[70] Derrida emphasizes the indeterminacy—*absolute* indeterminacy—of justice "to come" in order to safeguard against the inevitable *hybris* which would want to identify a particular political system or policy with the very advent of justice. The way to avoid the wars of determinate, "messian*istic*" eschatologies is by adopting an absolutely indeterminate, messianic eschatology.[71] Unfortunately, this means that our hope is always deferred, that justice is *always* (i.e., structurally) "to come"—which is why we are always "waiting." Justice, we must remember, is impossible.

Before undertaking a critique of Derrida's "messianic hope," let me first note what is salutary about this account, viz., Derrida's critical concern and reminder of the injustices which can take place when we identify our particular regime with "Justice Itself." That, it seems to me, even from a Christian perspective, is an important point that triumphalist Christian (but not only Christian) politics can often forget and which we do well to recall. However, I think we can maintain this critical posture without adopting Derrida's fundamental logic regarding determination and violence which, to summarize, goes as follows: determination itself is violence and leads to violence; therefore, in order to avoid violence we must have a hope which is *in*determinate; and insofar as our hope—the way in which we intend the future—is *in*determinate, our mode of expecting must be "without horizon." Let me unpack my criticism by working back through these three components.

First, as we have noted in previous chapters, Derrida's premise, which equates determination with violence—what I've called his "logic

---

69   Derrida, "Force of Law," 24–26, also alluded to as the "law of finitude, law of decision and responsibility for infinite existences" in *Specters of Marx*, 87.
70   Caputo, *Prayers and Tears*, 74.
71   Derrida, *Specters of Marx*, 58–59.

of determination"—can and must be called into question. The determinate and finite would only be construed as violent and exclusionary if one assumes they were somehow escapable. Further, Derrida conflates what I have called "the historical production of violence" with the "necessary production of violence" in its relation to religion. Not all finite decisions produce injustice, unless one operates with a notion of "infinite" responsibility which faults humanity for being finite, which would be a Platonic or Neoplatonic move. In short, I think in order to accept Derrida's premise that all determination or finitude constitutes violence, one would have to adopt some version of a Neoplatonic ontology, or at least be haunted by its ghost.[72] And if one does not adopt this premise, then there is no logical inference that motivates the evacuation of all content from this messianic hope. In other words, one would not need a messian*ic* hope in order to avoid violence; rather, a determinate, "messian*istic*" hope could be adopted without implicating oneself in necessary or inevitable violence.

Second, turning to the question of the indeterminacy of the object-hoped-for, we would now note, given the rejection of the logic which equates determination and violence, there is no need to maintain the absolute indeterminacy of hope. But two further points must also be made: Based on our phenomenological analysis of hope above, hope cannot be "absolutely indeterminate," since then it would have no object, and since hope is an intentional mode of consciousness, if there is no object, there is no hope. One can only intend that which is constituted to some degree; therefore, hope can only be hope insofar as it has an object which admits of some degree of determinacy. This does not require, however, absolute determinacy either; rather, as in Christian eschatological expectation, there is a degree of determinacy and a degree of indeterminacy, or what we might more properly describe as "mystery." Even from the perspective of Christian hope, *over*-determination is problematic. And there is an important sense in which Derrida's messianic is *not* indeterminate but rather "does have *certain* determinable features."[73] For one, we know that it is a *democracy* to come; and we know enough about that to know that it is *not*, for instance, a *theo*cracy to come. Further, it is very heavily indebted to the biblical prophetic tradition of justice, not only in its rhythms and nomenclature but in its very structure and concern (mediated by Levinas). But once one admits this "content," the

---

72 This is what I have argued in *Fall of Interpretation*, 127–29.
73 Caputo, *Prayers and Tears*, 142.

gig is up: absolute indeterminacy has been compromised[74] (not that it was ever possible) and one either admits that deconstruction's messianic hope is also violent or concede my point above, that determination should not be equated with violence. This means that the door is also opened for other determinate hopes, since they can no longer be disqualified simply by virtue of their determinacy—and that has important implications for the viability of Christian hope.

Finally, hope, as a conscious mode of intending the future, cannot be without horizon. Recalling the phenomenology of hope above, and our conclusions regarding the necessary determination of the object of hope, it follows that such constitution of the object of hope must take place within determinate horizons of expectation. As Caputo comments, Derrida resists "the very idea of 'horizon,' for any horizon, be it that of a regulative idea or of a 'messianic event,' sets limits and defines expectations in advance."[75] Thus Derrida speaks of messianic hope as "[a]waiting without horizon of the wait, awaiting what one does not expect yet or any longer."[76] Phenomenologically speaking, this is impossible, simply *Unsinnig*, Husserl would say, since any mode of intentional consciousness, such as hope, cannot escape the conditions of horizonality.[77] And in this respect, I follow Derrida's own affirmation, in "Violence and Metaphysics,"[78] that the "wholly other" must appear within the horizons of our experience, otherwise it would never appear for us at all. This is due simply to the structure of intentional consciousness described above, which Derrida would not want to deny. Indeed, we might say that he has been more scrupulous about nothing else than the conditions which attend the constitution and appearance of the other. One cannot wait for (literally) nothing.

Waiting in Hope: Christian Expectation

On the basis of a phenomenology of hope, I have critiqued Rorty's hope for a liberal utopia as, at best, "wishful thinking," and Derrida's messi-

---

74 I have developed this point more fully in "Determined Violence" and "Re-Kanting Postmodernism?"
75 Caputo, *Prayers and Tears*, 117; cp. 73.
76 Derrida, *Specters of Marx*, 65; cp. 168.
77 In this respect, Derrida begins to sound remarkably like Levinas and Jean-Luc Marion, of whom he has been critical on just this point. For my own critique of Levinas and Marion, see chs. 11 and 12 below.
78 Derrida, "Violence and Metaphysics: An Essay on the Thought of Emmanuel Levinas," in *Writing and Difference*, trans. Alan Bass (Chicago: University of Chicago Press, 1978), 79–153.

anic hope as either impossible (in the straightforward sense) or in fact more indebted to the biblical prophetic and messianic tradition than he acknowledges. In both cases, the critique of these postmodern hopes has opened the space, I think, for a reconsideration of a robust, determinate Christian hope as not only viable in postmodernity but perhaps its only hope. So in this brief conclusion, I will consider the elements of Christian expectation in light of our phenomenology of hope above.

First, if we consider the subject as hop*er*, and the subject's *act* of hoping, we see that the Christian community expectantly, even if somewhat impatiently (cf. Jas 5:7) and anxiously (Jude 21), awaits in *eagerness* (Rom 8:19, 23, 25; 1 Cor 1:7; Heb 9:28). But this hope is one that is produced by and sustained in suffering, which produces perseverance, character, and ultimately hope (Rom 5:3-4). Thus it seems that the Christian has a certain *disposition* to hope—that hope is a certain "virtue." Thus the waiting and awaiting of the Christian community is anticipatory and confident, since "hope does not disappoint" (Rom 5:5). And given our expectation, the advent of our hope is not something that will take us by surprise, even though we cannot determinately know when it will be fulfilled (1 Thess 5:1-10).

But the sanctified impatience of Christian hope—which exclaims so loudly, "Come! *Viens!*" (1 Cor 16:22; Rev 22:20)—is markedly different from the awaiting that characterizes Derrida's "messianic hope," which seems to be a hope that is happy to always wait, which delights in waiting (which is a good thing, since it always will). On Caputo's accounting, "[t]he very idea of the Messiah is that he is *to* come, *à venir*, someone coming, not that he could actually arrive." In that respect, the best we can do and hope for is to wait. This, of course, is Blanchot's "idea" of the Messiah, not the biblical prophetic understanding, for which the "essence" of the Messiah is his *anointing* for justice for the poor and oppressed who have known nothing but injustice (Isa 61:1-2; Luke 4:14-21). There is, then, no virtue in waiting; rather, the biblical awaiting for the Messiah is characterized by just this impatience, out of which the cries of "Come, Lord Jesus!" resonate with the prophetic laments, "How long, O Lord!" (cp. Rev 6:10-11). Hope deferred makes the heart sick, and there is a certain dis-ease which attends Christian waiting for the eschaton and the advent of justice.[79]

---

79 On this tension between imminence and delay, see Richard Bauckham, *The Theology of the Book of Revelation* (Cambridge: Cambridge University Press, 1993), 157–59.

Second, with respect to the object-hoped-for, this space is hardly appropriate for working out a comprehensive vision and analysis of the telos of the Christian hope.[80] It is important to recall that given our analyses above, we know that the object of our hope must have some object, that object must be determined to a certain extent, and that such an object of hope is constituted or determined within particular horizons of expectation; in other words, ours is (as must be any hope) a waiting *with* horizon and a messianic hope *with* a Messiah. The horizons of expectation are those provided by the tradition and community (Scripture and Church). Further, a phenomenology of Christian expectation will note that, contra Derrida's "messianic hope," there is an important degree of determinacy; but also an important, and perhaps helpful, *lack*[81] of specification and *in*determinacy. In other words, we know what to expect, but do not have a comprehensive knowledge of such; thus with Derrida and Caputo, we could agree that a this degree of indeterminacy functions as something of a safeguard with respect to attempts to institute the kingdom on earth, retaining the important distinction between the eschatological kingdom and our attempts to establish justice in the here-and-now. Further, Christian eschatology expects a future advent of justice which is both *continuous* with the present order, as a redeeming of creation, but also *dis*continuous, insofar as it represents a revolutionizing of fallen structures. In this way, it is not a sheer "otherworldly" utopia as Rorty charged, but neither is it a realized eschatology which finds the resolution of injustice within the mechanisms of history itself. Thus, Christian hope is characterized by a fundamental *transcendence* which is not opposed to immanence but is opposed to the immanentization characteristic of modern eschatologies; further, Christian expectation is "open" in the sense that Derrida advocates, but open precisely to the necessary *grace* which alone can revolutionize a fallen world. Thus we markedly disagree with Rorty, and modernity, when it claims that humanity alone has the resources necessary for its own redemption. In short, we reject the myth of progress for a narrative of grace.

---

80   For this kind of comprehensive vision and exposition, see Moltmann, *The Coming of God*.
81   This indetermination might also be due to a certain "excess" and "fullness" which exceeds description and determination. On this point, see Pieper, *Hope and History*, 78–79. On this tension, and the apophatic strategies adopted in the book of Revelation, see Bauckham, *Theology of the Book of Revelation*, 44–45.

And if Christian eschatological hope counters the immanentization of the object of hope, so also does it resist any attempt to immanentize the *ground* of hope. Perhaps the most important discussions of Christian hope in postmodernity will concern this question of ground. What is the ground of Christian expectation, and how can such a hope be viable in postmodernity? Christian hope, I would argue, is grounded in the revelation of God's faithfulness and the promise of his continued faithfulness, particularly as grounded in God's revelation in the cross and resurrection of Jesus Christ. Most elemental to this account is that this ground is ultimately grounded in *revelation* (not as propositions, let alone detailed plans, but the revelation of God in Christ) and that this revelation reveals God's faithfulness to his creation, his identification with the struggles of creation, and his power and providence to bring about its restoration. Without what Pieper describes as "prophecy"[82] we are left in a position not unlike Rorty: speculating and positing a hope for the future without a genuine ground. Thus I think Christian hope can only properly be *hope* insofar as one accepts and believes this revelation. But with respect to the epistemology of hope, this is akin to any other kind of hope: the hoper must relate to the ground of hope via a fundamental trust and commitment; it is because hope is grounded in faith that hope does not yield apodictic guarantees.[83] On this score, even the hopes of modernity rest on faith: whether in the myth of progress, dialectical materialism, technology and the market, or the rationality of humanity. In any case, these hopes rest on a faith in a particular ground; so unless one wants to undo the idea of hope altogether, we cannot exclude Christian hope simply by virtue of its grounding by faith commitments in a particular revelation. This is not to say, of course, that one could therefore "demonstrate" the superiority of this ground (that would be to confuse faith and knowledge);[84] but one can certainly proclaim such a hope and demonstrate the integrity and

---

82 Though there is a tendency for Pieper to reduce this to prophetic "statements" and "divinely authenticated information." See Pieper, *Hope and History*, 44, 78.
83 Space does not permit me to develop this any further here, but I would argue that hope is not "known" in a cognitive or rational sense, but rather "believed" and known "affectively"—known otherwise. As such, how hope is communicated or proclaimed should be via modes which communicate affectively, particularly the aesthetic, and perhaps even more particularly via images, activating the imagination. On this point, see the discussion in Bauckham and Hart, *Hope Against Hope*, 72–73.
84 As Pieper notes, "those reasons can convince only one who accepts the truth of Christian doctrine" (*Hope and History*, 87).

coherence of its ground. Finally, because of the Christian's commitments to God's revelation in Christ and his faithfulness to creation, a Christian eschatology must argue that, ultimately, God is our only hope. In that regard, the question of the viability of Christian hope in late modernity differs little from the context of Augustine's *De civitate dei*: it represents both a scandal and good news. My hope is that the demise of modern eschatologies, and the critique of postmodern hopes above, indicates an open space for Christians to unapologetically proclaim a hope that does not disappoint.

8

Beyond Epistemology

Derrida and the Limits of the "Limits of Knowledge"

> Teach me so that I may act, not just know how I ought to act.
>
> Augustine, *Discourses on the Psalms*, Ps 119, Daleth (on v. 27), 10.3

Derrida's Epistemological Reductionism: An Overview of the Argument

My aim in this chapter is to read the early Derrida against the later Derrida: to deconstruct Derrida's "religion without religion" by a confrontation with the trenchant critique of modernity in Derrida's earliest work. I will do so by focusing on Derrida's later fixation on epistemology (knowledge and the lack thereof).[1] In particular, I will argue that Derrida's (later) work on ethics and religion constitutes an epistemological reductionism in which ethical challenges always boil down to problems of *knowledge*—specifically the limits and lack thereof. So ethics is a problem because we cannot *know* what justice requires (e.g., in "Force of Law"); and classical orthodoxy is a problem because we cannot *know* God (e.g., in "Faith and Knowledge"), etc. This epistemological fixation, and epistemological reductionism, is a significant factor for explaining a related trend in certain sectors of theology and continental philosophy of religion that remain trapped by a binary imagination: *either* we know

---

1   In the next chapter I will read Derrida's later logic of determination against an almost tacit logic of incarnation in his earlier work.

God *or* we don't; *either* orthodoxy *or* negative theology; *either* certainty *or* skepticism; *either* law *or* anarchy. To put this otherwise, I think the epistemological fixation and reductionism of these trends indicate the extent to which the conversations remain haunted, and in fact governed, by the ghost of Cartesian certainty on the one hand, and the ghost of dogmatic fundamentalism on the other.

In contrast, I will argue that the early Derrida's critique of such binaries makes problematic the late Derrida's either/or with respect to religious and ethical knowledge—and that, in fact, the early Derrida articulates an account that resists such a binary epistemological reductionism. In other places[2] I have critiqued the account of *knowledge* that drives this mode of critique; here I want to critique the epistemological reductionism itself. Rather than playing by the rules of epistemology, I want to argue that what's wrong is precisely the focus on knowledge (and the philosophical anthropology it assumes). The challenge in ethics is not primarily knowing or not knowing what to do, but rather mustering the *will* to do it. Thus the epigraph invokes the wisdom of St. Augustine, who prays with the psalmist: "Teach me so that I may act, not just *know* how I ought to act" (on Ps 119:27). In other words, the question of *knowing* is not the central question in matters of ethics and religion.

After an exposition of Derrida's epistemological reductionism, I will offer a brief exposition of a key passage in *Confessions*, book 8, as an alternative. The burden here will be to point out that what is lacking in Derrida is any account of *virtue*. Finally, and following from this, I will briefly suggest that religion should not be thought primarily in terms of knowledge and ideas, but in terms of *practices*, habits, and disciplines. So Derrida's fixation on epistemology is a category mistake and indicates a persistent (or resurgent) modernism in Derrida's later work.

Overall, I want to argue that Derrida's fixation on knowledge, and the "limits" of knowledge, can offer only a limited, and ultimately reductionistic, account of both religion and justice. My argument has a couple of "layers" to it and goes something like this:

(1) For Derrida, the aporias of ethics, justice, hospitality, etc., are always aporias of *knowledge*—or rather, the lack thereof. Since we cannot know perfectly, completely, fully, comprehensively, or certainly, we are in a

---

2   E.g., James K. A. Smith, *Who's Afraid of Postmodernism? Taking Derrida, Lyotard, and Foucault to Church* (Grand Rapids: Baker Academic, 2006), ch. 5.

situation of challenge or aporia. Injustice, then, comes down to not knowing enough; our injustice stems from the limits of our knowledge. Thus the aporias of ethics, justice, and hospitality stem from the "conditions" of knowing, and more particularly the *limits* of knowing. Of course, this does not excuse us from *deciding*, from having to make a choice, from having to act: that is the point of undecidability. We are constrained to choose, decide and acts *sans savoir*, without all the data.

But Derrida never seems to problematize the *ability* to choose or decide or act. He seems to assume that if we *could* have complete knowledge or access to all the data, then we would know exactly what to do *and would do it*. The obstruction of justice comes down to matters of knowledge—of epistemic conditions—not an inability of the will. This is a wholly inadequate phenomenology of our moral landscape. Derrida's focus on the conditions and limits of knowledge (what I am calling his epistemological fixation) indicates a reductionistic moral psychology that is inattentive to other, more significant aspects of injustice. Is it really the case that we act unjustly because we lack *knowledge*? Is it not, more often than not, because we lack the *will* to act justly? Consider just one example of injustice: Is it the case that global warming and the desecration of the environment by consumer capitalism stems from the limits of our knowledge or our lack of certainty? Is the matter of injustice here a matter of knowledge or the lack thereof? Is it not rather the case that we do have sufficient (though not complete) knowledge, and what we *lack* is the "political *will*" to do otherwise? Playing this out on the register of epistemology would be a category mistake. Thus I want to suggest—following the ancient wisdom of St. Augustine—that knowledge is not the issue. Unlike Derrida, Augustine argues that even if we had "all the data," the question of our injustice looms large because we lack the *will* to choose or act justly. By merely focusing on the "limits" of knowledge, Derrida's epistemological fixation fails to be attentive to the other, more significant sources of our injustice: our malformed loves and desires. This stems, I think, from Derrida's assumption of a philosophical anthropology that remains still largely Cartesian, rationalist, and cognitivist. It is this rationalist anthropology that yields Derrida's stunted moral phenomenology. His moral landscape looks like the heady world of "quandary ethics" frameworks that one finds tied to the modernist traditions of both deontology and utilitarianism, and fails to be attentive to issues of habits, practices, and virtue formation.[3] So Derrida's fixation on the limits of knowledge yields a limited and stunted moral psychology.

(2) If the first layer of my critique focuses on Derrida's reductionistic fixation on the limits of knowledge, the second layer of my critique concerns his identification of the conditions of finitude *as* the conditions of injustice. Let us call this the aporia of the "double bind."[4] It assumes a basically Levinasian account of infinite responsibility to the Other, which is then demanded by every other Other, and therefore cannot possibly be met. At issue in these cases are not so much limited knowledge, but rather the limits of time and the finitude of our moral energies. Now, on this account of the double bind, Derrida is more attentive to the particularities of an embodied moral psychology. However, rather than actually embrace an unapologetic phenomenology of moral embodiment, he continues to be haunted by a disembodied ideal (just as he continues to be haunted by a Cartesian account of knowledge). So in contrast to Derrida, I want to embrace and affirm the conditions of finitude all-the-way-down, as it were, and thus not hang on to an ethics of infinity. In contrast to Derrida's logic of determination, I commend working from a logic of creation, incarnation, and resurrection. In doing so, our accounts of justice ought to affirm the situation of embodiment and "limits"[5] and thus affirm a situation of an-economic reciprocity.[6] To the extent that Derrida's

---

3   For a critique of the inadequacy and artificiality of quandary ethics, see Edmund Pincoffs, "Quandary Ethics," in *Revisions: Changing Perspectives in Moral Philosophy*, ed. Stanley Hauerwas and Alasdair MacIntyre (South Bend: University of Notre Dame Press, 1983), 92–111.

4   See Jacques Derrida, *Paper Machine*, trans. Rachel Bowlby (Stanford: Stanford University Press, 2005), 92 (henceforth cited in the text as PM). The "double bind" is a common theme since the earliest part of Derrida's corpus.

5   On my reservation with the language of "limits" in relation to finitude, see James K. A. Smith, *The Fall of Interpretation: Philosophical Foundations for a Creational Hermeneutic* (Downers Grove, Ill.: InterVarsity Press, 2000), 31, 151.

6   My thinking on this point is shaped by James H. Olthuis, "Face-to-Face: Ethical Asymmetry or the Symmetry of Mutuality," reprinted in *The Hermeneutics of Charity: Interpretation, Selfhood, and Postmodern Faith*, ed. James K. A. Smith and Henry Isaac Venema (Grand Rapids: Brazos, 2004), 135–56; and John Milbank, "The Soul of Reciprocity, Part One: Reciprocity Refused," *Modern Theology* 17 (2001): 341–43, and idem, "The Soul of Reciprocity, Part Two: Reciprocity Granted," *Modern Theology* 17 (2001): 486ff. See also Milbank, *Being Reconciled: Ontology and Pardon* (London: Routledge, 2003), 138–61. Cp. also David Wood, "Much Obliged," in *Thinking After Heidegger* (New York: Polity, 2002), 125–34.

account remains captive to a modern, abstract, dis-embodied penchant for "infinite" justice, I think he remains captive to a binary ethical imagination in which the "limits" of finitude make the "tragic" essential (PM 129) and justice simply impossible. But Derrida is backed into this corner precisely because he doesn't question the underlying assumptions of this Levinasian paradigm, which is basically an inversion of Hobbes. There are limits to this kind of focus on "limits," and it is precisely this reductionism that I want to contest.

We might say the first aporia is a matter of comprehension, whereas the second is a matter of extension. The first concerns the perspectival limits of knowledge, whereas the second concerns the finite limits of "moral energy" or the ability to discharge one's responsibilities. However, both still come down to a matter of knowledge: In the first case one knows not what to do; in the second case one knows not *to whom* one should respond. Given the first aporia, it seems that the second only supervenes upon the first. Even if one could *know* in such a way as to rightly discern *to whom* one should respond (which would still be essentially unjust), one then still would not know *what to do*.

The Injustice of Not Knowing: Derrida's Epistemological Fixation

Let me now try to make this case against Derrida by turning our attention to some texts where we see this embodied. I think the same logic can be seen in a number of texts from the "later" period (discussed in earlier chapters). Here I want to specifically consider the seminal essay "Force of Law,"[7] while also making reference to some related themes in *Paper Machine* (PM). While "Force of Law" is one of the earliest articulations of Derrida's account of justice, it seems clear that it is not revised or changed in the later works, only expanded and deepened.

The Aporias of Justice: Working without a Net of "Knowledge"

Consider first Derrida's careful account of justice and law in "Force of Law" and the organizing role that knowledge—or the lack thereof—plays in Derrida's account of the "impossibility" of justice, which depends upon

---

[7] Jacques Derrida, "Force of Law: The 'Mystical Foundation of Authority,'" in *Deconstruction and the Possibility of Justice*, ed. Drucilla Cornell, Michel Rosenfeld, and David Gray Carlson (New York: Routledge, 1992), 3–67 (henceforth abbreviated as FL).

Derrida's (not very novel[8]) distinction between "law" (which is deconstructible) and "justice" (which is not).[9] It is in this context that Derrida argues that an experience of *aporia* is essential to justice because "justice is an experience of the impossible" (FL 16). Why is this? Because justice is on the order of the *incalculable*. "Law," he says, "is the element of calculation," whereas "justice is incalculable, it requires us to calculate with the incalculable" (FL 16). The experience of justice is that of a decision made without the safety net of calculation, "moments in which the decision between just and unjust is never insured by a rule."

But why this link between justice and *in*calculability? Or why this collusion between law and calculation?[10] Is there a connection between the focus on "rules" and the fixation on "knowledge?" This link becomes clear, I think, when Derrida analyzes three aporias of justice, or the three aspects of the "one aporia" (FL 22). We will need to give some careful attention to this analysis in order for me to make my argument stick. To briefly rehearse his analysis, Derrida considers three aporias of justice vis-à-vis law: (1) the suspension of rules; (2) the inescapability of undecidability; and (3) the urgency of the decision to be made without knowledge. Let's

---

8   I say "not very novel" because the move here so clearly parallels quite classical natural law theory (as noted also by Westphal in *Overcoming Onto-theology: Toward a Postmodern Christian Faith* [New York: Fordham University Press, 2001], 219–28), though Derrida's is a natural-law-like position without knowledge. But nonetheless, the distinction functions in exactly the same way. In fact, when Derrida links his discussion with the question of civil disobedience, he sounds remarkably similar to Martin Luther King, Jr.'s account in "Letter from Birmingham City Jail," which explicitly appeals to the natural law theory of Augustine and Aquinas. See PM 116: "Law is deconstructed in the name of justice. Take for example 'civil disobedience,' in the United States or France. It's about objecting to a particular positive and national legality in the name of a superior law (such as the universality of the rights of man), or in the name of a justice that is not yet inscribed in law. . . . At any given time juridical limits can always be contested in the name of a justice yet to come." (This would seem to require that one knows *enough* about this justice to come that a particular, given, positive law does not measure up to "justice." In other words, this "justice-to-come" must be determinate enough to know when a given positive law is unjust. In this context, and contra Derrida's critique of "eschatology" and the "determinate" messianisms, I would point out that it is precisely the determinate vision of the eschaton that motivates and governs critique of the current [fallen] cultural order, but we cannot pursue this further here.)
9   See FL 15.
10 It's hard to ignore the echoes of Heidegger's critique of "calculative" thinking and extolling of "meditative" thinking (in *Discourse on Thinking*, trans. John M. Anderson and E. Hans Freund [New York: Harper & Row, 1966]), particularly given Derrida's invocation of the "mystical" in this context (FL 16).

consider these in reverse order, in order to track back to the "root" of Derrida's claims.

In the third aporia, Derrida emphasizes that there is an urgency of decision that "obstructs the horizon of knowledge" (FL 26). Justice is a demanding Other that doesn't wait for us to sort out all the options, gather all the data, and then confidently make a rational decision. "A just decision," Derrida emphasizes, "is always required *immediately*, 'right away.' It cannot furnish itself with infinite information and the unlimited knowledge of conditions, rules, or hypothetical imperatives that could justify it" (FL 26). This means that justice demands a decision that "has no horizon of expectation" (FL 27). In short, justice demands an *event*: "and there is no justice except to the degree that some event is possible which, as event, exceeds calculation, rules, programs, anticipations, and so forth" (FL 27). Justice demands an event, and an event *qua event* is without horizons and without calculation. In sum, justice demands a decision that constitutes an event precisely because it is without knowledge, "acting in the night of non-knowledge and non-rule."[11] So it is also these demands and requirements that prevent a "law" from ever being just, because laws and rules operate on the order of knowledge—within the comfortable bounds of horizons that function as a sort of safety net or what Derrida will often refer to as a "guarantee." To work within the comfortable confines of a horizon is to remain confined by a "limit" (FL 26), and more specifically, limited knowledge. And it is just such limited knowledge that precludes justice. One of the worst things that can happen for the cause of justice is for someone to think he *knows* what justice requires (FL 27–28). Then we're all in trouble. Justice requires deciding without a net, working in the dangerous arena of "non-knowledge and non-rule." Justice requires that we decide and act "without *norm*, with no *horizon* of anticipation—so with no established *criteria*, with no given *rules* for knowledge or determinant judgment, with no assurance" (PM 38).

But analyzing this backwards, we need to ask: Why should we assume that justice is incommensurate with rules, with knowledge? Why should horizons of expectation or the "limits" of knowledge be considered an "obstruction" of justice? This takes us back to Derrida's second aporia: the ghost of the "undecidable." Undecidability, of course, does not in any way

---

11 "If all that arises is what is already possible, and so capable of being anticipated and expected, that is not an event." An event "deprives us of all certainty" (PM 74; cp. 90).

refer to some sort of inability to decide. However, neither does it refer to a vacillating confusion in the face of competing goods or obligations, or "merely the oscillation or the tension between two decisions" (FL 24). Undecidability is not just the difficulty of trying to make up one's mind; rather, "it is the experience of that which, though heterogeneous, foreign to the order of the calculable and the rule, is still obliged" (24). Justice requires a decision, but that decision is undecidable, not just because we are confused or conflicted (phenomena still on the plane of knowledge and calculation), but because justice is heterogeneous to the very order of calculation or the register of knowledge. If justice demands a decision that is made without knowledge, this is because of what Derrida takes to be the nature of an authentic decision, viz., that it be made under the conditions of undecidability. "A decision that didn't go through the ordeal of the undecidable," he contends, "would not be a free decision, it would only be the programmable application or unfolding of a calculable process" (FL 24). In the same way that the infinite demands of justice haunt every law, so undecidability is a ghost that haunts every decision. Its "ghostliness deconstructs from within any assurance of presence, any certitude" (FL 24–25). The ghost of undecidability that entails "the deconstruction of all presumption of a determinant certitude of a present justice" operates on the basis of an "infinite justice"—a justice that obligates me to the other, "without calculation and without rules, without reason and without rationality" (FL 25). Thus justice is a kind of "madness," and "deconstruction is mad about this kind of justice" (FL 25).

So justice is incommensurate with knowledge/rules precisely because justice requires a *decision* that is an *event*, and the only decision worthy of the name is one that is made under the conditions of undecidability. But why should we assume that a decision is only a decision if it is undecidable? In other words, what is it that requires a just decision be undecidable? This brings us, finally, to the first aporia of justice: the *epoché* or suspension of the rule. And here, at the beginning, Derrida emphasizes the nature of *responsibility*. Notice carefully how his analysis begins: Derrida starts with "our common axiom," as he calls it, "that to be just or unjust and to exercise justice, I must be free and responsible for my actions, my behavior, my thought, my decisions" (FL 22). Responsibility requires *freedom*. "But if the act simply consists of applying a rule, of enacting a program or effecting a calculation, we might say that it is legal, that it conforms to law, and perhaps, *by metaphor*, that it is just, but we would be wrong to say that the decision was just" (FL 23, emphasis added). Why? Because if the decision is made by the application of preexisting rules—if it is made as the outcome of calculation—then it is not really free, and therefore not really *responsible*. Indeed, it wouldn't even really be a decision. "A decision that I *can* take, the decision *in my power* and that manifests the taking of action or the deployment of what is *already possible* for me, the actualization of my possibility, and decision that is dependent only on me—would that still be a decision" (PM 87)? Not according to Derrida. So "[t]o be just," Derrida emphasizes, the decision must be a "fresh judgment," "as if ultimately nothing previously existed of the law, as if the judge himself invented the law in every case" (FL 23). If the judge merely applies a given rule, then he has become simply "a calculating machine" and "we will not say that he is just, free, responsible" (23). Why? Because *machines* do not have responsibility. Only free agents are responsible, according to "our axiom," and thus "[e]ach case is other, each decision is different and requires an absolutely unique interpretation, which no existing, coded rule can or ought to guarantee absolutely" (FL 23).

So we can now run the tape forward: A just decision, in order to be just, must be *free*; in order to be authentically "free," such a decision or act must be an *invention*, and not just the application of a preexisting rule. In other words, it cannot be a decision made with the assurance or comfort of knowledge/rules. It must be undecidable, incommensurate with the register of knowledge and rules. And therefore it must be a decision made in the "night of non-knowledge" (FL 26). The limits of knowledge, embedded in rules, preclude justice because they preclude real decisions, and therefore preclude responsibility. No responsibility, no justice. No freedom, no responsibility. So, with respect to what I am calling Derrida's epistemological fixation, it should be noted that justice is inextricably linked to non-knowledge; or, conversely, what makes "law" essentially *un*just is the fact that it is inextricably linked to knowledge, to presumptions of "certitude" (FL 25) and "assurance" (FL 24). The issue is not simply that laws are finite, and therefore violent (they are, as discussed in chapter 6); it is that laws and rules are linked to *knowing*, and claims to knowledge represent an obstruction of justice, which is incommensurate with knowledge. From Derrida's analysis, it would seem that what is most traumatic and terrifying thing about my obligation to the other and the demands of justice is that they require me to work without a net of assurance. The trauma of obligation is an epistemic one: I do not *know* what to do; I *cannot* "know" what to do. *What am I going to do?* The ethical subject is marked by fear and trembling, not because of *what* is being demanded, but because she can't "know" what is demanded. The dark night of the soul for this Derridean subject is a night of epistemic wrangling with questions of warrant and justification, not a night of wrestling with demands that traumatize my selfishness, egoism, and comfort.

This terrain of justice and injustice is mapped in a strange way, as if Derrida, making a foray into the landscape of morality, takes note of the oddest landmarks. Charged with talking about justice, Derrida's analysis remains fixated on the themes of knowledge, rules, certainty, assurance, and decision-making. This seems a bit like someone visiting Paris and spending their time looking at street signs and failing to take notice of the Champs-Elysées. Imagined scenes of injustice, on this account, are scenes of epistemological hubris—as if, looking over the killing fields, what Derrida sees are agents who are guilty, first and foremost, of thinking that they *know* what they ought to do.[12] I do not mean to suggest that Derrida is not concerned about the killing fields, but only that his way of being concerned with them in these analyses betrays a moral psychology that remains fixated on knowledge and autonomy, and thus haunted by a ghost of rationalism. Let me restate my critique this way: Derrida's account of in/justice exhibits an epistemological fixation precisely because it is informed by a stunted and narrow moral psychology, which is itself a symptom of a lingering rationalist philosophical anthropology at work in Derrida. Let me now turn to unpack some of these claims.

Descartes' Ghost: Features of Derrida's Moral Psychology

I would note several features of what I am calling Derrida's moral psychology—the picture he paints of the moral "agent" (I use the word advisedly in this context). First, if we step back and perhaps try to shake

---

12   This might also be the effect of adopting an overly formalist account of justice that precludes any specificity, and therefore tends to preclude any judgment about "specifics." Without appeal to a determinate vision of justice, it becomes hard to say, "That's not the way it's supposed to be." One is left only with saying, "Don't be so sure that you *know* how it's supposed to be." In an account that can't admit any specified virtues, the cardinal sin becomes epistemic *hubris*.

off what we think Derrida *should* say, I think we will be surprised to note the centrality of *autonomy* in his account—indeed, what we might call a kind of *hyper*-autonomy. What gets the ball rolling in his analysis of these aporias is the unquestioned axiom that the condition of responsibility is freedom. I would not question that axiom at this point;[13] however, I think it important to ask what is being assumed in the notion of "freedom" here. While Derrida clearly calls into question Kantian paradigms of autonomy, he does so, it seems to me, in the name of an even more autonomous autonomy, a kind of hyper-autonomy that imagines the ethical agent as an inventor from nothing, a kind of microcosmic *creator ex nihilo*.[14] Justice demands that I make a "fresh judgment" in every case, generating a unique interpretation in every instance "as if ultimately nothing previously existed of the law, as if [I] invented the law in every case." And not only does justice demand that I *invent* the law in each instance, it demands that I come up with such unique interpretations without being subject to any horizons of expectation or anticipation. This is an essential feature of what Derrida calls the "structural finitude" of the decision vis-à-vis knowledge:

> even if it did have all that at its disposal, even if it did give itself the time, all the time and the necessary facts about the matter, the moment of *decision, as such,* always remains a finite moment of urgency and precipitation, since it must not be the consequence or the effect of this theoretical or historical knowledge, of this reflection or this deliberation, since it always marks the interruption of the juridico- or ethico- or politico-cognitive deliberation that precedes it, that *must* precede it. (FL 26)

But what is Derrida asking for here? What kind of a subject could *be* such a creature—a creature without memory, history, or tradition? What sort

---

13   For a provocative argument that does call into question this axiom, see Derk Pereboom, *Living without Free Will* (Cambridge: Cambridge University Press, 2003).
14   This would confirm the persistent *modernity* of Derrida's account. See David Burrell's description of the modern "libertarian" subject as a new creator *ex nihilo* in Burrell, *Faith and Freedom: An Interfaith Perspective* (Oxford: Blackwell, 2004), vii. My suggestion here is the opposite of caricatures of Derrida that see him portraying the human subject as merely a slave subject to external forces (e.g., Vanhoozer).

of ego has no history?[15] It seems to me that this demand (this "must") is calling for the ethical subject to be a kind of monstrosity, an ahistorical ego without memory and unconditioned by a tradition and history of formation—an ego not so different from the Cartesian cogito who thinks he is able to erase an entire history and legacy of belief on a quiet Friday night and reinvent the world from scratch.[16] But what does it say about Derrida's account of "justice" that it requires such a picture of the ethical subject? Should this rather Cartesian picture of such a history-less and tradition-less ego—a picture of the ego that Husserl, Heidegger and Derrida taught us to reject (and which we should also reject on theological grounds)—not make us question Derrida's related account of justice? In other words, if such a picture of the ahistorical "inventive" ethical subject is not viable, does that lack of viability not wash back onto the account of justice that generated from this picture? Why should we think that justice is incommensurate with the particularities of history, and the particularities of a historical subject? I would contend that Derrida's allergy to particularity and determinacy stems in no small part from a lingering philosophical anthropology that sees the ethical subject as primarily a *decider*, a decision-maker, and more specifically, an *unconditioned* decision-maker whose pedigree remains Cartesian and Kantian.

This spills over into a second feature of Derrida's moral psychology that we should note: across his corpus, it seems that Derrida's ethical subject is on her own. That is, the picture that Derrida paints of one subject to the Other is a very lonely scene: the subject of obligation is standing alone, trembling, naked before the Other's command from on high. The inventive decision that is required by justice—without the safety net of knowledge or the assurance of rules—is a decision I have to make on my own; no consulting, no friendship, no counsel, no community. Indeed, the requirement that I jettison my history and tradition requires me to sever ties to others who have gone before and forget, as it were, the relationships that have formed my imagination and molded my horizons of expectation.

15   Even Husserl was eventually attentive to this (and the young Derrida drew our attention to this). See especially Husserl, *Cartesian Meditations*, Med. V and the *Krisis* texts. For a discussion of Huserl's (later) generative phenomenology, see the excellent analysis in Anthony Steinbock, *Home and Beyond: Generative Phenomenology After Husserl* (Evanston, Ill.: Northwestern University Press, 1995).
16   Of course the burden of Gilson's reading of Descartes was to show precisely how Descartes' radical doubt remained marked by the categories of medieval thought.

The solitary ethical subject is left to fend for herself in the face of the accusation of the Other, detached from community.[17] But how persuasive or illuminative is such a phenomenology of our moral situation? Does this really resonate as a viable description of our moral experience? Or does it again feel like a description governed a priori by a rather Cartesian picture of the lonely ego? Could we not envision an alternative moral phenomenology that eschewed such assumptions about the solitary subject?

Third, and finally, consider carefully the embedded assumptions in Derrida's account of "knowledge" and the way in which it functions as an obstruction of justice. It is here that I think Derrida falls into the confines of a binary imagination: an all-or-nothing logic that runs against the best aspects of his own corpus. In "Force of Law," it seems clear that "knowledge," for Derrida, is always already identified with "certainty" and "assurance." Because we do not have "infinite information" or "unlimited knowledge," according to him, we are therefore in "the night of non-knowledge" (FL 26). And since rules or criteria are on the order of knowledge, they are taken to be instances of "assurance" (24) and "certitude" (25). Notice the all-or-nothing: either "unlimited" knowledge *or* non-knowledge. That, it seems clear, is a false dichotomy that is driven by a reductionistic conception of knowledge which simply reduces knowledge *to* Cartesian certainty. And since that is precluded, we are left not knowing. If knowledge is simply equated with certainty, then to lack certainty means to lack knowledge. In fact, in *Paper Machine*, Derrida goes so far as to identify "misunderstanding, failure of comprehension, making a mistake" with "evil" (PM 89).

Since I have criticized this binary, reductionistic equation of knowledge with certainty elsewhere, I will not belabor the point here.[18] Instead, as I have already noted, what most interests me here is not how Derrida (mistakenly) conceives knowledge, but that he construes the ethical situation as primarily an *epistemic* situation. This is indicative of a moral

---

17 I am not alone in finding this isolationism in Derrida. In a recent article J. Hillis Miller, against the tide, argues that "Jacques Derrida is unusual, if not unique, in explicitly denying that *Dasein* is *Mitsein*" and that Derrida, in his last seminars, affirmed "the fundamental and irremediable isolation of each *Dasein*." See Miller, "Derrida Enisled," *Critical Inquiry* 33 (2007): 248–76.
18 See *Speech and Theology: Language and the Logic of Incarnation* (London: Routledge, 2002), ch. 5, where I invoke the careful medieval distinction between "understanding" and "comprehension," between "touching" and "grasping"; and *Who's Afraid of Postmodernism? Taking Derrida, Lyotard, and Foucault to Church* (Grand Rapids: Baker Academic, 2006), 118–21.

psychology that is still playing on a basically Cartesian plane. As a contrast, let's consider briefly Augustine's account of moral struggle in book 8 of the *Confessions*.

Virtue, Vice, and Choice: An Augustinian Moral Psychology

In *Jacques Derrida: Live Theory* I argued that in order to understand Derrida well, it is crucial to locate his project within the phenomenological tradition.[19] While I stand by that, my critique here is that Derrida offers a very unnuanced phenomenology of the moral landscape. In other words, his "moral psychology" is remarkably thin and reductionistic, precisely because it remains so fixated on issues of knowledge and lack thereof. For Derrida, it seems that if the moral agent experiences a kind of anguish and angst, it is because she is in a situation of *non*-knowledge.[20] Moral crisis, in this Derridean landscape, always seem to be some modality of not knowing what to do, but having to make a *decision* anyway. (Even the priority of *decision* over action is yet another symptom of the rationalism of Derrida's account, which remains within a paradigm that gives us something like "deontology.") For example, I do not have any rules or guidelines or criteria to help me *know* what hospitality should look like in immigration reform—but I have to reform the law anyway. In any case, the challenge, even trauma, of the situation is epistemic. Though I lack knowledge, I have to make a decision. What we do not see Derrida grappling with, despite the centrality of decision-making in his account, is any careful attention to the dynamics of decision-making—except for his (rather outlandish) stipulation that the decision be a "fresh judgment" made without reliance on any prior knowledge (FL 26). But this is to reduce the ethical to the stage of individual decision-making (what I have referred to above as "quandary ethics"), and then submerge the dynamics of decision in a kind of "black box" with little attention to the mechanics of ethical agency. In sum, despite all his disavowal of calculation and

---

19 See James K. A. Smith, *Jacques Derrida: Live Theory* (London: Continuum, 2005), 135n57 and passim.
20 And it seems to me that this is an important point of difference between Levinas and Derrida. I would not say that Levinas' phenomenological description of the moral situation is characterized by the same epistemic fixation. Rather, "I" am traumatized by the Other precisely because of the involutional spiral of my own egoism. Questions of knowledge, justification, and warrant are really not in the foreground for Levinas.

his rejection of the judge as a "calculating machine" (FL 23), it seems to me that Derrida's moral psychology still assumes that the ethical agent is a kind of decision-machine. Admittedly, this would be a machine without algorithms, but still machine-like insofar as he gives no attention to the dynamics of the *formation* of the moral agent, and further assumes (requires) that the decider makes a one-off decision in every case.[21] There is no linkage between decisions; each is *sui generis*, *ex nihilo*, and without memory. We might say that the decision-maker lacks any *story*.

I think this picture needs to be contested on both levels: first, I think it is reductionistic to treat ethics, justice, and morality as instances of discrete decisions and acts; instead, I think a more persuasive and attentive moral phenomenology needs to see the ethical terrain as one of *character*, not simply discrete "acts" or "decisions." The currency of ethics is not individual decisions, but a life ("one swallow does not make a spring"). Second, and because of this, I think a persuasive moral phenomenology needs to provide an account of the *formation* of the moral subject, and especially the formation of habits (virtues/vices) that then play a significant role in an account of decision-making attentive to these dynamics. This will also require making intersubjective dependence ("community") central to any account of justice or ethics. The result of such a moral phenomenology of ethical life will be something very different from the picture bequeathed to us by Derrida. To put this starkly, Derrida's account has no room for virtue—or even vice.

Contrast this with Augustine's account of ethical crisis in book 8, the conversion narrative of the *Confessions*. In the middle of book 8, we find Augustine in an intriguing situation, particularly vis-à-vis our discussion of Derrida. He is ardent to follow the example of Victorinus' example of discipleship (*Conf* 8.5.10); to map this onto our prior discussion, let's say that Augustine is *convinced* of his obligation here—he *knows* that he owes it to the Other (in this case, God) to turn from his self-absorption and respond to the Other. He also knows what this requires (e.g., abandoning his post as an imperial rhetor). By this point in the narrative, after the epistemic anguish of books 2–7, and the drama of *not* knowing what is true, here in book 8 Augustine reaches the point where that epistemic struggle is settled. But that is hardly the end of the drama. In fact, it is the

---

21 In this respect, Derrida's ethical agent is akin to the *homo economicus* of classical economics, and thus subject to the same sort of critique laid out by behavioral economists such as Richard Thaler.

beginning of a more intense consideration of the mechanics (or perhaps better: "organics") of decision that we find nowhere in Derrida.

In broad strokes, for Derrida the moral landscape—the terrain of justice and ethics, and even religion—is primarily an epistemic landscape. Central to his analysis of the ethical situation is an analysis of the epistemic conditions of that situation, and the lack of certainty that characterizes it. Now if, by a hypothetical thought project, we could imagine a scenario where the ethical subject did somehow possess certainty or "infinite knowledge," the Derridean analysis would have to end. Since the drama of the Derridean ethical subject is largely the drama of one who doesn't know what to do, *knowing* what to do (fully, completely, certainly) marks the limits of this Derridean account.[22] That is, in the face of a situation where the ethical subject would *know* what to do, Derrida has nothing left to deconstruct. What gets deconstructed in his account are the conditions of rules, laws, knowledge, etc.; if we could imagine a scenario where such limits did not apply, Derrida has little to say. In fact, he himself does entertain such a scenario: recall that in "Force of Law," Derrida extrapolates and says, "*even if* it [the decision] did have all that ["infinite information and unlimited knowledge"] at its disposal, *even if* it did have the time, all the necessary time and facts about the matter, the moment of *decision*, *as such*, always remains a finite moment of urgency and precipitation, since it *must not be the consequence or the effect of* this theoretical or historical knowledge" (FL 26, emphases added). In other words, even if the ethical subject was furnished with all the data, had all the necessary and relevant information, had "certain" knowledge about the situation, she would only be making a *just* decision—or a decision pretending to justice—if she decided *as if* she had none of it. The ethical field only remains interesting on this Derridean register so long as we lack knowledge; and even if we imagined possessing all the knowledge needed, justice demands that we act *without* that knowledge playing any role or having any effect on our decision. In short, the whole scene remains linked to issues of (non-)knowledge, and Derrida's moral phenomenology has little to say beyond these matters of epistemic concern.

In contrast, the nuance of Augustine's moral psychology is indicated by the fact that even beyond questions about the limits of knowledge his

---

22 Not entirely, of course, since we still have the issue of *extension* (the distribution of moral finite energies), which will be addressed below.

account still has much to explore. In other words, Augustine's account takes us beyond epistemology—and beyond this epistemic fixation—by plumbing the depths of will, desire, love, and habit. When we move beyond epistemology Derrida has little to say about ethics, whereas for Augustine, once we get beyond epistemology, we are just getting started. This is because Augustine's moral psychology accords a prominent and influential place to the dynamics of desire or love, rooted in the will. It is on this complicated terrain that we find him in book 8 of the *Confessions*. It is not an epistemic situation: "I no longer had my usual excuse to explain why I did not yet despise the world and serve you, namely, that my perception of the truth was uncertain. By now I was quite sure about it. Yet I was still bound down to the earth. I was refusing to become your soldier" (8.5.11). The ethical dynamics of obligation here are not reducible to questions of knowledge, or the lack thereof, but a different order of desire and the will. As Augustine continues, "Though at every point you showed that what you were saying was true, yet I, convinced by that truth, had no answer to give you except merely slow and sleepy words: 'At once'—'But presently'—'Just a little longer, please.' But 'At once, at once' never came to the point of decision" (8.5.12). What precludes a "genuine" or "authentic" decision here is not the obstruction of knowledge or the interference of rules, but a dynamics of *vice* that Derrida's account nowhere entertains. What prevents "justice" in this case—what prevents a just "decision"—is not the violence of finitude per se, or captivity by "horizons of expectation," but rather the "violence of habit by which even the unwilling mind is dragged down and held" (8.5.12). Whereas Derrida's survey of the moral landscape still accords a quasi-Cartesian priority to mind and epistemology, Augustine's moral psychology goes beyond (through) epistemology to consider the dynamics of habit and desire precisely because Augustine's own philosophical anthropology accords primacy to love before reason. What we see in this episode is an account of the ethical subject in which will overrides reason—and that is true not only for the deformed or malformed self. In contrast to Plato, it is not only the unhealthy self that is governed by the will, whereas in the "healthy" self the intellect rules over the will. Rather, for Augustine, this is a structural feature of the human creature: we are *erotic* animals, creatures of desire who are defined by *love*. What is at stake, then, is not whether rationality is governed by love (the will), but rather what direction our will/love takes—what our love is aimed at. The account of the self in book 8 is not castigating the self for being habitual, but for being governed by *bad* habits animated by a *mis*directed love/will.

My central point is to emphasize that Augustine's moral psychology offers a much more nuanced account of justice and injustice precisely because he is more attentive to the dynamics of the will—the dynamics of love, desire, and habit-formation that does not even seem to appear on Derrida's moral landscape. In fact, more critically, Derrida's requirement that the just decision be made without a history, *sui generis* in each instance, and that the ethical subject pretend to justice just insofar as she erases the history of her formation, structurally precludes any place for habits (and therefore virtues and vices) precisely because habits are the traces of the formation of desire by embodied practice. It is surely ironic that Augustine, long (and wrongly) castigated as ancient despiser of all things bodily, in fact offers a moral phenomenology that is attuned to the embodied conditions of moral formation, whereas Derrida, paragon of postmodern difference, offers a moral psychology that treats us as decision-machines whose relationship to the body seems inconsequential, even "Cartesian." If Derrida's epistemological fixation yields a stunted moral psychology, I think this is because it is a symptom of a reductionistic philosophical anthropology which still tends to construe the human person as primarily a "thinking thing," a choice-machine.

9

A Principle of Incarnation in Derrida's *(Theologische?) Jugendschriften*

Towards a Confessional Theology

In previous chapters, I have contrasted the "logic of determination" with the "logic of incarnation." In this chapter, we will consider the way in which something like the latter—affirming embodiment and finitude—is latent in the early Derrida's critique of Husserl and Plato, even if the later Derrida in some way replays the logic of determination. If it is not too cute to say so, this is an exercise in deconstructing Derrida as a faithful reading of Derrida.[1]

In pursuing the question of incarnation, it must be noted from the beginning that what is at stake is Platonism. More specifically, our concern will be the relationship of Christian theology to Platonism. It is a curious phenomenon that, into the twenty-first century, the question of Christian theology's relationship to Platonism remains an orienting and fundamental theme of reflection. Replaying an Augustinian challenge,[2] the question has been raised anew by two revivals of Platonism

---

1   With this chapter's title, I am playing with descriptions of Hegel's early writings (as edited by Dilthey [1907]) and Gadamer's similar description of Heidegger's early work. See Hans-Georg Gadamer, "Heideggers 'theologische' Jugendschrift," *Dilthey-Jahrbuch* 6 (1989): 228–24, and Merold Westphal, "Heidegger's '*Theologische*' *Jugendschriften*," *Research in Phenomenology* 27 (1997): 247–61.
2   Few questions in Augustinian studies have generated more discussion than Augustine's relationship to Plato, Platonism, and Neoplatonism. For a lucid and helpful survey of the state of the question, see Robert Crouse, "*Paucis mutatis verbis*: St. Augustine's Platonism," in *Augustine and His Critics: Essays in Honour of Gerald Bonner*, ed.

which serve as catalysts: first, and most recently, a movement in theology which valorizes their identification, sketching a "Platonism/Christianity,"[3] and publishing a manifesto which promises—at the same time—"a more incarnate, more participatory, more aesthetic, more erotic, more socialised, even 'more Platonic' Christianity."[4] The second revival is one that takes place under the tent of phenomenology, as pointed out in Derrida's early critique of Husserl: concluding that Husserl's "determination of being as ideality is properly a *valuation*, an ethico-theoretical act that revives the decision that founded philosophy in its Platonic form,"[5] we might even suggest that Derrida's critique of Husserl is precisely a critique of Husserl's Platonism—in the name, I will argue, of a certain theory of incarnation. These two revivals collide in Catherine Pickstock's curious critique of early Derrida (particularly "Plato's Pharmacy"[6]), where she suggests an inversion of what we might have suspected, first arguing that Plato is in fact an "incarnational" philosopher who values the sensible as sacramental, and hence values writing (the *Phaedrus* notwithstanding), and second that it is Derrida, not Plato, who "suppresses embodiment and temporality" and is, in the end, a purveyor of the quintessential Parisian

---

Robert Dodaro and George Lawless (New York: Routledge, 2000), 37–50. I have also addressed the question in my "Staging the Incarnation: Revisioning Augustine's Critique of Theater," *Literature and Theology* 15 (2001), 123–39, and *The Fall of Interpretation: Philosophical Foundations for a Creational Hermeneutic* (Downers Grove, Ill.: InterVarsity Press, 2000), ch. 5.

3 John Milbank, *Theology and Social Theory: Beyond Secular Reason* (Oxford: Blackwell, 1990), 290. Similar formulations include the identification of "Platonism and Christianity" (290), "the Platonic/Christian shepherding ideal" (293), and an identification of "the neo-Platonic/Christian infinitization of the absolute" (295). Correlative to this is a critique of any who would seek to "de-Platonize" Christianity (294–95).

4 John Milbank, Graham Ward, and Catherine Pickstock, "Introduction—Suspending the Material: The Turn of Radical Orthodoxy," in *Radical Orthodoxy: A New Theology* (New York: Routledge, 1999), 3.

5 Jacques Derrida, *La voix et le phénomène: Introduction au problème du signe dans la phénoménologie de Husserl* (Paris: PUF, 1967), 59 / *Speech and Phenomena*, trans. David Allison (Evanston, Ill.: Northwestern University Press, 1973), 53.

6 Jacques Derrida, "Plato's Pharmacy," in *Dissemination*, trans. Barbara Johnson (Chicago: University of Chicago Press, 1981), 63–171. It is important to see the critique of the privileging of "speech" in this essay as analogous to the critique of Husserl in *Speech and Phenomena*; this will serve as further evidence that the object of critique in the latter is Husserl's Platonism.

heresy—a "metaphysics of presence."[7] In short, she suggests to us that Derrida is a Platonist.[8]

My overall project contests Pickstock's theses on two fronts: first, elsewhere, by arguing that it is precisely on an incarnational register that Platonism and Christianity are incommensurable—in short, to demonstrate once again that Plato is a Platonist.[9] In this chapter, my goal is on the second front, demonstrating that Derrida is not a Platonist, but rather offers a critique of Platonism[10] (in Husserl) and argues for what one might describe as an incarnational (or, at least, quasi-incarnational) account of language as constituted by both presence and absence—a "manifestation" (*Kundgabe*) which both "announces" and "conceals." And it is just such an incarnational account of language, I would argue, which is the condition of possibility for theology. Research on Derrida and theology has tended to travel several (now well-worn)

---

7   Catherine Pickstock, *After Writing: On the Liturgical Consummation of Philosophy* (Oxford: Blackwell, 1998), 4, 21, and passim. My goal here is not a sustained critique of Pickstock (for such, see ch. 5 of my *Speech and Theology: Language and the Logic of Incarnation* [London: Routledge, 2002]). At stake is an entire history of interpretation, which could be summarized as follows: the "traditional" reading of Plato's *Phaedrus* has concluded that Socrates devalued writing as sensible, temporal, and external; further, the tradition has *agreed* with that evaluation (this is Derrida's point in *Speech and Phenomena*, *Of Grammatology*, and other early works). In "Plato's Pharmacy," Derrida continues to uphold the "traditional" interpretation of the *Phaedrus*, but unlike "the tradition," calls this evaluation of writing into question (for reasons we will explore momentarily). Finally, Pickstock enters the fray, attempting to argue that Derrida is a nihilist and a modernist who has misread the *Phaedrus*, as indeed, has the entire "tradition" since, she argues, in the dialogue we find that Socrates in fact values sensibility, temporality, and hence, writing. If we follow Pickstock, it is *Derrida* who is the "Platonist" (in the "traditional" sense of the term). Permit me here to just note that I would argue Pickstock is mistaken on both scores, regarding her reinterpretation of Plato and her first interpretation of Derrida: first, Platonic participation differs fundamentally from Christian incarnation (this is argued elsewhere); second, as I will suggest in this chapter, Derrida's early project is funded by an understanding of embodiment and language which is much closer (perhaps too close to see) to Pickstock's "incarnational" and "liturgical" account. So in the end, Pickstock and I agree about the importance of an incarnational ontology, but we *dis*agree as to the resources for its development: she finds it in Plato and *not* Derrida; I am locating it in Derrida and *not* Plato (or Husserl).
8   Not a *real* Platonist, since the burden of her work is to argue that Plato is *really* a quasi-incarnational and sacramental philosopher; so Derrida is a "Platonist" in the "traditional" sense, an "apparent" Platonism.
9   See my *Speech and Theology*, ch. 5.
10 In other words, I think "metaphysics" and "Platonism" are basically synonymous in early Derrida.

paths: his relationship to negative theology, the possibility of theology after his critique of ontotheology and the metaphysics of presence, his understanding of the relationship between faith and reason, the impact of deconstruction on hermeneutics, or the role of "religion" and justice in his later thought—all of which I have explored elsewhere.[11] In this chapter, I want to tread a road less traveled, in two senses: first, rather than engage in a negative apologetic vis-à-vis deconstruction,[12] I want to enlist Derrida in a *constructive* theological project—even a *confessional* theology; second, I want to return to the *early* Derrida—and in particular, his work on phenomenology—as the foundation for a revisioning of theological method which is *incarnational* both in its account of how God can be known and how we can speak about God.

I will first briefly map the issues of language and alterity with a specific application of these currents to theological discourse. Then I will unpack Derrida's analysis of language in *Speech and Phenomena*, demonstrating that his is a latently incarnational account of language which is the fund for the conclusion: a constructive proposal for the development of a confessional theology, both as a theology *of* confession and a theology *based on* confession. Indicative of what Dominique Janicaud described as the "theological turn" of contemporary French philosophy, recent phenomenological debates have revolved around the question of transcendence (as seen in the work of Levinas, Marion, and Derrida). At stake here is, first of all, the matter of how that which is transcendent can make an appearance,

---

11   Respectively, on the question of negative theology see my "How to Avoid Not Speaking: Attestations," in James Olthuis, ed., *Knowing Other-wise: Philosophy on the Threshold of Spirituality*, Perspectives in Continental Philosophy Series (New York: Fordham University Press, 1997), 217–34, and "Between Predication and Silence: Augustine on How (Not) to Speak of God," *The Heythrop Journal* 41 (2000): 66–86 (esp. 80–84, where I develop a theology of "praise" in dialogue with Derrida and Marion, returning to Augustine); on the relationship between faith and reason, see ch. 10 below; on deconstruction and hermeneutics, see my *The Fall of Interpretation*, 115–29; and on questions of religion and justice in later Derrida, see chs. 5 and 6 above. One should also consult Guy Collins, "Thinking the Impossible: Derrida and the Divine," *Literature and Theology* 14 (2000): 313–34, and John D. Caputo, *The Prayers and Tears of Jacques Derrida: Religion without Religion* (Bloomington: Indiana University Press, 1997).
12   Such apologetic strategies usually begin from the premise that Derrida is a "nihilist" or, in Pickstock's terms, "immanentist." See, for example, Milbank, *Theology and Social Theory*, 302–15, and Pickstock, *After Writing*, 47–48. For an antidote, see Collins, "Thinking the Impossible."

and then following from this, how a discourse on transcendence could be possible—both of which are foundational questions for theology. Having tackled the first question elsewhere,[13] the focus of this chapter is how language, which is finite, can indicate that which is transcendent—and more particularly, how theological language can function in the modality of "confession" and "praise."

In particular, I want to consider the way in which a "confessional" theology is confronted by the challenge of transcendence.[14] By a "confessional" theology, I mean a theology which begins from an experience of the divine—a theology of *testimony*, for which we might look to Augustine or Kierkegaard for a paradigm.[15] For both Augustine and Kierkegaard, one of the fundamental challenges of any theology (or proclamation in general) is the incommensurability between the radical interiority of the God-relationship and the public traffic of language. In this sense, the interiority and privacy of the God-relation is incommensurate with language which is exterior and public. With respect to the "making present" of language, such an incommensurate interiority must remain absent. But how, then, could one speak of God, confess God? How could one "reveal" or "manifest" one's interiority to another? Would the theologian be consigned to silence? What is needed is an account of language and expression which can do justice both to the imperative of confession but also the incommensurability, even transcendence, of this interiority. This would be an account of language which accounts for a modality of "speaking" which can both "make present" and "conceal." In this sense, I would argue that it would be an account of language analogous to the Incarnation itself, which is a mode of manifestation that both makes God present to the immanence of human perception but also retains the transcendence of the Wholly Other. In short, it is a non-reductive manifestation.

It is just such an incarnational account of language, I will argue, which we find latent in Derrida's critique of Husserl—to which we now turn.

---

13   See James K. A. Smith, "Respect and Donation: A Critique of Marion's Critique of Husserl," *American Catholic Philosophical Quarterly* 71 (1997): 523–38.
14   A similar challenge would confront a "revelational" theology, which grapples not with the challenge of a heterogeneous *interiority* but a radical *exteriority*—the Wholly Other. However, these two challenges are not mutually exclusive; in Augustine, for instance, both challenges are at work. For a discussion, see my "Between Predication and Silence."
15   I have discussed this further in my "How (Not) to Tell a Secret: Interiority and the Strategy of 'Confession,'" *American Catholic Philosophical Quarterly* 74 (2000): 135–51.

Presence, Absence, and Husserl's Docetism
The Critique of Metaphysics as a Critique of "Platonism"

We might describe Husserl's phenomenology as a process of decontamination whose goal is the distillation of "purity"—even a "pure" metaphysics. But in this process, it is precisely materiality and embodiment which constitutes a contamination. It is for this reason that Derrida locates at the heart of phenomenology—intended to be a radical critique of metaphysics—a latent but persistent "Platonism" (i.e., metaphysics). Thus Derrida's project in *Speech and Phenomena* (hereafter SP) is to raise the question: Does the phenomenological reduction itself—which attempts to bracket metaphysics—in fact conceal metaphysical presuppositions (SP 3/4)? Does it "not harbor a dogmatic or speculative commitment which, to be sure, would not keep the phenomenological critique from being realized, would not be a residue of unperceived naïveté, but would *constitute* phenomenology from within, in its project of criticism and in the instructive value of its own premises?" (SP 3–4/4–5). That is, could it be that phenomenology is *at root* (i.e., *radically*) metaphysical? In pursuing this question, it is not a matter of finding mere vestiges of metaphysics in phenomenology, like unintended stowaways in the good ship phenomenology, but rather seeing at the heart and mission of phenomenology a metaphysical project—just what phenomenology sets out to "deconstruct." What other "degenerate" metaphysical speculations consistently missed, Husserl argued, was "the authentic mode of *ideality* . . . what may be infinitely *repeated* in the *identity* of its *presence*, because of the very fact that it *does not exist*, is *not real* or is *irreal*" (SP 4/6, emphases original). This ideality is ultimately "the *living present*, the self-presence of transcendental life" (SP 4–5/6). Metaphysics here represents the determination of being as presence purified of materiality which is infected by absence.

As a kind of case study, Derrida locates these operations in the opening discussion of the "sign" in Husserl's early work *Logical Investigations*,[16] where we "see the phenomenological critique of metaphysics betray itself as a moment within the history of metaphysical assurance" (SP 3/5). Phenomenology, Derrida will demonstrate,

---

[16] Edmund Husserl, *Logische Untersuchungen*, 2 vols. (Tübingen: M. Niemeyer, 1900–1901; 2nd ed., 1913) / *Logical Investigations*, 2 vols., trans. John Niemeyer Findlay (Milton Park, UK: Routledge, 1970).

A Principle of Incarnation in Derrida's *(Theologische?) Jugendschriften* 177

> seems to us tormented, if not contested from within, by its own descriptions of the movement of temporalization and of the constitution of intersubjectivity. At the heart of what ties together these two decisive moments of description we recognize an irreducible nonpresence as having a constituting value, and with it a nonlife, a nonpresence or nonself-belonging of the living present, an ineradicable nonprimordiality. (SP 5/6–7)

The phenomenological ego is haunted by a nonpresence, an absence, perhaps even a *transcendence*—another, an Other. And more so: the phenomenological ego is in fact *constituted* by such non-presence. In this sense, Derrida's analysis of the constitution of the ego by an absence or otherness could be read as a kind of poststructuralist "Third Meditation" like unto Descartes, where the Other disturbs the solitude of the ego (as emphasized in the reading of Descartes in Marion and Levinas).[17]

Here we must appreciate the correlation of three key terms: first, *absence* or *nonpresence* (which is consistently opposed to presence); second, *alterity* or *otherness*; and finally, *transcendence*. The first two are regularly employed by the early Derrida, the latter more frequent in later Derrida. But they are functional synonyms since, phenomenologically speaking, that which is "transcendent" is precisely that which lies outside of consciousness, that which cannot be made present within the sphere of immanence and thus remains absent. In other words, the transcendent is the *alter*, the other. Once we appreciate these connections, Derrida's early arguments regarding the primordiality of absence and nonpresence have significant theological implications. Further, the critique of metaphysics lies precisely in metaphysics' penchant to valorize "full presence" and hence exorcise any vestige of absence—which, given the correlation just noted, constitutes a fundamental exclusion of *transcendence*. Derrida is

---

17 We might recall and compare the interruption and displacement of the Cartesian cogito in the *Third Meditation* ("I am not alone"), particularly in light of the analysis of the "summons" (*revendication*) in Jean-Luc Marion, *Reduction and Givenness: Investigations of Husserl, Heidegger, and Phenomenology*, trans. Thomas A. Carlson (Evanston: Northwestern University Press, 1998), 204–5. Contrary to the standard "subjectivist" reading of Descartes' *Meditations*, close attention to the text will see that the *ego* is in fact constituted by this Other—that God is the very condition of possibility for the ego, both epistemologically and ontologically.

thus offering an apologia for transcendence, particularly in our account of language.

What exactly is meant, however, by the "concept of metaphysics?" Here Derrida suggests that in fact what is at stake is a traditional theory of language that posits the priority of logic over rhetoric, which Husserl assumes—determining the essence of language by reference to its supposed logical telos (SP 6/7). "That this telos is that of *being as presence* is what we here wish to suggest" (SP 6–7/8, emphasis added). Hence the project of SP is to demonstrate the way in which language itself is haunted by—indeed constituted by—an absence, a non-presence (a transcendence). Incessantly in Husserl, this "presence" of self-presence is elusive, slips away and is deferred; and in such cases, where "presence becomes threatened" (SP 8/9), Husserl recalls it as a telos or ideality (in the Kantian sense of an "Idea") which can be infinitely *repeated*—but for that reason Irreal. Derrida argues that "language is properly the medium for this play of presence and absence" (SP 8–9/10); in fact, what is at stake is a *spiritual* matter:

> But we ought to consider, on the one hand, that the element of signification—or the substance of expression—which best seems to preserve the ideality and living presence in all its forms is living speech, the spirituality of the breath as *phōnē*; and, on the other hand, that phenomenology, the metaphysics of presence in the form of ideality, is also a philosophy of life. (SP 9/10)

Or to put it differently: Derrida seeks to demonstrate that the "soulless consciousness" of the phenomenological ego "is still a *living* transcendental consciousness" (SP 9/10). Husserl posits a radical heterogeneity between "empirical (or in general, worldly) life and transcendental life," a distinction that Derrida questions (SP 9–10/10–11). Husserl accounts for the relation between the empirical and transcendental egos by recourse to a "parallelism" (SP 12/13); but "we must notice," Derrida observes, "that this parallelism does more than release transcendental ether; it renders more mysterious still (as it alone is capable of doing) the meaning of the *mental* and of mental *life*; that is, of a *worldliness* capable of sustaining, or in some way nourishing, *transcendentality*, and of equaling the full scope of its domain, yet without being merged with it in some total adequation" (SP 12/13). Thus could we not suggest that what is at stake here, in a sense, is the relation between soul and body? Or the relation between the transcendent and immanent? Further, insofar as he critiques this framework, might we not conclude that Derrida is seeking an account which avoids the reduction of the one to the other? And what would that be but an incarnational account? In other words, Derrida seeks to demonstrate a more holistic, incarnational account of the relation between body and soul, presence and absence, immanence and transcendence. Below we will see that it is precisely the relation between soul and body, the question of ideality and materiality, which orients Husserl's phenomenology. But Husserl takes this in a Platonic direction, seeking to decontaminate the ideal of any connection to embodiment.

The Word without Flesh

This metaphysical (i.e., Platonic) penchant of phenomenology is traced in Husserl's discussion of speech and expression. In the opening of the first of the *Logical Investigations*, Husserl seeks to clarify a fundamental distinction between two different concepts of the "sign" (*Anzeichen*): (1) "expression" (*Ausdruck*) and (2) "indication" (*Anzeichen*).[18] Indications are signs that "express nothing because they convey nothing one could call . . . *Bedeutung* or *Sinn*; they are deprived of 'meaning,' but not of signification" (since there can be no sign without signification) (SP 17/17). Indications, in other words, are characterized by *absence*. Expressions are expressive insofar as they are linked to "the ideality of a *Bedeutung*" and thus tied to "the possibility of spoken language (*Rede*)" (SP 18/18). What distinguishes spoken language as expression from "indication" is *meaning* (*vouloir-dire*): "a speaking subject, 'expressing himself,'" as Husserl says, "'about something,' *means* or *wants to say* something" (SP 19/19). Only speech is "expressive" in this sense.

However, this distinction between expression and indication is more functional than substantial: "One and the same phenomenon may be apprehended as an expression or as an indication, a discursive or nondiscursive sign depending on the intentional experience which animates

---

18 We should be reminded that what is at stake in a Christology and doctrine of the Incarnation is a certain semiotics, an account of the way in which Christ constitutes an "icon" of the invisible God (Col 1:15). In a sense, I am arguing for the formulation "Christ, the *indication* of God."

it" (SP 20/20). In other words, it is a question of how it is constituted by the subject. As such, the distinction sometimes leads Husserl to describe the relation of expression and indication as an "entanglement" (*Verflechtung*)—an "interweaving," or "contamination"—and even that such an entanglement is a "*de facto* necessity." In fact, the distinction between the two is only effected *de jure*, and *in language*—which is itself always already "infected" by the "contamination" of the two (SP 21/20–21). The implication of this would be that "[e]very expression would thus be caught up, despite itself, in an indicative process" (SP 21/21). As such, the expressive sign would be a species of the genus "indication"; and then "we would have to say in the end that the spoken word, whatever dignity or originality we still accorded to it, is but a form of gesture [a kind of indicative sign characterized by absence]. In its essential core, then, . . . it would belong to the general system of signification and would not surpass it. The general system of signification would then be coextensive with the system of indication" (SP 21–22/21).

But *this is just what Husserl contests*. Husserl wants to maintain the "purity" and privilege of spoken language, reserving a privileged presence in speech. This demand for "presence" is also an exclusion of "absence," and hence alterity. In other words, Husserl's account of language leaves no room for the manifestation of a transcendence which cannot be made fully present.[19] And it is here that Derrida wants to point out the contamination and infection of absence—the inescapable interweaving of alterity in language. In order to retain a privileging of expression and speech, Husserl must demonstrate that "expression is not a species of indication" (SP 22/21). In order to make this case, Husserl would have to find a case in which expression is disentangled from indication, "a phenomenological situation in which expression is no longer caught up in this entanglement, no longer intertwined with the indication" (SP 22/22). Insofar as all communicative expression ("colloquy") would always already be infected by "indication" (because [a] "expression indicates a content forever hidden from intuition, that is, from the lived experience of another" and [b] "the ideal content of meaning and the spirituality of the expression are here

---

19   This is also why Derrida suggests that Husserl's analysis of the appearance of the Other signals a discontinuity in this regard—a key moment of interruption. See SP 6/7, but also "Violence and Metaphysics."

united to sensibility" [SP 22/22]), Husserl must locate a "pure" expression in *soliloquy*, a "language without communication, in speech as monologue" as found in "solitary mental life" (SP 22/22). For in this private sphere of solitary mental life we would have located both a site of full presence and a site uncontaminated by sensibility. "By a strange paradox, meaning would isolate the concentrated purity of its *ex-pressiveness* just at that moment when the relation to a certain *outside* is suspended" (SP 22/22). Thus it is demonstrated by a kind of reduction to interiority which brackets all exteriority, and hence all communication/colloquy.

But can this be sustained? Will not the privacy of this "sphere of ownness" be interrupted by another, an Other?

The metaphysical attachment of phenomenology is evidenced in Husserl's attempt to lay down an *extrinsic* relation between indication and expression, thus attempting to maintain a "pure presence" in soliloquy. In order to retain the privileging of "expression" as the only site of "meaning," the treatment of "indication" is *reductive*: "Indication must be set aside, abstracted, and 'reduced' as an extrinsic and empirical phenomenon, even if it is in fact closely related to expression, empirically interwoven [entangled] with expression" (SP 28/27). In fact, "Husserl's whole enterprise—and far beyond the *Investigations*—would be threatened if the *Verflechtung* which couples the indicative sign to expression were absolutely irreducible, if it were in principle (*de jure*) inextricable and if indication were essentially internal to the moment of expression rather than being only conjoined to it, however tenaciously" (SP 28/27). It is precisely this irreducibility of the "interweaving" that Derrida seeks to demonstrate.

Husserl, on the other hand, makes a docetic move which seeks to purify expression of any material attachment. Expression, he argues, is always inhabited and animated by a meaning because it never takes place outside oral discourse (*Rede*) (SP 36/34). "What 'means,' i.e., *that which* the meaning means to say—the meaning, *Bedeutung*—is left up to whoever is speaking, insofar as he says what he *wants* to say, what he *means* to say" (SP 36/34). Thus Husserl concludes that all speech counts as expression—and this is the case whether or not such speech is actually uttered.[20] So all the aspects of the "physical incarnation of the meaning" ("the body of speech") is "if not outside discourse, at least foreign

---

20 Husserl, *Logical Investigations*, 275.

to the nature of expression as such, foreign to that pure intention without which there could be no speech" (SP 36/34). In short, the physical, material incarnation of meaning is relegated to indication and "retains in itself something of the nature of an *involuntary* association" (SP 36/34). The bodily manifestation of intentionality in the flesh of words—seen or heard—exceeds the control of the speaker; once I have spoken, my words take on a life of their own and I can no longer control their meaning.

What is excluded by Husserl's phenomenological reduction, then, is "the whole of the body and the mundane register, in a word, the whole of the visible and spatial as such" (SP 37/35)—such as facial expressions and gestures. Thus I have described this as Husserl's Docetism (or Platonism). What is at stake is an *opposition* between body and soul: "The opposition between body and soul is not only at the center of this doctrine of signification, it is confirmed by it; and, as has always been at bottom the case in philosophy, it depends upon an interpretation of language" (SP 37/35). Visibility and spatiality, on Husserl's terms, would represent the death of self-presence.[21] Bodily indications such as gestures and facial expressions lack meaning: "Nonexpressive signs mean (*bedeuten*) only in the degree to which they can be made to say what was murmuring in them, in a stammering attempt" (SP 38/36); indication lacks *vouloir-dire*.

Husserl has excluded indication from expression in order to guarantee a "pure presence" (indeed, a bodiless soul); however, he must exorcise a still "considerable sphere of the nonexpressive in speech itself" (SP 39–40/37); in other words, further "decontamination" is still needed to achieve purity. In order to do so, Husserl will bracket from "expression" "everything that belongs to the *communication* or *manifestation* of mental experiences [to another]" (SP 40/37). This will require a reduction to privacy and the exclusion of all intersubjectivity; in other words, the elimination of all "nonpresence"—which here represents all otherness, all alterity (SP 40/37). Recalling that "the difference between indication and expression was functional or intentional, and not substantial" (SP 40/37; cf. 20), Husserl can now exclude as 'indications' elements of substantial speech; in particular: "*All speech <u>inasmuch as it is engaged in communication</u> and*

---

21 This "incarnation" would represent the "death" of self-presence only insofar as we conceive presence as "full presence," as complete presence without absence; then any spatialization or temporalization would represent a *loss*. But could we not think presence differently? Could it not be a matter of both presence and absence, immanence and transcendence?

manifests[22] *lived experience operates as indication*" (SP 40/37-38, emphasis added). Excluded, then, are all forms of discourse which are intersubjective; even though Husserl concedes that expression is originally intended to serve the function of communication, it is not *pure* in functioning this way: "only when communication is suspended can pure expression appear" (SP 41/38). Thus all the "goings-forth (*sorties*) effectively exile this life of self-presence in indications," indicating, in fact, "the process of death at work in signs. . . . As soon as the other appears, indicative language—another name for the relation with death—can no longer be effaced" (SP 41/38).

Manifestation, Revelation, and Absence

Why is communication bracketed in the attempt to distill "pure" expression? What is it about communication that supposedly "contaminates" expression? What happens in communication? For Husserl, communication represents a *loss* of pure presence: "Sensible phenomena (audible or visible, etc.) are animated through the sense-giving acts of a subject, whose intention is to be simultaneously understood by another subject. But the 'animation' cannot be pure and complete, for it must traverse, and to some degree lose itself in, the opaqueness of a body" (SP 41/38).[23] The intersubjectivity of communication demands a mediation which constitutes a loss of full-presence. "Manifestation," for Husserl, is always "inadequate." We need to appreciate—as Levinas has suggested—that what is at stake here is a concept of revelation and incarnation (since the Incarnation is the revelation of the invisible God *par excellence* [Col 1:15]); indeed, what is at issue is the *possibility* of revelation and incarnation.[24]

As Derrida notes, this evaluation and analysis revolves around a notion of "presence" as "full" and "immediate":

> If communication or intimation (*Kundgabe*) is essentially indicative, this is because we have no primordial intuition of

---

22 To place this in a broader discussion, we should recall the connection between "manifestation" and "revelation" as unconditioned in Marion and Levinas.
23 Husserl, *Logical Investigations*, 277.
24 Ultimately, I think Levinas (and, for that matter, Jean-Luc Marion) offers us only an inversion of the Husserlian schema—not something like an "incarnational" account. For my criticism of Levinas and Marion on this score, see ch. 5 of my *Speech and Theology*.

the presence of the other's lived experience [i.e., the other is "absent" to me]. Whenever the immediate and full presence of the signified is concealed, the signifier will be of an indicative nature. (This is why *Kundgabe*, which has been translated a bit loosely by "manifestation" . . . , does not manifest, indeed, renders nothing manifest, *if by manifest we mean* evident, open, and presented "in person." The *Kundgabe* announces and at the same time conceals what it informs us about.) (SP 43/40, emphasis added)

For Husserl, "manifestation" indicates a presentation *without remainder*; as such, we must note that manifestation (*Kundgabe*) would in fact represent a *reduction* of the alterity of the other to the sphere of the same—a reduction of the transcendence of the other (here in a rigorously phenomenological sense) to the immanence of the perceiver/receiver. Thus it seems that Husserl leaves us with two (heretical) options: the other's subjectivity is either merely indicated and thus not *really* present, or it is fully present and thereby presented without remainder and reduced to immanence. This is both based on a theory of "purity" and contributes to it. Theologically speaking, we might say that the options are either Docetism or Arianism.

Christ, the Indication of God: Discerning Derrida's Incarnational Account of Language

As we have noted above, Husserl's devaluation of the embodiment of indication stems from his conception of presence as "full" presence (without lack, without remainder) and the correlate demand for the purification of expression in order to maintain such full presence. In other words, Husserl seeks to eradicate the *Verflechtung* of expression and indication, soul and body, by guarding a pure presence which is uncontaminated by materiality. On an incarnational register, Husserl will not jeopardize presence (being as ideality) by exposing it to sensibility or embodiment which are necessary for communication.

But does God maintain the same protections? Does God refuse to risk full presence? Does God refrain from communication in order to guard presence? Indeed, is it not precisely the Incarnation which would be the catalyst for a radically different notion of "manifestation" (*Kundgabe*)? Could we not conceive "manifestation" in different terms, meaning by it not *full* presence, but *real* presence?[25] And would not such a notion of real presence *retain the "remainder"* and thus transcendence? Could we not thus evaluate "manifestation" (*Kundgabe*) more positively?

It is just such a notion of the interweaving (*Verflechtung*) of presence and absence which grounds Derrida's critique of Husserl's "Platonism." Derrida insists that the intertwining[26] of presence and absence, ideality and materiality, is inescapable and constitutes the very conditions of language, discourse, and communication. Manifestation indicates both an announcement and a concealment—a "making present" which also retains an element of absence or transcendence. In other words, language operates as the Incarnation, which is its condition of possibility.[27]

The Incarnation ruptures the two things which Husserl's Docetism/Platonism seeks to put out of play: it is *communicative* and thus communicates by means of *embodied signs*. In the same way, what I have described above as a "confessional" theology both seeks to express or manifest transcendence and seeks to do so *for another* (i.e., it is communicative—its goal is communication). Such a "method" of theology begins with the *testimony* or "experience" of the believer and the believing community as the primary locus or site for theological reflection.[28] Thus it is a "confessional" theology in two senses: first, it begins from the confession of the believer testifying to her experience of God, and second, it is informed by participation in the believing community and tradition (and so, dialectically, also

---

25 Derrida uses the term "real presence" (57/52), but basically as a synonym for "full presence"; I would argue a fundamental difference.

26 I think this opens new horizons for the theological consideration of Merleau-Ponty, "The Intertwining—The Chiasm," in *The Visible and the Invisible*, ed. Claude Lefort, trans. Alphonso Lingis (Evanston: Northwestern University Press, 1968), 130–55. For developments of this, see Phillip Blond, "The Primacy of Theology and the Question of Perception," in *Religion, Modernity, and Postmodernity*, ed. David Heelas (Oxford: Blackwell, 1998), 285–313 and idem, "Perception: From Modern Painting to the Vision in Christ," in *Radical Orthodoxy*, 220–42.

27 I have developed this intuition, sparked by Augustine, in much more detail in *Speech and Theology*, 114–49.

28 The Pentecostal filiation of this notion of theology will be evident; however, the same can be found in David Kelsey's *To Understand God Truly: What's Theological about Theological Education?* (Atlanta: Westminster John Knox, 1992), and Edward Farley, *Ecclesial Reflection: Anatomy of Theological Method* (Minneapolis: Fortress, 1982).

informs and nourishes the community and tradition). As such, it is also a *relational* theology, again in two senses: first, it begins from the relationship between God and the believer, and second, it is both informed by and nourishes the believer's relationship to the believing community. It is the first element of *confession* or *testimony*, which requires "manifestation" or "expression," and it is the second element of *relationality*, which demands "communication." And both of these are summoned in response to a primary *communication* of God to humanity in the Incarnation, reconstituting a *relation* engendered by creation.

The condition of possibility for both confession and communication is language, and in order for such manifestation and communication to take place, we must break with a Platonic or metaphysical account of language that privileges "full" presence, because such an impossible full presence would preclude the possibility of manifestation, and hence the possibility of communication. As such, it would preclude, first of all, the very possibility of *revelation* and so the Incarnation; and insofar as the Incarnation is the condition of possibility for language, especially theological language, such a Platonic or Husserlian account of language would also preclude the possibility of theology in the mode of "confession."

Instead, theology must operate with an incarnational account of language which entails a notion of "real" presence—a presence which includes an absence, an excess or remainder which remains transcendent. The Husserlian criterion of "complete" or "adequate" presence would demand the complete absorption of alterity into the sphere of the same; more concretely, it would demand an Incarnation in which all transcendence is denied or given up—an appearance *without remainder*. But the result would be to permit only an "apparition" (no real appearance or giving, only an illusory presence) or an immanentizing "appearing without remainder" which shuts down any transcendent excess—neither of which are genuine Incarnation. But we need not adopt Husserl's logic on this score: an appearance can be "real" without being completely "adequate," exhausting the phenomenon's transcendence. Thus one can speak of the Incarnation as a genuine appearance—a *real presence*—which is nevertheless attended by inadequation, indicating a reference to a transcendence which exceeds the appearance, but is also embodied in the appearance. Such an incarnational logic will be the condition for both

God's confession and communication,[29] which evokes from the believing community a theology which is a mode of confession, involving—like the Incarnation—both manifestation and communication in words that *embody* the experience of God (1 John 1:1-3).[30]

---

29   We might think of the revelation of God in the Incarnation as a kind of "confession" or "testimony" of God, wherein God speaks "in Son" (Heb 1:2) and thus communicates to humanity (Heb 1:1-3).
30   For further discussion of Derrida and Incarnation, see James K. A. Smith, "Limited Inc/arnation: The Searle/Derrida Debate Revisited in Christian Context," in *Hermeneutics at the Crossroads: Interpretation in Christian Perspective*, ed. Kevin Vanhoozer, James K. A. Smith, and Bruce Ellis Benson (Bloomington: Indiana University Press, 2006), 112–29 (now included as ch. 7 in Smith, *The Fall of Interpretation*, 199–221).

10

Deconstruction—an Augustinian Science?

Augustine and Derrida on the Commitments of Philosophy

Said Reason: "God, to whom we have committed ourselves, will doubtless lend his aid and deliver us from these difficulties. Only let us believe and ask him with the greatest devotion."

Augustine, *Soliloquies* 2.6.9.

Suspicions

Jacques Derrida has left many in tears, including his mother, who, like St. Monica, wept over her wandering and wayward "son of these tears"[1] who had broken the covenant and would, by his own (cir)confession, "quite rightly pass for an atheist."[2] And now the prodigal son stands as a father to a most transgressive movement whose filial bonds to Nietzsche

---

1   Augustine, *Confessions* 3.12.21, where Monica's tears are in fact prayers which do not go unheard. Tears, including Augustine's tears, are important for Derrida's analyses in *Memoirs of the Blind*. For a close analysis, see also Kim Paffenroth, "Tears of Grief and Joy: Confessions Book 9: Chronological Sequence and Structure," *Augustinian Studies* 28 (1997): 141–54.
2   Jacques Derrida, "Circumfession: Fifty-Nine Periods and Periphrases," in Geoffrey Bennington and Jacques Derrida, *Jacques Derrida* (Chicago: University of Chicago Press, 1993), 155. For a commentary on Derrida's "religion without religion," see John D. Caputo, *The Prayers and Tears of Jacques Derrida: Religion without Religion* (Bloomington: Indiana University Press, 1997), 308–29 (henceforth abbreviated as PT). For a discussion of Augustine's *Confessions* and Derrida's *Circumfessions*, see Robert Dodaro, OSA, "Loose Canons: Derrida and Augustine on Their Selves," in *God, the Gift, and Postmodernism*, ed. John D. Caputo and Michael J. Scanlon (Bloomington: Indiana University Press, 1999), 79–97.

haunt its most suspicious and rigorous questioning and criticism such that deconstruction, if we are to believe William Bennett or Allan Bloom, is reason to weep and lament, ushering in the end of metaphysics, the closing of the book, the loss of the self, and the death of God. Derrida's incessant questioning marks a suspicion, it is assumed, that negates every commitment in a Dionysian celebration of *différance*; as such, deconstruction would signal the collapse of commitments and function as the nemesis to faith. Deconstruction would see through the facade and ruthlessly expose any grounding or primordial trust as inevitably a construction and myth, as a bluff. Derrida would be yet another master of suspicion pledged to questioning every commitment, committed only to questions and questioning.

Or so the story goes. "Do you believe this? (*Vous croyez?*)"[3] Are we to believe this? Are we to believe that deconstruction is intent on eliminating belief, that its probing criticism upsets every trust? Are we to give credit (*credere*) to this tale of deconstruction's dismantling of commitment? Is this reading of Derrida and deconstruction beyond question, or should we perhaps be suspicious of such a reading which would have Derrida committed to distrust? Could it in fact be the case that Derrida, and even deconstruction, has a certain faith, a certain commitment to commitment? Is there not a specter of this trust—this secret—which haunts deconstruction? Could it be that deconstruction, far from questioning every commitment, is in fact a celebration of commitments which revels in prayer and praise? Could deconstruction be an Augustinian science, which both acknowledges and even confesses that one must believe in order to understand?[4] "You better believe it (*il faut croire*)" (MB 32).

Derrida's Formalization of Augustine

In this chapter, I will argue that deconstruction, rather than being characterized by a spirit of suspicion, is concerned with the primordial

3   Jacques Derrida, *Memoirs of the Blind: The Self-Portrait and Other Ruins*, trans. Pascale-Anne Brault and Michael Naas (Chicago: University of Chicago Press, 1993), 1 (henceforth abbreviated as MB). Numbers in square brackets refer to selections from the sketches and drawings chosen by Derrida for an exhibition at the Louvre in 1990–1991, of which he was the guest curator. The pieces and Derrida's commentary constitute *Memoirs of the Blind*.
4   We are playing here on Derrida's reading of Freud in *Archive Fever*, the question of whether psychoanalysis is a "Jewish science," and Caputo's transposition of the question, whether deconstruction is a Jewish science (see *The Prayers and Tears of Jacques Derrida*, 263–64).

trust which sets questioning in motion, and thus is itself always already committed. That is to say, what we locate in Derrida's critique of reason is a fundamentally Augustinian structure which points to the commitments (trust, faith) which precede knowledge—the pledges which precede philosophy. With Augustine, Derrida would confess that "[u]nless one believes, one will not understand."[5] "I don't *know*," Derrida responds, "one has to *believe*" (MB 129, emphasis added). Despite rumors and caricatures, deconstruction does not side with any secularism. Instead, Derrida insists that a fundamental faith or trust must precede knowledge; on his account, the very structure of knowledge—and thus philosophy—points to a faith or trust which makes knowledge possible. "This is to take a fundamentally Augustinian, religious, and biblical position," Caputo comments, "for on this point Augustine himself is just being a good student of the biblical and prophetic tradition rather than of Plotinus" (PT 311). Rather than proceeding without presuppositions, previous commitments are the very condition of possibility for knowing.

However, though arguing that this is a fundamentally Augustinian structure, we must also recognize that it is also a formalization of Augustine. As discussed in chapters 6 and 7 above, the primordial faith that precedes knowledge as its condition of possibility is not, for Derrida, a contentful, determinate religion. For Augustine, the faith which issues in knowledge is ultimately very particular and contentful: faith in Christ the interior Teacher.

> Regarding each of the things we understand, however, we don't consult a speaker who makes sounds outside us, but the Truth that presides within over the mind itself, though perhaps words prompt us to consult Him. What is more, He Who is consulted, He Who is said to dwell in the inner man, does teach: Christ—that is, the unchangeable power and everlasting wisdom of God, which every rational soul does consult, but is disclosed to anyone to the extent that he can apprehend it, according to his good or evil will.[6]

---

5   See, for example, *De magistro* (CSEL 77) 11.37.
6   *De magistro* 11.38 in Augustine, *Against the Academicians and The Teacher*, trans. Peter King (Indianapolis: Hackett, 1995), 139.

Thus for Augustine, this structure is wedded to a particular content: the faith which precedes knowledge is precisely a commitment to the Origin and Creator, who is also the inner Teacher, the One who was "in the beginning" and "enlightens every person" (John 1:1, 4-5). In *De vera religione*, Augustine emphasizes that knowledge is possible only insofar as our diseased eyes (of the mind) are healed; and it is precisely faith which is the condition of possibility for healing, which is the condition of possibility of knowledge.[7] This is why, for Augustine, "philosophy, i.e., the pursuit of wisdom, cannot be quite divorced from religion."[8]

In Derrida, however, this Augustinian structure is divorced from its determinate content: the faith which precedes knowledge is merely structural, a commitment to something—like one's language—which makes knowledge, philosophy, and science possible. While the structure is universal (which must be qualified, based on deconstruction), the content or object of commitment is contingent.[9]

Derrida's Pledge: Of Spirit

Deconstruction, then, is doubly committed: it is committed, before criticism, by a certain trust and affirmation, but it is also committed to pointing out these commitments which precede every discourse or theoretical framework, suggesting that thinking entrusts itself to something Other than itself—to the guidance of the Spirit, or let us say *l'esprit*. Thus the site of this commitment to commitment, this pneumatic discourse, may be located in Derrida's little treatise on spirits: *ruah*, *pneuma*, *esprit*, and especially, *Geist*. Derrida's *Of Spirit* is a discourse on both "spirit" and

---

7   Augustine, *De vera religione* 3.3–4.
8   Augustine, *De vera religione* 5.8.
9   Thus elsewhere I have linked Derrida's discourse with Kuhn's notion of "paradigms," which are also fundamental commitments to frameworks that are contingent. For a discussion, see James K. A. Smith, "The Art of Christian Atheism: Faith and Philosophy in Early Heidegger," *Faith and Philosophy* 14 (1997): 71–81; and James K. A. Smith and Shane R. Cudney, "Postmodern Freedom and the Growth of Fundamentalism: Was the Grand Inquisitor Right?" *Studies in Religion/Sciences Religieuses* 25 (1996): 41–44. I think the same kind of "structural" commitment is glimpsed in Calvin's notion of the *sensus divinitatis*, and its development in Dooyeweerd; for both Calvin and Dooyeweerd, it is not the case that all human persons believe in God, but rather that humans are essentially religious—they need to believe in something. This structural belief can, however, take an apostate direction. For an especially helpful discussion, see Herman Dooyeweerd, *In the Twilight of Western Thought: Studies in the Pretended Autonomy of Theoretical Thought*, ed. James K. A. Smith, Collected Works B/4 (Lewiston: Edwin Mellen Press, 1998), ch. 2, "The Concentric Character of the Self."

"avoiding," or more specifically, *Geist und vermeiden* and how Heidegger (unsuccessfully) attempted to avoid this spirit in his work and life. A life and work haunted by ghosts—is this Heidegger or Derrida? Of course within Heidegger's *Gesamtausgabe* there lurk a number of disturbing specters: spirits which both disturb this corpus but also arise from this corpus to disturb us.[10] Derrida's goal in his little spirit-filled treatise is to reveal that, despite all of his protests and attempts, Heidegger failed to avoid this tormenting *Geist*:

> *Geist* is always haunted by its *Geist*: a spirit, or in other words, in French [and English] as in German, a phantom, always surprises by returning to be the other's ventriloquist. Metaphysics always returns, I mean in the sense of a *revenant* ("ghost"), and *Geist* is the most fatal figure of this *revenance* ("returning," "haunting"). . . . Is this not what Heidegger will never finally be able to avoid (*vermeiden*), the unavoidable itself—spirit's double, *Geist* as the *Geist* of *Geist*, spirit as the spirit of the spirit which always comes with its double?[11]

But again we may ask: is there not also a spirit, let us say *l'esprit*, which Derrida cannot avoid, which is the unavoidable? Is there not a specter lurking behind and underneath Derrida's corpus, his body (of writings), his writing body?

We need not consult the witch of Endor to conjure up this spirit, for it is sighted in a startling way later in the text, when Derrida considers the origins of language as promise, a passage hovering between commentary and autobiography.[12]

---

10   Not least of which is the spirit of Augustine, particularly as glimpsed in the publication of Heidegger's lecture course from the summer semester of 1921, published as "Augustinus und der Neuplatonismus," *Phänomenologie des religiösen Lebens*, Gesamtausgabe Bd. 60 (Frankfurt: Klostermann, 1995).
11   Jacques Derrida, *Of Spirit: Heidegger and the Question*, trans. Geoffrey Bennington and Rachel Bowlby (Chicago: University of Chicago Press, 1989), 40–41 (henceforth abbreviated as OS).
12   What Derrida observes regarding Heidegger's relation to Trakl could also be said of Derrida's relation to Heidegger: "Statements like those I have just cited and translated . . . are obviously statements of Heidegger. Not his own, productions of the subject Martin Heidegger, but statements to which he subscribes apparently without the slightest reluctance. On the one hand, he opposes them to everything which he is in the process of opposing, and which forms a sufficiently determining context. On the other hand, he supports them in a discourse of which the least one can say is that it does not bear even

> It remains to find out whether this *Versprechen* ("promise") is not the promise which, opening every speaking, makes possible the very question and therefore precedes it without belonging to it: the dissymmetry of an affirmation, of a yes before all opposition of yes and no . . . . Language always, before any question, and in the very question, comes down to the promise. This would also be a promise of spirit. (OS 94)

Following on the heels of this passage is an extended note (which, not without significance, he offers as a pledge)—an attempt to understand this uninvited visitation of (the) spirit. Here the spirit of promise, of the "pledge," returns, as that which must precede any question. Thus before any hermeneutics of suspicion (which is, at heart, a hermeneutics of radical questioning), one must place one's trust in the promises of language.

> Language is already there, in advance at the moment at which any question can arise about it. In this it exceeds the question. This advance is, before any contract, a sort of promise of originary allegiance to which we must have in some sense already acquiesced, already said yes, given a pledge, whatever may be the negativity or problematicity of the discourse which may follow. (OS 94)

This pledge, he goes on to say, is a "commitment" to what is given in the promise itself. Questioning—the heart and soul of suspicion—does not have the last word, precisely because it does not have the first word, because it is itself grounded in trusting a promise (OS 130). This pledge happens before the question, even before language, in time immemorial: "before the word, there is this sometimes wordless word which we name the 'yes.' A sort of pre-originary pledge which precedes any other engagement in language or action" (OS 130).

As Derrida notes, then, there is a trust which is more primordial than suspicion, precisely because, Augustine (though not Derrida) would suggest (and he is quite committed to this), goodness is more primordial than evil. The state of affairs composed of deception and false consciousness is

---

the trace of a reservation. It would thus be completely irrelevant to reduce these statements in ontological form to 'commentaries.' Nothing is more foreign to Heidegger than commentary in its ordinary sense" (OS 85).

an accidental way of being, not an essential one. The *pharmakon*[13] is not original nor constitutive, but rather a contingency resulting from the brokenness of a fallen world. But before this fall, and now in spite of this fall, there is a primordial "yes": a "wordless word," a living logos who was "in the beginning," who tabernacles with us in flesh, and whose spirit resides within us (John 1:1-18). It is this wordless Word, this Who, that we name "yes": "For the Son of God, Christ Jesus, who was preached among you by us—by me and Silvanus and Timothy—was not yes and no, but is yes in Him. For as many as may be the promises of God, in Him they are yes" (2 Cor 1:19-20). That is why *parole*, Derrida urges, "must first pray, address itself to us: put in us its trust, its confidence, depend on us, and even have already done it" (OS 134). And this pledge, he continues, this "already," is essential because it reaches back to a moment of already-having-trusted, an older event, part of a past which never returns, and never "was."

In this regard, the fundamental movement of deconstruction is a celebration of commitments, pointing out the pledges and promises that ground discourse—and the academy. Thus the university, any university, is founded on faith: before the work of scholarship happens every scholar says a little prayer, whispers her pledge, commits and entrusts herself to language.[14] The university, we might suggest, is quite religious, even if it has not been founded by priests; and it is this grounding commitment which deconstruction is sworn to celebrate.

Confessions of the Blind: Derrida's Memoirs

We could say this otherwise, as Derrida does in *Memoirs of the Blind*, his running commentary on the exhibition he hosted at the Louvre. Here his hypothesis is that drawing proceeds from a certain structural blindness, begins where it cannot see and hence, where one cannot "know."[15] As the

---

13   Derrida plays with the term *pharmakon* (from Plato's *Phaedrus*) in order to show that language—like the meaning of *pharmakon* itself—can be both "poison" and "cure," and is both always already. There is a violence which is equiprimordial with goodness. See Jacques Derrida, "Plato's Pharmacy," in *Dissemination*, trans. Barbara Johnson (Chicago: University of Chicago Press, 1981).
14   See Derrida, "The University without Condition," in *Without Alibi*, trans. Peggy Kamuf (Stanford: Stanford University Press, 2002), 202: "faith in the university."
15   As Augustine notes, "what I understand I also believe, but not everything I believe do I also understand. Again, everything I understand I know; but not everything I believe I know," *De magistro* 11.37 (trans. modified). Cp. also *Soliloquies* 1.3.8 and *De vera religione* 25.46.

Western tradition has come to understand, to know is to have an "idea" (*eidos*), hence to "see" (*oida*) (MB 12). Based on this occidental privileging of sight, one who is blind cannot know. But Derrida, along with the New Testament, wants to problematize this, suggesting that knowing or seeing is predicated upon a certain blindness, upon what one does not see; knowing, as such, would proceed from a commitment to that which is beyond seeing, the "unbeseen" as absolute invisibility, to which one is entrusted.[16] In this blind economy of faith, to see is in a sense not to see, such that Jesus' opponents are blind precisely because they claim to see (John 9:40-41). On the other hand, those who are blind nevertheless see, walking by faith, not by sight (MB 18). To see is not to believe, whereas blindness is a kind of faith such that one must rely on others for direction, often walking with outstretched arms, as in prayer [1, 4, 6].[17] "Look at Coypel's blind men," Derrida suggests as an example. "They all hold their hands out in front of them, their gesture oscillating in the void between prehending, apprehending, praying, and imploring" (MB 5).

The movement of modern thought and technology is precisely to probe beyond the limits of sight "with instruments—anoptic or blind—that sound out, that allow one to know (*savoir*) there where one no longer sees (*voir*)" (MB 32). To (technologically, prosthetically) expand one's vision is to eliminate faith, to undo the commitment which blindness necessitates. But because of the structural invisibility of the absolutely other than sight, the probes can never sound deep enough, can never plumb the depths of blindness, or faith. Derrida sees this structure outlined in the healing of Tobit's blindness by his son [12-14], behind whom stands an angel as the condition for the possibility of Tobit's healing, who also announces a commandment: "acknowledge God (*rendez grâce à Dieu*)" (MB 29). The story is a chain of acknowledgments: Tobit thanking his son, who points to the angel Raphael, who in turn indicates that Tobit's debt is to God. His healing is a gift for which he must render thanks, in writing (Tobit 12:20): "In order to give thanks (*rendre grâce*), the memory of the event must be inscribed. The debt must be repaid with words on parchment" (MB 29).

Thus the healing, and more precisely the story of the healing, begins by and from a debt: "What guides the graphic point, the quill, pencil, or

---

16   Derrida describes this unseen as the "unbeseen" and the "absolutely invisible" in order to emphasize that it is that which is radically heterogeneous to sight, which can never be seen. "To be the other of the visible, absolute invisibility must neither take place elsewhere nor constitute another visible" (MB 51). Structurally it is the invisible, the *tout autre* ("wholly other") of sight.

17   Numbers in square brackets refer to numbered images in MB.

scalpel is the respectful observance of a commandment, the acknowledgements before knowledge, the gratitude of the receiving before seeing, the blessing before knowledge" (MB 29–30). The angel, then, indicates the place of faith, of acknowledgment, of commitment, and of trust. In works such as Bianchi's [13], the angel stands boldly in the center. The debt is acknowledged. But in Rembrandt's rendering [15], for example, the angel is withdrawn, marginalized, and the human actors are now engaged in what appears to be simple surgery, such that the sketch was originally but mistakenly referred to by the title Surgeon Bandaging a Wounded Man—a recovery of sight by knowledge, by more seeing. Thus we may locate a movement of a certain secularity with the move to a modern era—an exclusion of the angel and a denial of one's debts. And this denial represents, in sum, a denial of commitment: an Enlightenment claim to neutrality and objectivity, freed from prejudice, which is just the kind of prejudice deconstruction is determined to expose.

Such a (modern) construal, on Derrida's accounting, fails to give credit to the role of faith (*credo*), to the commitments which make such seeing possible. Writing, drawing, speaking are all indebted, committed, owe credit to that which is originally other, such that

> at the origin of the *graphein* there is debt or gift rather than representational fidelity. More precisely, the fidelity of faith matters more than the representation, whose movement fidelity commands and thus precedes. And faith, in the moment proper to it, is blind. (MB 30)

To translate this into a rather classical idiom, Derrida is offering another way to think of the relationship between faith and reason; however, he would see any disjunction or opposition between the two as untenable, precisely because reason is grounded, structurally, in commitments, trust, a pledge. Before knowledge there is acknowledgment; before seeing there is blindness; before questioning there is a commitment; before knowing there is faith.[18]

While blindness is the condition for the possibility of faith, there is also a sense in which faith is blinded because it sees too much, blinded by bedazzlement, "the very bedazzlement that, for example, knocks Paul

---

18   On this question, I am arguing (as does Caputo [PT 328]) that Derrida would side with Augustine and the Franciscan tradition over against the Thomistic tradition from Thomas to Gilson. For a discussion, see my essay "The Art of Christian Atheism," 76–79, and 81n26.

to the ground on the road to Damascus" (MB 112) [67–68]. And if faith is linked to blindness, it is also associated with madness; or, as Derrida remarks, the "clairvoyance of the all-too-evident is Paul's madness" (MB 117). Paul is mad, Festus asserted (Acts 26:24), or as we sometimes say, he should be "committed," to Bellevue, perhaps. He is one who should be committed because of his mad commitments—because of his faith. Thus deconstruction, if it is a celebration of commitments, is also a celebration of a certain madness—the madness of faith.[19] Further, deconstruction is committed to pointing out the place of this madness within and before the academic community (the madness of reason), as that which is the very condition for its possibility—which often enough makes people (like Richard Rorty) a little mad.

Derrida the Augustinian: Contra Caputo

Having sketched the Augustinian structure of Derrida's account of the relationship between faith and philosophy, which Caputo has also suggested (PT 311, 328), permit me to conclude with just two questions for Caputo in this regard.

First, while suggesting that we find an Augustinian moment in Derrida's understanding of the commitments of philosophy, I wonder whether Caputo does not continue to read this through something of a Thomistic lens, which might undercut the radicality of Derrida's account. When commenting on this aspect of Derrida's thought, we will often find Caputo taking recourse to a Kantian maxim, from the second preface to the first critique: "I have found it necessary to deny knowledge, in order to make room for faith" (PT 312, 328). But is this an Augustinian maxim? For Kant, of course, faith marks the limits of reason, that boundary beyond which philosophy (and knowledge) cannot venture, the final frontier where philosophy cannot tread. This, it seems to me, preserves the scholastic, and specifically Thomistic understanding of the relationship between faith and philosophy: faith goes beyond philosophy, speaks where philosophy is lost for words. Faith, in a sense, picks up where philosophy left off.

But for Augustine, faith is not the boundary or limit of philosophy, but rather the fountain out of which philosophy springs. Faith is not "beyond" philosophy, but "before" philosophy—the condition of possibility of philosophy and knowledge. Rather than faith picking up where philosophy

---

19   This would also be seen in Derrida's meditation on Kierkegaard's Abraham in *The Gift of Death*, trans. David Wills (Chicago: University of Chicago Press, 1995).

left off, Augustine emphasizes that philosophy would be speechless without the first word of faith—what Derrida describes as "this sometimes wordless word which we name the 'yes'" (OS 130). While describing this Derridean structure as "more Augustinian and Franciscan than Thomistic and Dominican" (PT 328), it seems to me that Caputo continues to read this through a Thomistic, or at least Kantian, lens, which undoes the radicality of the Augustinian position.

Second, if Derrida is right about the relationship between faith and philosophy—and if this is an Augustinian rather than Thomistic structure—then it also seems that Caputo would need to revise a distinction which has run through his work from *Radical Hermeneutics* to the present. I refer to his distinction between what he describes as the (Kierkegaardian) "religious" and (Nietzschean) "tragic" responses to suffering.[20] Undecidability, he remarks, prevents the privileging of either. But it seems that, ironically, Caputo privileges the Nietzschean by describing the religious response as a "construal," a hermeneusis based on faith which "has looked down the dark well of suffering and found there a loving power which takes the side of suffering."[21] More recently he says,

> Faith is a matter of a radical hermeneutic, an art of construing shadows, in the midst of what is happening. Faith is neither magic nor an infused knowledge that lifts one above the flux or above the limits of mortality. Faith, on my view, is above all the hermeneia that Someone looks back at us from the abyss, that the spell of anonymity is broken by a Someone who stands with those who suffer, which is why the Exodus and the Crucifixion are central religious symbols. Faith, does not, however, extinguish the abyss but constitutes a certain reading of the abyss, a hermeneutics of the abyss.[22]

Faith is only a construal which is enveloped and haunted by undecidability; Abraham is haunted by Zarathustra's laughter. The construal of the religious response is simply a faith-ful way to cope with the cold reality of the flux by construing it as something warm.

---

20   John D. Caputo, *Radical Hermeneutics: Repetition, Deconstruction, and the Hermeneutic Project* (Bloomington: Indiana University Press, 1987), ch. 10.
21   Caputo, *Radical Hermeneutics*, 279.
22   John D. Caputo, *Against Ethics* (Bloomington: Indiana University Press, 1993), 245.

But does not this characterization already deny undecidability? Is not his characterization of the flux as "cold" already a privileging of Nietzsche? Is not the tragic also a construal, a faith-ful hermeneusis which is also exposed to undecidability? It seems that in this (rather Thomistic) distinction, Nietzsche speaks as a philosopher; Kierkegaard, on the other hand, goes beyond philosophy, making an affirmation of faith which one cannot admit "philosophically." However, though Abraham certainly hears the echo of Zarathustra's laughter, I wonder if Zarathustra ever lies awake at night wondering if Abraham is right. Is that not a more insistent understanding of undecidability? If Augustine and Derrida are right about the commitments of philosophy, then does not Nietzsche have his faith, too? Caputo seems to put the burden of proof upon the religious response, which must answer to Nietzsche, but does not Nietzsche also have some explaining to do? Both the religious and the tragic responses are construals: interpretations of factical life grounded in faith-ful commitments. Caputo continually insists on the frigidity of the world while seeing the necessity of a religious response; but this privileging of the tragic interpretation seems to convey that Nietzsche knows what the world is really like (which is a very realist notion). Only a hermeneutic which recognizes the creational nature of faith can truly recognize the all-the-way-downness of undecidability. That, it seems to me, reflects a more Augustinian understanding of the commitments of philosophy—an understanding which Derrida also affirms.

This is Derrida's promise: to announce the promise which precedes us, the commitment which is older than us, the "yes" to which we always already have acquiesced. That is deconstruction's prayer and in-vocation, echoing the prayer of reason in Augustine's *Soliloquies* (2.6.9); as such, it might seem appropriate to close with a prayer, but Derrida's (and Augustine's) request is precisely that we recognize that it is with prayer that we begin.[23]

---

23   *Sols.* 1.1–6.

11

Picturing Revelation

Idolatry and the Aesthetic in Marion and Rosenzweig

Introduction

The Incarnation is the locus of God's self-revelation—the primary site of God's self-giving. Thus the logic of incarnation is fundamentally an account of *what gives*, of how difference and otherness is revealed—whether that is the "horizontal" revelation of ourselves to one another or, paradigmatically, the revelation of divine transcendence in the region of immanence that is creation. Hence the logic of incarnation is an account of revelation, which also means that how we think about revelation impinges on whether we are operating with a logic of determination (per Derrida, Caputo, and others) or what I'm calling the "Nicene option" when it comes to understanding difference and its unveiling.

It is not surprising, then, that questions of revelation and incarnation lead us to matters of idolatry. In both Jewish and Christian traditions, the prohibition of images provides an important frame for critique of sites both conceptual and aesthetic. More specifically, the concern in postmodern religious thought is to avoid a reduction of the transcendent to an immanentized stasis, a finite measuring of the infinite. The poststructuralist concern with difference, I would argue, is really a concern about maintaining transcendence. At stake, then, is a kind of *ethics* of representation: can images and concepts do justice to the alterity of the Wholly Other? Or is the image, and the concept, linked to an economy of reference which necessarily entails a reduction—and hence *violation*—of alterity? Would all images and concepts be characterized by an inextricable violence? In the twentieth century, this proscription of images, and its attendant ethical questions, were intensified: while traditionally linked to both questions of conceptuality and art in the classical sense, the twentieth century saw a new advent of images first in photography and then cinema. Here the question of idolatrous images replays itself, now in terms of a critique of "the gaze" (*le regard*), which subjects the Other to the confining conditions of the perceiver. Elements of this theme in Levinas were then taken up and developed by Luce Irigaray to formulate a feminist critique of the gaze which we can understand as a kind of critique of idolatry, leaving us a new critical question: can there be a non-idolatrous gaze? The stakes of this question regarding the "propriety" of images and critique of idolatry were heightened in the latter part of the century in a post-Holocaust context. The question of how this horror could be imaged, already an ethical question, gave way to the more fundamental question of whether it ought to be imaged at all. In this respect, should not the proscription of images once again resound, prohibiting any possible representation of the unimaginable?

The Second Commandment, then, is a formative Western legacy. While it is true that the proscription of images generates a critical tradition in both Judaism and Christianity, it is also certainly true that the Christian tradition's understanding of and response to the Second Commandment is markedly different from the Jewish tradition. It is almost a truism that, if we were to consider the history of images in respective traditions, one could much more easily discern a tradition of "Christian art" than a legacy of "Jewish art." While the Christian tradition has, in a sense, affirmed the Hebraic prohibition of graven images, it is nevertheless the Christian tradition which also affirms that Christ is the "image (*eikon*) of the invisible God" (Col 1:15). Thus, though still attended by iconoclastic episodes, the Christian religious tradition also developed a rich legacy of iconography which operated on a more affirmative valuation of images—particularly as a means of revelation. In contrast, the Jewish tradition, including rabbinic sources and into modernity, has been more consistently iconoclastic and suspicious of the visual, fueled by a primal valuation of the *aural*. God is not *seen*, the tradition goes, God is *heard*. Thus this Jewish tradition of reflection tended toward a hermeneutics of speech rather than a semiotics of the image.

However, there is another side to the Jewish religious tradition in which a logic of vision is more fundamental to both religious thought and practice. As Daniel Boyarin, Elliot Wolfson, and others have demonstrated, there is both a biblical and rabbinical affirmation of visuality with respect to the divine. In fact, one might argue that rooted in a (theophanic) logic of revelation in the Hebrew scriptures, such an affirmation of the visual is a more consistently Hebraic insofar as it is rooted in an affirmation of the goodness of creation. For at stake in the question of idolatry and the proscription of images are three related concepts: *vision, materiality*, and *finitude*. Iconoclastic traditions—from Plato to Protestant fundamentalism—ground their suspicion of the visual and the aesthetic in a more fundamental negation of materiality and embodiment, and hence a certain desire to overcome finitude because finitude is construed as a lack. So conversely, a positive evaluation of images and the aesthetic as a medium of revelation must be grounded in a fundamental affirmation of embodiment and finitude. In this chapter, I argue that the Jewish thinker Franz Rosenzweig offers a more affirmative "creational" (even "incarnational") aesthetic than that offered by a contemporary Christian theorist, Jean-Luc Marion. In particular, I will argue that, despite his "iconic" account of revelation, Marion nevertheless retains a very iconoclastic (perhaps even Platonic) aversion to finitude and embodiment, in contrast to the very tradition of revelation he means to appropriate. In contrast, Rosenzweig's thought revolves around an account of creation and revelation which fundamentally affirms finitude and embodiment, hence providing the framework for an affirmative aesthetic—perhaps even a Jewish iconography. I will first briefly unpack Marion's critique of idolatry and his constructive account of the "icon," demonstrating how his notion of the icon nevertheless remains linked to an aversion to finitude. I will then turn to Rosenzweig's analysis. My goal is to sketch a "creational" (i.e., "Rosenzweigisch") critique of Marion and provide a constructive account of a religious aesthetic founded on an affirmation of embodiment and materiality.

The Image as Icon: Marion's Kenotic Aesthetic

The Essence of the Idol

In the wake of the madman's pronouncement regarding the death of God, Jean-Luc Marion finds some ambiguity in the obituary of the divine: Just who or what has died? Is this the death of God, or merely the death of "God," a god—the god of modernity? If so, is that much of a loss? Is this cause for mourning—or celebration? Should we not rejoice at the toppling of an idol? Might we not then celebrate the advent of atheism as the requiem for an idol? "If what one names 'God' passes into the emptiness of a death," Marion argues, "then that 'God,' from the very first, was not one. For a 'God' who can die harbors already, even when he[1] is not yet dying, such a weakness that from the outset he falls short of the idea that we cannot not form of a 'God.'"[2] Thus Marion takes Nietzsche as an ally in his critique of idolatry (ID 45–105/27–78) precisely because he announces the death of an idol and opens the space for a non-idolatrous revelation of the divine.

The idol whose wake both Nietzsche and Marion attend was a distinctly modern production, though with medieval filiation. But why an "idol?" What constitutes "idolatry" for Marion? I think we could suggest that Marion follows the Second Commandment in linking idolatry to a certain domestication of God's transcendence and alterity which is the result of "the subjection of the divine to the human conditions for experience of the divine" (ID 20/6).[3] Here we locate the core of Marion's concern: in the idol, God's appearance is constrained by *conditions* of finite human experience. In other words, the idol is constituted by the horizons of human experience rather than revealed from the divine. In this way, the idol confirms a Feuerbachian thesis: the god of its production is a reflection of humanity's image (ID 21/6).[4] Thus the idol functions as

---

1   Neither Marion nor Rosenzweig problematize their gendered references to God, despite that fact that both of their "theologies" should call this into question.
2   Jean-Luc Marion, *L'idole et la distance: Cinq études* (Paris: B Grasset, 1977) / *Idol and Distance: Five Studies*, trans. Thomas A. Carlson (New York: Fordham University Press, 2001), 15/1 (henceforth abbreviated as ID, followed by French and English pagination). In the last clause Marion alludes to a certain Anselmian notion of God which he later developed in more detail in "Is the Ontological Argument Ontological? The Argument According to Anselm and Its Metaphysical Interpretation According to Kant," *Journal of the History of Philosophy* 2 (1992): 201–18.
3   Here Marion repeats the Levinasian critique of horizonality and constitution in Husserl's phenomenology, which would be developed much more explicitly in Marion's later thought. For a discussion and critique, see my "Respect and Donation: A Critique of Marion's Critique of Husserl," *American Catholic Philosophical Quarterly* 71 (1997): 523–38, and *Speech and Theology*, ch. 5.
4   Here Marion suggests the political idolatries which can also result: "This is indeed why politics always gives rise to idols, even after paganism; 'Big Brother,' the 'Great Helmsman,'

an "invisible mirror" which returns the gaze of the perceiver, but at the same time masks its mirror function. As Marion later suggests, "[t]he idol thus acts as a mirror, not as a portrait: a mirror that reflects the gaze's image, or more exactly, the image of its aim and of the scope of that aim. The idol, as a function of the gaze, reflects the gaze's scope. But the idol does not at once manifest its role and status as a mirror."[5] At stake here is a semiotics—the way in which the idols "signals" or functions as a sign (GWB 16-17/8-9), or better, *fails* to function as a sign, precisely because the idol does not refer beyond itself. Rather than being a "sign" (*signum*), the idol functions as an end in itself which absorbs the gaze.[6] As such, this semiotic failure of the idol results from the fact that it does not preserve any distance or difference between the sign and the referent. There is, then, an element of substitution which characterizes the idol.

"What is peculiar to the idol," Marion concludes, "has to do with this: the divine is fixed in it *on the basis of* the experience of the divine that is had by man" (ID 20/5, emphasis added). It is not only the *fixation* of the divine (this will return in Rosenzweig) but the conditions of this fixation—that the fixation *is* conditioned. In the terms of his later work, the appearance or revelation of the divine is "measured": "in the idol, the divine actually comes into the visibility for which human gazes watch; but this advent is measured by what the scope of particular human eyes can support, by what each aim can require of visibility in order to admit itself fulfilled" (GWB 23/13-14). The idol is the product of the gaze precisely because the gaze is satisfied with this measured and conditioned representation of God. In this sense, even the deity which emerges out of Heidegger's critique of onto-theo-logy remains yet another idol because it remains

---

the *Führer*, the 'Man we love best' must be divinized: made into gods, they conjure the divine or, more vulgarly, destiny. . . . Idolatrous temptation for Israel always depended on political necessities. Conversely, it is to politics first that our time owes the fact that we are not lacking for new idols" (ID 21/6; cp. 32/17, 39/23). This linking of politics and idolatry in Marion (which I hope to pursue elsewhere) also bears important analogies to Rosenzweig's critique. See Franz Rosenzweig, *The Star of Redemption*, trans. William W. Hallo (Notre Dame: University of Notre Dame Press, 1985 [1970]), 402ff. (henceforth abbreviated as SR).

5   Jean-Luc Marion, *Dieu san l'être* (Paris: PUF, 1991), 21 / *God without Being*, trans. Thomas A. Carlson (Chicago: University of Chicago Press, 1991), 12 (henceforth abbreviated as GWB followed by French and English pagination).

6   I have analyzed this phenomenology of the idol in terms of the Augustinian distinction between "use" (*uti*) and "enjoyment" (*frui*) in my "Between Predication and Silence: Augustine on How (Not) to Speak of God," *Heythrop Journal* 41 (2000): 66–86.

subservient to *conditions*: "God is only 'God' [in Heidegger's account]; if he no longer intervenes except as a supreme being [as in onto-theo-logy], this is in order to appear all the more as an inferior being; 'God,' under this second condition, is subjected entirely to an idolatrous precondition that deduces him ... on the basis of (*à partir de*) Being" (ID 259/209; cp. GWB 58-75/37-49).[7] But this conditioned fixation of God is an undoing of God's *un*conditioned transcendence—a violation of God's absolute alterity. Rather than being the site of revelation, the idol is a project, a construction, even an invention.

For Marion, the idol is not illusory or a mere simulacrum; quite the contrary, the idol is a spectacle which gives itself to the worshiper—which is precisely what makes it a domestication of God's irreducible transcendence (ID 23/8). "The idol does not deceive," he remarks; "it apprehends the divinity," "identifies" it, granting to us a figure of the divine which is "familiar, tamed" (ID 21/6). By collapsing any "distance" between finite and infinite (precisely by shutting down the semiotic operation of reference), "[t]he idol therefore *delivers* us the divine, wherefore it neither deceives nor disappoints. It delivers the divine to us to the point of enslaving it to us" (21/6). Delivered into our hands by the idol, God's transcendence is captured and thereby subdued—and ultimately denied. Rather than being that which eludes or exceeds us, the idol makes God "available,"[8] ready-to-hand to be manipulated (often for political ends). Marion thus asks: "by establishing such an availability of the divine within the fixed, if not frozen, face of the god, does one not deceitfully but racially eliminate the lofty irruption and the undeniable alterity that properly attest the divine" (22/7)?

The Artistic Idol

This shutting-down of "distance" or collapsing of alterity is, then, what marks the artistic idol. Constituted by the same gaze that "allows the divine to occur only in man's measure, man can consign the idolatrous experience to art" (GWB 25/15). The artistic idol (i.e., the work of art which functions as an idol) is characterized by a semiotic failure of ref-

---

7   Marion's critique of Heidegger here parallels Levinas' critique of Heidegger's "Letter on Humanism" in Levinas, "God and Philosophy," trans. Alphonso Lingis in Emmanuel Levinas, *Of God Who Comes to Mind* (Stanford: Stanford University Press, 1998), 55-78.
8   When Marion describes God as being made "available" I think we should hear echoes of Heidegger's analysis of *Zuhandenheit* in *Sein und Zeit*, §16.

erence: it becomes an end-in-itself which absorbs the gaze. However, this critique of the idol, even the artistic idol, does not lead Marion to a wholesale rejection of images, unlike more aniconic interpretations of the Second Commandment, whether in Jewish or Christian traditions. Instead, Marion provides an alternative phenomenology of the image which functions as *icon* and thus provides an alternative iconic or "kenotic" aesthetic which, it would seem, affirms the role and value of the image. In order to make sense of this alternative aesthetic theory and its valuation of images, we need to first unpack Marion's careful phenomenological distinction between the idol and the icon.

In offering what he describes as a "comparative phenomenology of the idol and the icon" (GWB 17/9), Marion observes that the difference between them is a "manner of being" (15/7); I think it is helpful to think of this as a semiotic distinction between their "sign" functions. The idol, it will be recalled, failed to function as a sign precisely because it failed to refer beyond itself; in contrast, the icon does function as a *signum*: first, because it is characterized by an operation of "transpiercing" by which the gaze does not rest upon the visible, but crosses *through* it, as though transparent (GWB 20/11). Rather than functioning as a mirror, absorbing the gaze into itself and returning it to itself (as in the idol), the icon functions as a *prism* (ID 23/8) that deflects or redirects the gaze beyond itself to a Referent which exceeds the sign. Thus the icon makes visible the invisible (cp. Col 1:15); it "attempts to render visible the invisible as such, hence to allow that the visible not cease to refer to an other than itself, without, however, that other ever being reproduced in the visible" (GWB 29/18). Second, this rupturing of the visible that enables the operation of "transpiercing" also opens a space for the reversal of intentionality; in other words, the icon, rather than being the product of the perceiver's gaze, is instead the site where the worshiper/perceiver finds herself subject *to* the gaze of an Other. Echoing Levinas, Marion suggests that the icon is the site where (Husserlian) intentionality is reversed and what appears is not a construction but a *revelation*: "the gaze no longer belongs here to the man who aims as far as the first visible, less yet to an artist; such a gaze here belongs to the icon itself. . . . If man, by his gaze, renders the idol possible, in reverent contemplation of the icon, on the contrary, the gaze of the invisible, in person, aims at man. The icon regards us" (GWB 31/19). In the icon, I am subject *to* the gaze of a "face" which envisages me (GWB

32/20). Finally, the structure of the icon—characterized by the operation of transpiercing and the reversal of the gaze—is also the site for an *un*conditioned revelation.[9] "The icon recognizes no other measure than its own and infinite excessiveness" (GWB 33/21), giving itself *from itself* (*à partir de lui*). Marion describes this as a "kenotic" paradigm for understanding revelation (ID 262–64/213–15): "The kenosis sets no condition for revealing itself, because in that revelation it gives itself and reveals nothing other than this unconditional gift" (264/215). This revelation, far from conceding to or being measured by the perceiver, instead overwhelms and saturates the horizons of the perceiver/receiver. Rather than conceding to "the idolatrous primacy of a human point of view" (GWB 120/81), the revelation of the icon proceeds purely from the divine, without condition, and in fact, outside of the chain of signifiers—operating *hors-texte*, "outside of the text."[10]

Conditions of Creaturehood: A Critique of Marion

But why must this be the case? Why must revelation be *un*conditioned? And why would a revelation which concedes to the conditions of human perception be idolatrous? Is there not an important difference between domestication and condescension? I would argue that Marion requires an "unconditioned" revelation because of a more fundamental devaluing of finitude per se. To put this in terms that we have employed thus far, for Marion, the logic of prohibition operating behind the Second Commandment is understood to stem from finitude itself. Or, in language that will anticipate our discussion of Rosenzweig below, Marion posits a notion of revelation which must structurally counter "creation" insofar as it is the finitude and materiality of "creation" which precludes God's appearance. This is due to a conflation of finitude with "sinfulness": "the condition that is as much finite as it is 'sinful' situates us at an infinite distance from *agapē*" (GWB 158/109). There is, according to Marion, an incommensurable "gap" between the Creator and creature which pre-

---

9   In the space of this chapter, I will not be able to critically engage Marion's (non)hermeneutic which emerges from this. Permit me to just note that I have serious concerns about Marion's claim to locate a "revelation" which is unmediated (*hors-texte*), as he suggests in GWB, ch. 5. For my critique of such a hermeneutics of immediacy, see my *The Fall of Interpretation: Philosophical Foundations for a Creational Hermeneutic*, 2nd ed. (Grand Rapids: Baker Academic, 2012), chs. 1 and 2.

10 Here Marion is obliquely contesting Derrida's contention that *il n'y a pas de hors-texte*, "there is nothing outside of the text" (*Of Grammatology*, trans. Gayatri Chakravorty Spivak [Baltimore: Johns Hopkins University Press, 1976], 158).

cludes "contact"—a gap that "is inscribed in the *constitutive* distance of the creator" who is "*inconceivable* to the creature" (GWB 158/109, emphasis added).[11] God's revelation must be a "crossing of being" precisely because "[w]e fall—in the capacity of beings—under the government of Being. We do not accede—in the capacity of 'sinners'—to *agapē*" (GWB 157/108). Note again this conflation of creatureliness with sinfulness, and in turn, with finitude in what he describes as "the (sinful) 'economy' of the creature": "Of this crossing [of Being in revelation] we would know nothing, in whatever sense this nothing should be expressed, since *finitude*, as well as the status of *creature* and the ignorance of *agapē* implied by the condition of *sinner* forbid us access to it" (GWB 158/109, emphasis added). In this account, revelation—the very condition of possibility for establishing any "relation" between Creator and creature—must run counter to the structures of creation itself, viz., finitude, materiality, and embodiment.

So despite Marion's rubric of "kenosis" and even "incarnation" (ID 262/213), in the end this revelation entails an overwhelming of the conditions which attend embodiment. And it is precisely here that I would launch a critique of Marion's "kenotic" aesthetic—a critique which is nourished by Rosenzweig's more "creational" model. Recall my thesis above: that a positive or affirmative account of vision (and hence images) must be grounded in a fundamental affirmation of the *conditions* of vision, viz., finitude, materiality, and embodiment. Conversely, aniconic and iconoclastic thought which disparages images usually does so on the basis of a deeper negation of finitude as such. If this holds, then Marion presents a strange case, for on the one hand, he wants to offer the possibility for an affirmation of images as "icons"; but on the other hand, we have seen that he lays a groundwork which negates finitude as such. Does this disprove my thesis? I would argue that it does not, and that Marion demonstrates its consistency by, in the end, not really valuing images as such. In other words, I think that Marion's supposedly "iconic" rescuing of images still, in the end, negates a positive role for images and harbors a logic of prohibition which can affirm only those images which erase themselves—that is, precisely those images that cease to be images.[12]

---

11 Below I will suggest that, on Rosenzweig's register, this would make Marion's God quite "pagan"—a "concealed God." For Marion, God is, as Creator, always already *deus absconditus*.
12 To put this otherwise, Marion's notion of incarnation is "docetic," per my philosophical deployment of this category in ch. 9 above (vis-à-vis Husserl).

Conceptually, we see this in the link between the operation of "transpiercing" and the "transparency" that characterizes the icon. Apart from the intervention of the idol which halts the gaze, "the gaze transparently transpierced the visible. To be exact, the gaze did not see the visible" (GWB 20/11). The icon manifests the invisible precisely because, in the end, it makes itself invisible: it becomes transparent. The gaze sees (and is seen) *through*. . . . The image, then, can only be affirmed insofar as it is self-effacing: "The self-affirmation of the image, like all others, yields only in front of an abandonment: it is precisely because the icon is not given for itself, but rather *undoes* its own prestige, that is perhaps demands veneration—veneration that it does not seize but rather lets pass through it to the invisible prototype."[13] Marion describes this as the *kenosis* or self-impoverishment of the image (CV 113). What this entails is an undoing of the very material conditions of the work of art—an undoing of the art's embodiment.[14] This is confirmed in the explicit "kenotic aesthetic" (CV 111) which Marion develops out of his phenomenology of the icon in *La croisée du visible*. In a very telling example (which I would like to cite at length), Marion contrasts the idolatries of "great art" with the kenotic icons of mass-marketed religious kitsch:

> If such poverty characterizes art insofar as it is Christian, one can draw a surprising but probable conclusion: the often indisputable meanness (*la laideur*) of art said to be "sulpician" (*sulpicien*)[15] ought not to be discredited. For as Andre Frossard remarked one day, in front of a *Virgin* by Raphaël, "A Raphaël!," but in front of a sulpician *Virgin*, one recognizes the

---

13   Jean-Luc Marion, *La croisée du visible* (Paris: PUF, 1996), 111 (henceforth abbreviated in the text as CV).
14   It is here, I think, that one could activate a feminist critique of Marion's account.
15   This descriptive term (*sulpicien*) is derived from a unique Parisian context: in the nineteenth century, a number of shops selling mass-produced religious artifacts (cards, statues, etc.) developed in the area surrounding Saint-Sulpice church in Paris. We might understand these "works of art" as akin to contemporary religious "merchandise" which is mass-produced for the devotion of the faithful, but considered by others, from an artistic perspective, to be representative of poor taste (or what we might describe as "kitsch"). Marion is here obliquely affirming the function of such art as an example of images which negate themselves and refer the observer to the prototype. Because we have no equivalent term in English (except, perhaps, "Barclay Street art," referring to a comparable market in Manhattan in the nineteenth century), I have opted to simply anglicize the term. For further discussion, see Colleen McDannell, *Material Christianity* (New Haven: Yale University Press, 1995), 167–73.

> Virgin herself. Thus sulpician art practices, more than "great art," the impoverishment of the image and the transfer of veneration from the image to the original. Its unintentional *arte povera* assures that, less than ever, it seizes veneration for the sake of the image, thus protecting it against every tyranny of the image. This paradox of sulpician art is obviously not sufficient to compensate for the obvious bankruptcy of religious art in the twentieth century; it explains why this is the case even less, seeing especially that the contribution of notable artists has done nothing to change this defeated situation. In their[16] chapels, it is simply a matter of recognizing that "That is by Matisse!," "That is by Cocteau!,"—thus, it is a place to *see*; but it is not a place of prayer—that is, of *being seen*; or better, it is necessary to forget (*oublier*)[17] that these are "by Matisse" or "by Cocteau"—to forget the visible. These chapels celebrate their painters, not the addressee [the object of worship]—they play the role of simple idols, not of icons. (CV 113–14)

The work of art which is to function as an iconic means of revelation, then, is precisely the work which makes itself invisible—in other words, when it ceases to be a work of art. So despite the rubric of iconography, it would seem that, in the end, Marion sticks close to a very aniconic understanding of the Second Commandment which ties the logic of prohibition to the very conditions of finitude—which is to say, to the very conditions of creatureliness itself.

The Image as *Pharmakon*: Rosenzweig's Creational Aesthetic

Jewish Iconoclasm: Maimonides to Levinas

How one understands the Second Commandment depends upon an interpretation of just *what* is prohibited and, more importantly, *why*. What is the logic of prohibition that is operative here? As I have suggested above, Marion ties this prohibition to finitude itself; in this respect, he follows a

---

16   The Chapelle Matisse, or Chapelle du Rosaire du Dominicaines du Vence, was designed and decorated by Henri Matisse between 1947 and 1951; Jean Cocteau completed the decoration of Chapelle Saint-Pierre (in Villefranche-sur-Mer) in 1957.
17   The word also carries the connotation of "overlooking"; thus such a forgetting might be understood as an "oversight."

long line of Jewish thinkers who have understood the prohibition in a similar way—and which, in many respects, has been taken to be something like the official "party line."[18] Indeed, Lyotard argued that this proscription of images stems from a deeper suspicion: "The Hebraic law forbidding images is not some artistic or ritualistic idiosyncrasy, but a declaration of suspicion concerning the 'visible.'"[19] This can be confirmed in even a cursory analysis of the works of several major Jewish thinkers. While we might go back to Philo,[20] consider first the apophatic[21] logic which informs Maimonides rigid construal of the Second Commandment. As Batnitzky aptly summarizes, "[f]or Maimonides, the problem of idolatry and representation points to two central human limitations. The first is the human inability to represent God's essence, the second, the inability of language to represent anything true about God."[22] In a manner similar to Marion, Maimonides understands the problem of images (and the impossibility of God's "representation" in them) to stem from the very structure of finitude, construed negatively as "limitations." Thus the constraints of materiality and embodiment themselves—constitutive of creatures—are precisely what preclude God's revelation *in* images. Images can only be idols precisely because their materiality precludes the revelation of God's transcendence within them.[23] The incommensurability between finite

---

18 ced This understanding then generates the mistaken historical notion that Judaism is "aural" while the Greeks are "visual," which is precisely what Boyarin and Wolfson are out to deconstruct (see, e.g., Wolfson, *Through a Speculum That Shines: Vision and Imagination in Medieval Jewish Mysticism* [Princeton: Princeton University Press, 2005], 13ff.). I think Derrida's work also calls into question this false dichotomy between the visual and the aural.

19 Jean-François Lyotard, "Letter to Eberhard Gruber," in Lyotard and Eberhard Gruber, *The Hyphen: Between Judaism and Christianity*, trans. Pascale-Anne Brault and Michael Naas (Amherst, N.Y.: Humanity Books, 1999), 59.

20 Wolfson, however, enlists Philo as the impetus for finding a Jewish tradition which values the visual (*Through a Speculum That Shines*, 50–51).

21 I would argue that those who tie the logic of prohibition to finitude itself must ultimately end up with a basically apophatic position, since in the end, it must be conceded that even *speech* is sensible and finite and thus, based on their logic, incommensurate with the infinity of God. Rosenzweig criticizes apophatics as the product of a pagan conception of the "concealed God" (SR 23). For my critique of apophaticism, see *Speech and Theology: Language and the Logic of Incarnation* (London: Routledge, 2002), chs. 1 and 5.

22 Leora Batnitzky, *Idolatry and Representation: The Philosophy of Franz Rosenzweig Reconsidered* (Princeton: Princeton University Press, 2000), 19.

23 And note that Maimonides is consistent here insofar as he includes *language* itself in this prohibition. As Batnitzky suggests, Maimonides always finds words and images "shameful" (*Idolatry and Representation*, 21).

and infinite which would consign every image (and word) to idolatry is inscribed into the very structure of creation (cp. GWB 158/109).[24]

The same logic is replayed in modern Jewish thought. Hermann Cohen argues that one of the conditions for monotheism is a critique of images: "prophetic monotheism is necessarily opposed to, necessarily contradicts *art*."[25] This is because art is a kind of Babel—a construction of human hands with a penchant for "deification."[26] And this then informs his critique of Christianity: "in every plastic image of God [there is] a contradiction of monotheism."[27] Theophanic revelations and Genesis 1:26-27 notwithstanding,[28] Cohen asserts that "[o]f God . . . there can be no likeness," therefore, "the assault on art becomes direct and explicit."[29] Once again, this logic of prohibition is rooted in an understanding of the rift between Creator and creature which constitutes finitude itself. In a manner completely subject to Heidegger's critique of onto-theo-logy, Cohen's "religion of reason" is predicated on the assertion that God's "uniqueness" can never be represented or positively known because of an "incomparability" between God and any concept or image of God[30]—which would seem to preclude the very possibility of revelation to finite perceivers.[31]

Finally, the same logic of prohibition seems to be operative in Levinas' critique of art; the work of art, as image, constitutes both an "evasion" and a "substitution" rather than a medium of revelation. Art, Levinas suggests, "is the very event of obscuring, a descent of the night, an invasion of shadow. To put it in theological terms, which will enable us to delimit however roughly our ideas by comparison with contemporary notions:

---

24 Would this not make creation the first idol?
25 Hermann Cohen, *Religion of Reason: Out of the Sources of Judaism*, trans. Simon Kaplan (Atlanta: Scholars Press, 1995), 53.
26 Cohen, *Religion of Reason*, 54.
27 Cohen, *Religion of Reason*, 54.
28 Committed to his rationalist monotheism, Cohen's explicit engagement with this text concludes that "[t]here can be no image of God. Therefore man cannot be an image of God" (*Religion of Reason*, 86). I would argue that the premise of this argument is not actually found in the Hebrew Scriptures but rather results from an *over*reading of certain passages such as Exod 20:3-4 and Isa 40:18 (which Cohen references).
29 Cohen, *Religion of Reason*, 54.
30 Cohen, *Religion of Reason*, 44.
31 Though I cannot address this in detail here, my concern is that Cohen's account of God's uniqueness and "incomparability," when coupled with his rationalism, actually tends towards a negation of God's transcendence. In other words, the radical assertion of equivocity actually slides toward univocity. This then gives birth to an immanentized conception of revelation as "the creation of reason" (*Religion of Reason*, 72).

art does not belong to the order of revelation. Nor does it belong to that of creation, which moves in just the opposite direction."[32] This is because the order of the image is idolatrous insofar as its opacity stops the "gaze": "The insurmountable caricature in the most perfect image manifests itself in its stupidity as an idol. The image *qua* idol leads us to the ontological significance of its unreality."[33] As in Marion, the image is an idol precisely because of its semiotic failure: it does not point beyond itself. Though "[t]he intention of one who contemplates an image is said to go directly through the image, as through a window [the classical Eastern description of an icon]," in fact the image does not function in this manner, which is why the image is not a *signum*. "In what does an image differ from a symbol, sign, or a word? By the very way it refers to its object: resemblance. But that supposes that thought stops on the image itself; it consequently supposes a certain opacity of the image. A sign [in contrast] is *pure transparency*, nowise counting for itself."[34] Thus the painting, he argues, does not lead us "beyond" itself, but only "to the hither side of it. It is a symbol in reverse."[35] For Levinas, because there is a direct and necessary link between images and idolatry,[36] he concludes with Cohen that "[t]he proscription of images is truly the supreme command of monotheism."[37] And this construal of the Second Commandment is understood to mean a critique of images in general, precisely because it is rooted in a deeper critique of the "gaze" and visuality as necessary violations of alterity (whether of God or the other "person").

But I would argue that linking the logic of prohibition to the very conditions of visuality, embodiment, and finitude contradicts the Hebraic logic of "creation"—or more specifically, the affirmation of the *goodness* of creation (Gen 1:31). Thus we can locate an alternative tradition of Jewish thought (ranging from theophanic traditions in the Hebrew scriptures, medieval mystical sources, midrash, and other rabbinic sources) which

32 Emmanuel Levinas, "Reality and Its Shadow," trans. Alphonso Lingis in *The Continental Aesthetics Reader*, ed. Clive Cazeaux (London: Routledge, 2000), 118.
33 Levinas, "Reality and Its Shadow," 123.
34 Levinas, "Reality and Its Shadow," 121, emphasis added, recalling Marion's criteria of transparency above.
35 Levinas, "Reality and Its Shadow," 122.
36 "To say that an image is an idol is to affirm that *every* image is in the last analysis plastic, and that every artwork is in the end a statue—a stoppage in time [a fixation]" (Levinas, "Reality and Its Shadow," 123). He goes on to argue that the introduction of "time" into images in cinema "does not shatter the fixity of images" (124).
37 Levinas, "Reality and Its Shadow," 126.

does not harbor this suspicion of the visible, but rather privileges the visible as the site/sight of revelation.[38] This tradition, running counter to the aniconic thesis of Maimonides, Cohen, and Levinas, is rooted in a fundamental affirmation of finitude, materiality, and embodiment—and it is precisely this creational affirmation that animates the project of Franz Rosenzweig, to which I now turn.[39]

Creation as Revelation in Rosenzweig

We must keep in mind that what is at stake here is an account of revelation, and the framework which determines such. For instance, in Marion and Levinas, revelation must run counter to the structures of created finitude, since it is precisely finitude which precludes the possibility of God's revelation. But behind this logic is what Rosenzweig would describe as a very pagan—and at the same time modern—conception of both God and revelation which makes God structurally "concealed" (SR 112) and resists any collusion between God and the world. From this pagan perspective, any such relation would "ensnare God once more in the passion of love," constituting a "constriction of God" (SR 39). The pagan logic of the concealed God bristles at such collusion, because "of course to this end it would be necessary for the infinite God to come more finitely close to man, more face-to-face with him, more proper-name to proper-name, than any sense of sensible men, any wisdom of wise men could ever admit" (SR 39). And it is just such a corporeal donation which this pagan logic of incomparability precludes: "He does not give of himself, does not love, does not have to love. For he keeps his *physis* to himself, and therefore remains what he is: the metaphysical" (SR 40). From Rosenzweig's perspective, it is this pagan logic which crept into modern religious thought, particularly in the guise of "historical theology" in the wake of Schleiermacher and Ritschl, resulting in an opposition between "creation" and "revelation," which translated into an opposition between "theology" and "philosophy." "The

---

38   Wolfson orients his thesis around Philo's claim that "Israel" is defined as the "one who sees God" (*Through a Speculum That Shines*, 50).
39   A note about my project here: I am not attempting to provide a mere exposition of what Rosenzweig describes as an "aesthetic theory" in the three books of part 2. Mine is a more constructive project, attempting to tease out the elements of a creational aesthetic from the logic of Rosenzweig's argument. Thus my project is more akin to what Zachary Braiterman describes as Rosenzweig's "aestheticism" in "Der Ästhet Franz Rosenzweig: Beautiful Form and Religious Thought," *The Journal of Jewish Thought and Philosophy* 10 (2000): 145–69.

school of Ritschl," Rosenzweig observes, "asserted a separation between theology and philosophy which involved the neglect of 'creation' and an over-emphasis on 'revelation'" (SR 103).[40] And this is because it has (perhaps unwittingly) adopted a logic of concealment which must posit an opposition between revelation and creation.

Thus Rosenzweig understands his project to be precisely a recovery of creation, challenging the logic of concealment with what we might call his logic of manifestation, beginning not from a "concealed God" but rather "the manifest God" (SR 116). In his words, "creation has once more to be placed next to the experience of revelation in the full gravity of its substantiality"; more specifically, "revelation itself . . . must once more be built into the concept of creation" (SR 103). Against the discontinuity posited by the pagan logic of concealment, Rosenzweig emphasizes a relation of continuity between creation and revelation because "as 'manifest' God he cannot do otherwise than create" (SR 116). Notice, then, that this logic of manifestation stems from fundamentally different conceptions of God (as "manifest" and Creator), of creation, and more specifically, of the *relation between* Creator and creature. For Rosenzweig, creation—and creatureliness—is not the site of concealment, not God's first hiding place; rather, it is the first revelation. To put it otherwise, creation does not *institute* an incommensurable "gap" between Creator and creature as suggested by Marion (GWB 158/109); on the contrary, creation is the first movement of manifestation and hence, relation. "God's creating," he argues, "is the beginning of his self-expression"—the site where "God's configuration . . . emerges into visibility" (SR 113).

Now, the relation between creation and revelation is, if not quite reciprocal, at least mutual: on the one hand, "revelation is providentially 'foreseen' in creation" (SR 108); on the other hand, creation is only seen *as* creation in light of revelation (SR 182–83).[41] But what difference does it make to see the world as creation? First, for Rosenzweig, the emphasis here is

---

40   It is in this context that Rosenzweig's "New Thinking" has much to say to contemporary discussions regarding the relationship between philosophy, theology, and religion, particularly as unpacked in Jean-Luc Marion, "Metaphysics and Phenomenology: A Relief for Theology," *Critical Inquiry* 20 (1994): 572–91. Rosenzweig conceives of revelation as a "bridge" between philosophy and theology which can generate both "new" philosophers and "new" theologians, "situated between theology and philosophy" (SR 106).
41   This is why philosophy (by which Rosenzweig generally means "idealism") which rejects revelation must find a substitute for creation in the notions of "emanation" or "generation" (SR 134ff.).

on *being* created or *being* a creature, not *having been* created (SR 120); it is not a question of origin but rather current status. Second, the notion of creation entails a fundamental *affirmation* of the world. The "first word" of creation, the "arch-yea," is an affirmation, a "positive evaluation" which says "Yes!" to the world, which is to say, "good!" (SR 127). Thus central to his "creational" account is the primordial *goodness* of creation as expressed in God's "utterly affirming valuation" (SR 153): "Creation consists of this divine affirmation of creaturely existence. . . . Existence is affirmed by God's pronouncing his own work 'good': he has made it and it is good" (SR 151). By emphasizing the status of the world as created, Rosenzweig means to communicate this affirmation of its goodness—a fundamental valuation of those conditions which constitute creaturehood: finitude, materiality, and embodiment.

So, in contrast to the "concealed God" of paganism and modernity (especially in the Kantian guise which Cohen inherited), revelation gives us "a manifest God." Even if the mythic God of paganism is revealed, it is an undoing of concealment; in other words, in paganism there is a *dis*continuity between "creation" and revelation. In contrast, in light of revelation, God as creator is the God that must be made manifest, whose nature impels manifestation: "in this sense we had to designate creation as already a becoming-manifest on the part of God" (159). Creation is the first moment of God's revelation.

It is with this link between creation and visibility that Rosenzweig makes a unique contribution that contrasts with the aniconic tradition of Maimonides, Cohen, and Levinas;[42] for Rosenzweig, God is "he who is visible in creation," and it is in creation that God "is in the process of becoming visible" (SR 114; cp. 113). If creation is the first moment of God's "visibility," then this must entail quite a different understanding of images, precisely because it is grounded in a different valuation of *vision* which undoes common assumptions about the primacy of the aural in Jewish thought.[43] In fact, Rosenzweig portrays vision as more primordial than speech, because "[t]hat which can be perceived is superior to speech

---

42 I would argue that Rosenzweig would see all of these figures adopting the pagan logic of concealment.
43 Based on the evidence below, I think that Wolfson's reading of Rosenzweig is mistaken (see *Through a Speculum That Shines*, 15–16). On the other hand, Batnitzky rightly discerns the centrality of this in Rosenzweig's work: "Vision, and not sound, is the culmination of knowledge of the divine, for Rosenzweig" (*Idolatry and Representation*, 86).

218   The Nicene Option

and exalted above it. Light does not discourse, it shines" (SR 295).[44] This is a remarkable inversion of the tradition of thought Rosenzweig inherited from Cohen, but also a bold affirmation that stems from his commitments regarding creation. In explaining why that which is "seen" ("Light" that shines) is superior, Rosenzweig offers a rich concept of revelation and the relationship between transcendence and immanence: "Light does not sell itself, it does not give itself away, like speech, when it expresses itself. Rather it is visible by remaining wholly in itself" (SR 295). In this sense, the transcendent gives itself in immanence, in a mode we might describe as a "real presence," and yet also retains its transcendence; the transcendent *inheres* in the immanent without being reduced to immanence. Thus the visible manifestation of God is precisely that mode which protects God's alterity. In fact, it is just this operation which allows creation to function as a *sign* since, to be a sign, it must at once participate in the reality it signifies, but also maintain a distance which preserves the otherness or excessiveness of that reality.[45] Thus that which is "perceived" ("Light") "gives itself" without giving itself *away*—it manifests itself without giving itself up.[46]

Now, it is precisely this semiotics of vision which also helps to explain Rosenzweig's understanding of the Second Commandment. First, as Batnitzky observes, Rosenzweig would assert that, despite this participation of the sign in the thing signified, there is also a certain poststructuralist caution in his theory because "a sign's possibilities of signification are infinite."[47] There is a *risk* that attends signs, opened by the distance or space which they traverse: they may point elsewhere, or fail to point at all. We could reify the sign so that it no longer functions as a sign, but instead absorbs the intention and becomes merely a "thing."[48] And

---

44   This is offered in a context where Rosenzweig discusses the way in which *liturgy* is paradigmatic for his account, precisely because liturgy traffics primarily in gestures, not speech (SR 294–95).
45   For a helpful discussion of Rosenzweig's semiotics, in comparison to Tillich, see Batnitzky, *Idolatry and Representation*, 147–49.
46   I have suggested that a similar structure can be found in the structure of "respect" which Derrida outlines in his seminal essay "Violence and Metaphysics: An Essay on the Thought of Emmanuel Levinas," in *Writing and Difference*, trans. Alan Bass (Chicago: University of Chicago Press, 1978), 79–153. For my discussion, see *Speech and Theology*, ch. 2.
47   Batnitzky, *Idolatry and Representation*, 148.
48   We might hear echoes of Buber's analysis of the "Thou" being reduced to an "It." In fact, Buber explicitly suggests that this is a risk which attends the work of art. See Martin

this risk is constitutive of creation itself. On the one hand, creation is the first expression and revelation of God "in visible form," guarding God from concealment (SR 160); on the other hand, once manifest in creation, there remains the danger that creation will fail to function as a sign. As such, something is necessary to "secur[e] the revelation which takes place in creation against retrogression into the night of mystery" (SR 161). Rosenzweig describes this as a "second revelation": "Precisely for the sake of its revelational character, the first revelation in creation thus demands the emergence of a 'second' revelation, a revelation which is nothing more than revelation, a revelation in the narrower—nay in the narrowest—sense" (SR 161).[49] This second revelation does not create, but rather transforms as a kind of *coup d'oeil*. It is the power to change—or better, recover—the created "thing" into a testimonial, a *sign*.

> The power to change the color of created being, which is illuminated by such a moment, from created "thing" into a testimonial to occurred manifestation resides in the effulgence of this *coup d'oeil*. Each thing is such a testimonial, if only because it is a created thing and because creation itself is already the first revelation. But precisely because it is a created thing from of yore, therefore the fact that it is testimonial to an occurred revelation remains behind it in the darkness of a first beginning. Only when it is once, somewhere in time, irradiated by the effulgence of a revelation taking place at that very moment—not of one which has taken place once and for all—only then will the circumstance that it owes its existence to a revelation become for it more than a "circum-stance"— the inner nucleus of its factuality. (SR 161)

This second revelation "liberates" creation from the danger of sliding back into mystery or concealment. "[R]evelation is thus the means for confirming creation structurally" (SR 161). The Creator God does not "retreat behind creation into the darkness" of an "origin"; rather, as manifesting and manifest, God is given *in the present*. "And by doing so, he lets God's concealedness sink into the past once and for all" (SR 162). "Revelation

---

Buber, *I and Thou*, 2nd ed., trans. Ronald Gregor Smith (New York: Scribner's, 1958), 10, 14.
49   We could perhaps suggest a parallel to this distinction in the Christian theological tradition's distinction between "natural" or "general" revelation and "special" revelation.

commences with 'I the Lord' as the great Nay of the concealed God which negates his own concealment" (178). This second revelation—functioning as an illumination—recovers the sign-function of a reified creation and thus restores the integrity of the visible.

This is how we should understand Rosenzweig's interpretation of the Second Commandment: obviously, it cannot be that all images are banned, since his own theory considers vision primordial and images ("visibility") as the site of God's revelation. If this is not a blanket prohibition of images, then how should this prohibition be understood? What "logic of prohibition" would Rosenzweig offer, in contrast to the logic of prohibition that we have seen in Marion, Cohen, and others, which ties it to finitude as such? For Rosenzweig, the prohibition is directed at a *danger*, a *risk* that attends images—the same risk that attends creation as the first revelation. Both are in danger of failing to function as signs. But this does not stem from being images as such, or because they are finite representations, or because the revelation takes place under "conditions" of finitude (as in Marion, Cohen, et al.); rather, such a danger resides in the perceivers insofar as it is the perceiver/worshiper who constitutes the image as either a sign (which refers to that which exceeds it while being present in it) or an idol. This is why Rosenzweig's account, which affirms vision and embodiment—and hence affirms images—nevertheless retains a critical function or power. It is the responsibility of the perceiver (worshiper), or better, the worshiping community, to not let the image be reified, reduced to a "thing" which then becomes a substitute. We might say that, for Rosenzweig, images are *pharmacological*, harboring the potential of both poison and cure.[50] The power of images stems from their affectivity and its resonation with the affective constitution of the creature; but that same affective power can also be a lure to become absorbed with the image. As Batnitzky summarizes, "Rosenzweig argues that images can authentically represent God. But to fixate on and worship any one image is idolatry. *Idolatry comes from the way in which an image is worshipped and not from the image itself.*"[51] Such a fixation would deny the semiotic function of the image (there is *reference* only where there is *distance*), constituting at once

50   I am drawing here on Derrida's analysis of the *pharmakon* in "Plato's Pharmacy," in *Dissemination*, trans. Barbara Johnson (Chicago: University of Chicago Press, 1981), 61–171, esp. 70–77. The interpretation of the Second Commandment in Marion, Maimonides, and Cohen would ultimately see images as only poison because of their finitude.
51   Batnitzky, *Idolatry and Representation*, 23, emphasis original.

a *substitution* of the image for the divine, as well as a denial of God's freedom to reveal God's self to the human being.[52] So Rosenzweig is still able to do justice to the (now qualified) proscription of images without adopting a general negation of images or the visual as such.

A Creational Aesthetic

Given his affirmation of creation and its conditions (finitude, materiality, and embodiment), coupled with his privileging of vision, and also his account of the "riskiness" of signs/images, we can briefly draw out the elements of what I would describe as Rosenzweig's "creational" aesthetic. First, art is a provocation which awakens the self of the spectator; as a language that is "prior to any real human speech, art creates, as the speech of the unspeakable, a first, speechless, mutual comprehension, for all time indispensable beneath and beside actual speech" (SR 81). Art "provides the ground on which the self can grow up everywhere," and it does this by opening the self to exteriority in a way that is analogous to—and a medium of—revelation (SR 81–82). Second, "the work of art thus supplies us with an analogy of creation" (SR 150) because art is a mode of expression, just as creation is God's self-expression. Rosenzweig considers art, and hence images, as a mode of communication: "art is the true language for the world prior to the miracle of revelation" (SR 147)—and will in fact be an avenue *of* revelation. Thus, third, art is that which irrupts the introversion of the "enclosed" pagan self (SR 167) and functions as "that language prior to revelation whose existence alone makes it possible for revelation to one day enter time as historical revelation" (SR 190). So "man possesses, in art, a language already when he is yet unable to pronounce what is inside him; art, then, is the language of what is otherwise still unpronounceable" (SR 190–91). This is because the image is a language which speaks otherwise than speech. Finally, since revelation is a "gift" (SR 162–63), it demands a consideration of its *reception* (the *per*ceiver is a *re*ceiver); in the work of art, this becomes a question regarding the role of "the spectator" in 'receiving' the work of art, giving it a "home." The work of art does not speak to its author; "it only 'speaks' to the beholder" (SR 243). I think we should hear in this question of reception a notion of responsibility on the part of the receiver in light of our discussion above regarding the risk of idolatry. The idol is the product of a gaze, therefore

---

52 Batnitzky, *Idolatry and Representation*, 23.

of the perceiver. So in emphasizing this role of reception in the spectator, Rosenzweig inserts the critical concern regarding the riskiness of images and their pharmacological character.

In contrast to Marion's "kenotic" aesthetic—which demands that the gaze pass *through* the image to a transcendence which is beyond it (to the point that we forget the image since it is merely transparent)—Rosenzweig's "creational" aesthetic affirms the possibility of a revelation of transcendence which inheres *in* the image without being *reduced* to immanence. The painting can be a site of "real presence" precisely because creation is the first picture of revelation.

12

The Call as Gift

The Subject's Donation in Marion and Levinas

> Loving—receiving and giving love—is not something, first of all, that we do. Love is who we are, as gift and call, as passion to be lived out. . . . It is in heeding the call of love—in making life-affirming connections—that we become human.[1]

In Ingmar Bergman's cinematic masterpiece *Persona*, the central character is the subject of a *gaze*—finding herself subject to a voyeuristic exhibition which is, at the same time, that which makes possible the construction of an identity. Like the adolescent boy in the prefatory sequences[2] in which Bergman explores the themes of voyeurism and the implication of his own camera in such subjugation, Sister Alma/Elisabeth Vogler finds herself subject to a gaze which is at the same time a *call*—a call to be subject. The observation of this gaze is at the same time a com-

---

1   James H. Olthuis, *The Beautiful Risk: A New Psychology of Loving and Being Loved* (Grand Rapids: Zondervan, 2001), 69.
2   The young boy finds himself the subject of a gaze but from an other who cannot be constituted or brought into focus—the gaze comes from a sort of shifting other who remains anonymous. This is part of an opening montage of what might be described as "case studies" in which Bergman places the viewer as the subject of a question: To what extent do I, like the director's camera, participate in such a voyeuristic gaze? And in what sense am I also subject *to* such a gaze? To what extent is my own "subjectivity" constructed out of response to a call that perhaps even the film evokes, and which is troubled by its breakdown (when the celluloid becomes tangled in the projector)?

mand, a decree, a call to respond by gathering oneself into a subject. The gaze as call thus grants subjectivity—the subjectivity of a respondent, perhaps even a "devoted one" (*l'adonné*).[3]

But who is looking? What calls? What gives (*ce que cela donne*)?[4] The play of the film leaves this ambiguous: Is she the subject of her own gaze? Is the care of Sister Alma for Elisabeth in fact a concern for herself? Is Elisabeth's supposed "study" of Sister Alma in fact a case of self-reflection and hence exhibition for an audience of the same? Is this gaze and call circulating only within a closed economy, in which case the only one "calling" is in fact oneself? If that were the case, according to Marion and Levinas, what we would have is a simply Heideggerian account of subjectivity which, despite its critique of the transcendental subject, nevertheless remains within a horizon of immanence where no one *other* calls to Dasein—Dasein simply calls to itself.[5] Being self-constituted, the "autarky" of Dasein remains intact.[6] As Levinas earlier observed, in Heidegger "Being is already an appeal to subjectivity," but this is always already an "egoism"—Dasein calling unto itself, never escaping the swirling eddy of the same, never interrupted by an exteriority.[7]

But in the play of *Persona*, and the play of personas within *Persona*, there remains the possibility for another account, what we might describe as a Levinasian thesis: the possibility that the gaze is neither Elisabeth's nor Sister Alma's—that the gaze, and hence the call, comes from outside, from another, an Other. Our focus here is not the film per se, but this warrants further

---

3   Jean-Luc Marion, *Étant donné: Essai d'une phénoménologie de la donation* (Paris: PUF, 1998²), 369–72 (henceforth abbreviated as ED). The word can also carry the connotation of an addict, one who is obsessed, which comes to characterize Sister Alma in *Persona*. Unfortunately, I don't think either sense is denoted by Jeffrey Kosky's translation of *l'adonné* as "the gifted." See Jean-Luc Marion, *Being Given: Toward a Phenomenology of Givenness*, trans. Jeffrey L. Kosky (Stanford: Stanford University Press, 2002), 268 and 369n22 (occasionally the pagination of this translation will be cited following the French).
4   Jean-Luc Marion, *La croisée du visible* (Paris: PUF, 1996), 80–81.
5   This, of course, would be no surprise, given Bergman's (deeply Lutheran) debts to existentialism.
6   Jean-Luc Marion, "The Final Appeal of the Subject [L'interloqué]," trans. Simon Critchley in *Deconstructive Subjectivities*, ed. Simon Critchley and Peter Dews (Albany: SUNY Press, 1996), 90–92 (henceforth abbreviated as FA).
7   Emmanuel Levinas, *Totality and Infinity*, trans. Alphonso Lingis (Pittsburgh: Duquesne University Press, 1969), 45–48. In other words, and here Marion merely echoes Levinas, Dasein is *self*-constituted. What both Marion and Levinas' account of the "subject" (the word is used advisedly) shares is the sense that the subject is constituted by the Other.

consideration. Any account of the evidence would have to consider the role of the fiancé and the lover—as well as the son (both the son who is and the son who was not permitted to be)—as instances of exteriority which constantly call upon Elisabeth/Sister Alma and, in the end, are perhaps the occasion for her gathering herself up into a responsible subject. These matters would be considered in light of Levinas' account of the domestic scene of fecundity, and in particular the child who is "the stranger" *par excellence*.[8] On this reading, the call is haunting but nevertheless *welcomed*, received as a gift that *gives* the subject *of* responsibility.[9] Rather than a constituting subject whose intentional gaze dominates its world, the called-self is a constitut*ed* self, subject *of* a gaze. And as such, the call is a gift that gives the subject.[10]

My goal in this chapter is to first consider the way in which Jean-Luc Marion's account of the subject repeats this Levinasian thesis, insofar as both Levinas and Marion provide an "analytic"[11] of the subject who comes "after the subject"—a subject *of* donation, including the sense in which the subject is both called and donated, both obligated and *graced*.[12] The second part of the chapter will then consider an important point of departure in Marion's account which, perhaps, grants a richer account of the post-metaphysical subject. Here I want to address the question of reciprocity, in dialogue with Olthuis and Milbank, suggesting that Levinas operates on the basis of an oppositional notion of difference (or "differential ontology") which means that an "ontology of violence" continues to undergird his project, even if it is offered in the name of peace.[13] In contrast, I think

---

8   Levinas, *Totality and Infinity*, 267ff.
9   Levinas, *Totality and Infinity*, 27, 84. For discussion, see Jacques Derrida, "A Word of Welcome," in *Adieu to Emmanuel Levinas* (Stanford: Stanford University Press, 1999), 15–123.
10   See, for instance, Levinas, *Otherwise than Being, or Beyond Essence*, trans. Alphonso Lingis (The Hague: Martinus Nijhoff, 1981), 10.
11   Marion remarks: "while *Dasein* indeed received an analytic (*Daseinanalytik*), the one who is claimed (*le revendiqué*) does not, explicitly at least, receive any" (FA 93).
12   The "claim" *gives* ("the claim imparts," FA 94); "I receive *myself* from the call or appeal which gives me to myself" (97).
13   In suggesting this, I am invoking the language of John Milbank's critique of Nietzsche, Foucault, Lyotard, and Derrida in *Theology and Social Theory* (Oxford: Blackwell, 1990), ch. 10. Interestingly, Levinas is not dealt with extensively there; this is corrected in his more recent "The Soul of Reciprocity, Part One: Reciprocity Refused," *Modern Theology* 17 (2001), esp. 341–43. My reading of Levinas (and especially the theme of "peace") owes much, even in disagreement, to Jeffrey Dudiak's masterful reading in *The Intrigue of Ethics* (New York: Fordham University Press, 2001).

Marion's account of the gifted subject is (or *should* be) undergirded by an "ontology of peace," which conceives of differential relations in a harmonious (i.e., analogous), rather than oppositional, way.[14]

Marion, Levinas, and the Gifted Subject

While the question of Marion's unpaid debts to Levinas remains a legitimate avenue of inquiry, my concern is not to sort out genealogical filiations. Instead, I want to first outline the parallels in Levinas and Marion regarding the subject. Like Levinas, Marion reverses the intentional arrow of the Husserlian ego (ED 367), arguing that, prior to the intentionality of consciousness (as well as prior to the *Anspruch des Seins*), the subject is the subject *of* and subject *to* a "claim" (*revendication*) and a "call" (*appel*) (ED 366–69): "the human being should thus be named *der Angesprochene*—the one who is claimed (*le revendiqué*)" (FA 93).[15] With this suggestion, Marion sets up a contrast between the analytic of Dasein in *Sein und Zeit* and the later Heidegger's account of the call of Being. Indeed, "anticipatory resoluteness" marks the way in which Dasein, far from coming "after" the metaphysical subject (Descartes, Kant, Husserl), is rather the culmination of the modern subject—its "last heir" (FA 91).[16] For the call that beckons Dasein in *Sein und Zeit* is merely an echo of Dasein's own voice. To the "they-self," the caller is "*something like* an alien voice"[17]—but it is not *really* alien, because in the end, "the caller is Dasein."[18] As such, Dasein is never opened up to alterity; as Marion puts it, "Dasein does not comport itself towards anything other, to any being, and therefore comports itself towards nothing" (FA 89). Never opened up to any exteriority, Dasein is never ruptured by any alterity; as such,

---

14 On an "ontology of peace," see Milbank, *Theology and Social Theory*, 279ff.
15 This subject is also designated "the interlocuted" (*l'interloqué*) and later, in ED, "the devoted" (*l'adonné*). In fact, in *Étant donné*, Marion tends to use the word "subject" to describe *the phenomenon*, in contrast to the "receiver" (*l'attributaire*) who "per/re-ceives" the phenomenon. Indeed, he argues that the phenomenon must be a kind of "self." See ED 343–44/248–49.
16 Earlier he remarks that "[t]he shadow of the ego falls across *Dasein*" (FA 90). This analysis of the Heideggerian subject is paralleled in ED 355–61/257–62. I think Marion would level the same charge against the Nietzschean "subject." See Marion, "The End of the End of Metaphysics," *Epoché* 2, no. 2 (1994): 1–22.
17 Martin Heidegger, *Being and Time*, trans. John Macquarrie and Edward Robinson (New York: Harper & Row, 1962), §57, 321 [H. 277], emphasis added.
18 Heidegger, *Being and Time*, 322 [H. 277].

Dasein "no longer admits any extrinsic relation" (FA 92). The result is an obfuscation of Being rather than a revealing.

But precisely "[s]ince anticipatory resoluteness, as a self-calling or auto-appeal, fails through neutralizing the question of Being," Marion comments, "it must be opened, *from the outside*, to an appeal or call that it no longer controls, decides, or performs" (FA 93, emphasis added). We find this irruption of an *outside*, Marion argues, in the later Heidegger (particularly the postface to *What Is Metaphysics?* and in the *Letter on Humanism*). It is in these later analyses of the "appeal of Being" that Marion launches his own analysis of the original "claim" (*la revendication*) of/upon the human being as an "analytic" of "the one who is claimed."

"The claim, then," he continues, "interpellates me. Before I have even said 'I,' the claim has summoned me, named me, and isolated me as myself" (FA 94). Rather than a constituting *je*, I already find myself a constituted *me*: the nominative gives way—"provisionally at least"—to the accusative. I am at the same time both recipient and subject of a call which makes me subject.[19] While this "dispossession" (ED 344/249) marks the "disaster of the I" (FA 95), it also signals another event: the *birth* of the subject as receiver, as gifted, as the *interloqué* (ED 361, 367/262, 266, cp. 289–90).[20] Thus, in contrast to the Cartesian (or Husserlian) ego, the subject as receiver is an inherently *relational* self; its identity is constituted by a relation whereby it is identified (FA 95).[21] As Marion summarizes:

> the relation precedes and produces individuality. And moreover, individuality loses its autarkic essence by being derived from a relation which not only is more originary than it, but is half unknown; for the claim delivers up to evidence only one of its two poles—*myself* or rather *me*—without necessarily

---

19 "[S]i j'ai à en répondre, j'ai aussi à lui répondre, j'ai donc reçu (et subi) un appel" (ED 368).
20 This metaphor of *birth* marks a development, I think, between the earlier "Final Appeal" and *Étant donné*. This could be considered in relation to Olthuis' consideration of the "matrix" and "womb" of love and perhaps the way in which birth is a product of *love*.
21 However, even the Cartesian subject's "isolation" is interrupted at its origin by its relationship to the Infinite (*Meditations*, III): "I am not alone in the world," he concludes. For a critical discussion, see Marion, "Does the *Ego* Alter the Other? The Solitude of the *Cogito* and the Absence of the *Alter Ego*," in *Cartesian Questions* (Chicago: University of Chicago Press, 1999), 118–38.

228   The Nicene Option

> or for the most part delivering up the other pole, namely, the origin of the call or appeal. (FA 95)

So, in a manner that echoes Levinas, Marion emphasizes the anonymity of that which calls.[22] The alterity of the other which alters the identity of the receiver comes *je ne sais d'ou*. This anonymity of the convocation entails a surprise for the interlocuted one: contradicting intentionality, the *interloqué* is called out of itself, "covered over (taken over [*sur*-prise]) by an extasis" (FA 96). But this exstasis is "a more originary affection which precedes metaphysical subjectivity" (FA 96). As soon as I awake, I find myself called—a called one. My subjectivity is a matter of donation.[23]

The Gift of Peace: Marion Contra Levinas?

When Marion moves on to consider the nature of the interlocution, we begin to detect a divergence from Levinas—or at least a moment in which Marion intentionally marks a distinction between his account and that of Levinas. For Marion, "interlocution"—the interlocutionary appeal[24]—effects a *reduction*: "the ultimate phenomenological reduction" (FA 97) or what he elsewhere describes as a "third reduction" to the pure givenness of a claimed self.[25] When describing such, he contrasts such a reduction with the reductions of Husserl, Heidegger, *and Levinas*:

> To determine the given as pure given demands the suspension [hence a reduction] within the *I* of everything which does not directly result from the claim itself, and therefore to reduce the *I* to the pure giving or donation of a *myself/me*. It is no longer a question of comprehending this giving according to the

---

22   This anonymity, akin to the slippage between *Il* and *il y a* in Levinas, is important for Marion, since he believes it preserves the properly "phenomenological" (rather than "theological") parameters of his account. This is also emphasized in his account of the "gift" in *Étant donné*, §10.

23   I use "subjectivity" tentatively to try to indicate a sense of identity which is not a (Cartesian) subjectivity. We might also appeal to Kristeva's account of a self in-process / on trial. For a discussion in a Levinasian context, see Olthuis, *Beautiful Risk*, 76–77.

24   Marion notes the legal universe of this metaphor (FA 96–97).

25   It is named such in Marion, *Reduction and Givenness: Investigations of Husserl, Heidegger, and Phenomenology*, trans. Thomas A. Carlson (Evanston: Northwestern University Press, 1998), 204. For my reservations regarding the possibility (or even desirability) of an "unconditional givenness," see my "Respect and Donation: A Critique of Marion's Critique of Husserl," *American Catholic Philosophical Quarterly* 71 (1997): 523–38.

> nominative case (Husserl) or according to the genitive case
> (of Being: Heidegger) *nor even according to the accusative case
> (Levinas), but rather according to the dative case*—I receive
> *myself* from the call or appeal which gives me to myself. (FA
> 97, emphasis added; cp. ED 371/269)

In a later formulation of this point, Marion continues by again invoking the metaphor of *birth*: "Receiving himself from the call that summons him, the gifted is therefore open to an alterity, from which the Other can be lacking, but who thus appears all the more.... Thus the gifted is delivered straightaway—with its birth—from solipsism" (ED 371–72/269). So we clearly have the elements of a Levinasian structure here: a primordial relationality which is the condition of a call which makes me subject—which calls forth my identity, not as a solipsistic individual but as a responsible "called one." Alterity is at the heart of identity, for Marion.

But what are we to make of this evaluation of and departure from Levinas? What does Marion mean to indicate by suggesting that the Levinasian subject is understood according to the *accusative* (my identity is *given*), whereas the interlocuted subject is understood according to the *dative* (my identity is given *to me*)? I want to (tentatively) argue that here Marion may be calling into question the thesis of *substitution* in Levinas; that is, I believe that we might see Marion as here rejecting the Levinasian axiom regarding non-reciprocity. In contrast, Marion's account of the interlocuted subject, while still maintaining some element of asymmetry, also tries to (or *ought* to) provide an account of *reciprocity* in intersubjective relationships. While my identity is given *for* the Other, it is nonetheless given *to* me.

My thesis rests on a particular reading of Levinas, which I should at least briefly lay on the table.[26] While I could concede that Levinas understands the relationship with the Other to be "primordial," it seems to me that it is at best *co*-primordial with egoism, which makes it *co*-originary. In other words, even if, as Levinas asserts, infinity is "as primordial as totality,"[27] this seems to still entail that totality is primordial. Hence, there is a way in which relationality is always already inscribed with war. Even if

---

26   I have articulated my concerns about Levinas' account in more detail in my *The Fall of Interpretation: Philosophical Foundations for a Creational Hermeneutic* (Downers Grove, Ill.: InterVarsity Press, 2000), 123–26.
27   See Levinas, *Totality and Infinity*, 23.

the swirling eddy of egoistic enjoyment is a kind of "second" moment, it seems to be one that grows out of this primordial war. (In other words, there is a sense in which "Cartesian dualism" is "rigorously preserved" by Levinas.[28]) It is against this backdrop that I understand the language and descriptions of *Otherwise than Being* pertaining to substitution, persecution, and hostage-taking. Don't we simply have here the inversion of egoism?[29]

While I have tried to note obvious echoes of Levinas in Marion's account of the post-metaphysical subject (which stems from their parallel accounts of a phenomenology of absolute revelation divined so well by Janicaud[30]), what are we to make of some obvious differences? First, let us note the striking difference in language, especially the notable absence in Marion of the Levinasian language of guilt and persecution, and the (intentional?) avoidance of a violent paradigm which construes the relation as one of hostage-taking. I think we need to do justice to this absence, since it is certainly not just a matter of semantics.

Second, we need to return to our earlier question regarding Marion's own suggestion that the devoted or gifted one (*l'adonné*) is to be understood not in the accusative sense of Levinas, but rather in terms of the dative. What does Marion mean to suggest by this? If we begin this question, we'll be in a place to account for the first set of questions regarding language.

If we look at Marion's suggestion carefully, we note that what distinguishes the accusative from the dative is the direction or *telos* of the giving, not the object given. In the dative conception, "I receive *myself*"; the call or appeal "gives me to myself" (FA 97). He goes on to suggest that perhaps "this strange dative case was not here distinguished from the ablative case (as in Greek), since the *myself/me* accomplishes, insofar as it is the first gift which derives from the appeal or call, the opening of all other donations or gifts and particular givens, which are possibly ethical" (FA 97). In *Étant donné*, this last aspect is further developed:

---

28   Milbank, "Soul of Reciprocity," 341.
29   I have suggested this in *Fall of Interpretation*, 125. Milbank suggests the same ("Soul of Reciprocity," 342).
30   I take up Janicaud's critique of Marion and Levinas (and basically take his side) in my *Speech and Theology: Language and the Logic of Incarnation*, Radical Orthodoxy Series (London: Routledge, 2002).

Fully offering himself to givenness, to the point that he delivers it as such, the gifted finally attains his ultimate determination—to receive himself by receiving the given unfolded by him according to givenness. Consequently, the gifted is defined entirely in terms of givenness because he is completely achieved as soon as he surrenders conditionally to what gives itself—and first of all to the saturated phenomenon that calls him.[31]

For Marion, the gifted, while recipient of subjectivity, is nevertheless also a certain giver—an "unfolder" of the givenness of phenomena. In other words, I hear in Marion a sense in which the call to be subject is a call to responsibility which at the same time affirms a certain *reciprocity* of giving—stemming from an iconic paradigm in which the gaze of the Other is an invitation to relation.[32] I think Marion recognizes that our conception of this relation is rooted in an ontology—more specifically, in how we conceive *difference*.[33] While I would concede that Marion is somewhat ambiguous on this score, there are at least suggestions in his corpus of an ontology which conceives of difference not as opposition (as in Levinas' differential ontology)[34] but as participatory, engendering an account of intersubjective relation which provides a positive account of mutuality.[35] If this is not immediately evident in *Being Given*,[36] we see the rudimentary lines of such an ontology in Marion's early work *Idol and Distance*. There, in the context of a critique of Levinas, Marion notes that when trying to think the "relation" with the Other, we need to think difference differently—a thinking which would "free itself . . . by ceasing to play on the

---

31 Marion, *Being Given*, 282–83.
32 I allude, of course, to Marion, *God without Being*, trans. Thomas A. Carlson (Chicago: University of Chicago Press, 1991); but see, in this immediate context, *Being Given*, 318–19.
33 See Marion's discussions of different notions of "difference" in ED 405–8/294–96.
34 Though I would concede that at times he appears to (and perhaps *does*) buy into the logic of oppositional difference and a differential ontology. See, for instance, Marion, *Prolegomena to Charity*, trans. Stephen Lewis (New York: Fordham University Press, 2002), 80–81.
35 Following Jim Olthuis, one could think of *relation* not only as "analogical" or "participatory," but also *covenantal*, in which case the marital relationship could be a model for thinking difference. See James H. Olthuis, *I Pledge You My Troth* (New York: Harper & Row, 1975; rev. ed., 1989), and idem, *Keeping Our Troth* (San Francisco: Harper & Row, 1986).
36 I am leaving open a dialogue that must take place regarding Milbank's reading of Marion in "The Soul of Reciprocity," 344–55.

field and with the terms of ontological difference, in order to reinterpret it, in situating it on another terrain of difference."[37] What we would ultimately need is what we might call a "Chalcedonian" *difference*, an account of analogical difference "without confusion or separation."[38] The Chalcedonian understanding of the Incarnation—what I have been describing as the "logic of incarnation"—provides an alternative way for understanding difference, or better, the *relation* between differences. In the Chalcedonian model we see a certain mutuality—a play of differences which permits relation without either reducing the terms to the Same, or asserting a radical incommensurability that precludes connection. In his phenomenology of the icon, one finds Marion taking this Chalcedonian model seriously, and we see hints of it spilling over into his anthropology—enough traces of an alternative to mark a difference between the philosophical anthropologies of Levinas and Marion.

Let me conclude by trying to get at this intuition of a difference between Levinas and Marion in another way. As Jeffrey Dudiak has amply demonstrated, there is a (very qualified!) moment of reciprocity in Levinas' account. In *Otherwise than Being*, Levinas remarks: "It is only thanks to God that, as a subject incomparable with the other, I am approached as an other by the others, that is, 'for myself.' 'Thanks be to God,' I am an other for the others."[39] As Dudiak comments, this is not a relation that is "deducible" from my assymetrical relationship, as though we were dealing with a kind of Kantian kingdom of ends; rather, *if* it happens that I am respected as an other by the other, it happens as a matter of *grace*. In this way, "[j]ustice as a society of equals, wherein I too am a citizen, already presupposes this grace."[40]

Marion also appeals to a role for grace; indeed, the very notion of being "gifted" entails a being "graced." "What do we have that we have not *received*?" Augustine would often ask, echoing St. Paul (1 Cor 4:7). So too in Marion: our identity itself, as gift, is a matter of grace. Thus he

---

37   Jean-Luc Marion, *Idol and Distance*, trans. Thomas A. Carlson (New York: Fordham University Press, 2001), 220. He goes on to conclude that as in Levinas, Derrida's *différance* really does not escape the problem: "One perhaps escapes the ontological difference as little through *différance* as through the Other" (231).
38   I concede that my argument might be normative, not descriptive: that perhaps Marion does *not* articulate an "ontology of peace," but that, given other commitments of his thought, he *should*.
39   Levinas, *Otherwise than Being*, 158.
40   See Dudiak, *Intrigue of Ethics*, 329–30.

concludes that "[g]race gives the *myself* to *itself* before the *I* even notices itself. My grace precedes me" (FA 104). In light of this role of grace in both Levinas and Marion, my concluding question is this: Is grace *original*? I would put the question to both. It seems to me that for Levinas, grace, in a way, supervenes upon nature. I am trying to argue for an *original* grace, perhaps not so common, which is more primordial than violence.

If Marion would consistently follow the logic of Chalcedon and Nicea,[41] then I would argue that he should adopt an ontology which accounts for difference (or "distance"), not oppositionally, yielding a paradigm of violence, but *analogically* or *incarnationally*, yielding an ontology of peace which undergirds an account of originary intersubjectivity. If this connection is not explicitly made in Marion, I would at least return to our earlier question regarding language: perhaps the absence of the language of violation (persecution, hostage-taking) can be explained in these terms. In that case we might suggest that Marion's account of intersubjectivity inscribes grace into the structure of creation. When we begin with this graced creation, the relationships of intersubjectivity need not be construed as acts of violence (as in Levinas), but rather can be described as a "dance"—a being-with that involves an erotics of mutuality, a giving-and-receiving which is an-economic. Olthuis describes this as "with-ing": "With-ing is a healing dance in the wild spaces of love, a meeting-in-the-middle to mark out space together."[42] It seems to me that Levinas' model of relations cannot account for the space where such with-ing is possible. Thus Olthuis emphasizes not just the *gift*, but also the *call* to identity and relation:

> God is love, and humans are made in God's image. Love, then, is who we are—love's agents. God is the giver, we are the gifted, love is the gift. God is the caller, we are the called, love is the calling. This is what I mean by the *gift/call* structure of humankind. Being and becoming lovers—the *gift* of being human and the *call* to become human—happen together, inextricably, simultaneously in a process of being and becoming.[43]

---

41   Marion does so in his *The Crossing of the Visible*, trans. James K. A. Smith (Stanford: Stanford University Press, 2004), ch. 4.
42   Olthuis, *Beautiful Risk*, 130.
43   Olthuis, *Beautiful Risk*, 68. Cp. idem, "Be(com)ing: Humankind as Gift and Call," *Philosophia Reformata* 58 (1993): 153–72.

This is why Olthuis criticizes Levinas' "ontologizing" of egoism such that the other always come to me as a violent interruption. In Levinas, Olthuis concludes, "there seems to be no room, ontologically, for the possibility of a self, of its own initiative, to reach out, attentive and open to the other."[44] Resisting the oppositional notion of difference that funds Levinas' understanding of relation, Olthuis also rejects the notion of asymmetry for a model of an-economic but nevertheless reciprocal mutuality.

Marion's account of intersubjectivity, unlike Levinas', at least glimpses this reality of an originary grace, a primordial love, which is then free to see relations as otherwise-than-violent (even if, in a broken world, all relations are susceptible to such violence). The genius of Olthuis' contribution to philosophical anthropology has been his consistent refusal to inscribe structures of violence into the fabric of creation.[45] For Olthuis, the advent of the Other can be an invitation to dance.

But here a final key theme comes to the fore: the deep eschatology of Olthuis' account, which recognizes the fallenness of creation,[46] both requires and engenders a hope for the final banquet, with lots of wine, where the dance of mutuality will no longer be tinged with the risk of refusal or exclusion. We hope to find ourselves dancing in the kingdom of love—in its redeemed wild spaces. The hope for this final dance, however, is not utopian; it is eschatological, and we are called to both occasion and testify to its inbreaking—its *ad-venire*—in the dances we find ourselves in. We are called to be subjects of responsibility and love, dancing agents of the kingdom who are gifted and called to be image bearers of the God who is love.

---

44   James H. Olthuis, "Face-to-Face: Ethical Asymmetry or the Symmetry of Mutuality?" in *Knowing Other-wise: Philosophy on the Threshold of Spirituality*, ed. James H. Olthuis (New York: Fordham University Press, 1997), 141. Olthuis attributes this to Levinas' acceptance of the traditional understanding of power as necessarily power-*over* (143–44).
45   This refusal, far from making him blind to the realities of violence, has in fact been the impetus for real, concrete concern about relational violence. See, for example, his research on family abuse in Olthuis, "Rethinking the Family: Belonging, Respecting, and Connecting," in *Towards an Ethics of Community: Negotiations of Difference in a Pluralist Society*, ed. James H. Olthuis (Waterloo, Ont.: Wilfrid Laurier University Press, 2000), 127–49.
46   It is crucial to recognize that Olthuis' "dance" model in no way expects all of our intersubjective being-in-the-world to be a party. Indeed, no one more than Olthuis emphasizes the dangers, risk, and vulnerability of relationships and love. But at the same time, for Olthuis this risk and danger is the product of the Fall—of sin—not the constitutive structures of finitude. See Olthuis, *Beautiful Risk*, 74–75, 78–79.

Afterword

An Incarnational Phenomenology

There is no philosophical standpoint that is not, at bottom, confessional. Despite the pretension of Enlightenment claims, there is no neutral, objective, "pure" reason. There are, of course, disciplines of thinking and debate, agreed-upon conventions for thoughtful discourse, and standards of rationality that constitute the "game" (in Wittgenstein's sense) we call "philosophy." But every philosopher who steps into that arena brings with them commitments that are *pre*-philosophical, even *ur*-philosphical. As Wittgenstein put it: "If I have exhausted the justifications I have reached bedrock, and my spade is turned. Then I am inclined to say: 'This is simply what I do.'"[1]

This does not preclude dialogue and debate with those who have a different take on what that bedrock is. Recognizing the confessional nature of philosophy does not abandon us to enclaves or proverbial choirs of monolithic agreement. But it does mean that productive philosophical debates need to unearth these commitments and bring them to the surface in order to foster genuine encounter. In such encounters, what we often do is offer our confessional "take" on phenomena as an explanation and account that others could "try on" and see whether (or not) it illuminates

---

1   Ludwig Wittgenstein, *Philosophical Investigations*, 2nd ed., trans. G. E. M. Anscombe (Oxford: Blackwell, 1958), § 217.

their experience.[2] This, I think, is at the heart of the phenomenological method. And it is just such an "offering" that animates what I'm calling an "incarnational phenomenology." A core challenge in continental philosophy has been to account for alterity and difference: How can we know the Other? How can we encounter that which transcends us without folding the Other into our sphere of perception, thereby reducing alterity to the sphere of the same?[3] Most bluntly: Is it even possible to really know someone else? Or are we locked inside an egoistic consciousness where others always appear on *our* terms?

How we answer such questions is constrained by all kinds of unstated assumptions, an "unthought" but assumed logic that constrains the way we imagine the relationship between same and other, identity and difference, me and you, humanity and the divine. These logics are more on the register of Wittgenstein's "bedrock" than evidenced positions. And too many accounts, I have been arguing, are constrained by the logic of determination, which can only imagine this relation as a zero-sum game, a binary logic with limited possibilities. In contrast, I have tried to suggest, there is an imagination carried in the (strange, perplexing, almost unthinkable) Christian doctrine of the Incarnation that offers an alternative, nonbinary way to understand the relationship between immanence and transcendence, self and other, humanity and God. This "Nicene option" is a logic nourished by a scandalous confession: that in the embodied Jesus Christ, "the only Son of God, begotten from the Father before all ages," we meet that human who is "God from God, Light from Light, true God from true God, begotten not made; of the same essence as the Father." The One through whom all things were made is born; the Creator is incubated in a womb; the God who precedes the cosmos appears in a manger.

In the Incarnation, the (transcendent) divine is given to (immanent) us without subtraction or loss. In the Formula of Chalcedon, identity and difference touch; same and other kiss in the person of Jesus of Christ— "truly God *and* truly man . . . of one substance with the Father as regards

---

2   For a lucid analysis of Charles Taylor's project as just such a strategy, phenomenological at heart, see Deane-Peter Baker, *Tayloring Reformed Epistemology: Charles Taylor, Alvin Plantinga, and the* de jure *Challenge to Christian Belief* (London: SCM Press, 2007), esp. 105–60.

3   The seminal articulation of this challenge is Edmund Husserl's "Fifth Meditation," in *Cartesian Meditations*, trans. Dorion Cairns (Dordrecht: Springer, 1960), 89–150. The corpus of Emmanuel Levinas is, then, the great ensuing challenge to the Husserlian account.

his Godhead, and *at the same time* of one substance with us as regards his humanity." Perhaps above all this is a picture of ontological abundance where something—Someone—is given without losing; something can both appear within immanence *and* remain transcendent: without confusion, without change, without division, without separation. The alterity of the divine can be both intimate and cosmic. The transcendence and Otherness of God is not compromised just because the Son is held by a young mother in a stable. In the Incarnation, the transcendent God refuses to be elusive; but that doesn't mean God's transcendence dissolves into comprehension. This is a meeting with mystery.

The paradox of the Incarnation bequeaths to us a newly elastic imagination for conceiving relationships we would have thought to be binary either/or relations. The wager of an incarnational phenomenology is that this starting point, this "bedrock," proves to be illuminating when we "try it on" as a way to account for our experience of alterity—not only encounters with the divine but also other modes of transcendence (phenomenologically speaking), including our encounters with others. The idea of incarnation, we might say, is also "horizontal" insofar as the other person is an alterity whose transcendence should not be reduced to my comprehension; neither would we want to conceive of interpersonal encounters as merely bumping into inauthentic stand-ins for the other, leaving the other effectively unknowable (and unlovable). The philosophical imagination that is primed by the Incarnation refuses such either/or binaries and thus prompts us to reconceive the interpersonal encounter as a revelation that also preserves mystery: I can meet you, know you, understand you, even if I will never plumb the depths of your alterity—in part, no doubt, because I also remain a mystery to myself.[4] While I hope an incarnational

---

4   Indeed, Maurice Merleau-Ponty argues that this mystery of my own selfhood is what makes it possible for me to be truly opened to an encounter with the other: "The plurality of consciousness is impossible if I have an absolute consciousness of myself. . . . If it is perfect, the contact of my thought with itself seals me within myself and prevents me from ever feeling that anything eludes my grasp; there is no opening, no 'aspiration' towards an Other for this self of mine, which constructs the totality of being and its own presence in the world, which is defined in terms of 'self-possession,' and which never finds anything outside itself but what it has put there. This hermetically sealed self is no longer a finite self" (Merleau-Ponty, *Phenomenology of Perception* [London: Routledge, 1962], 373). Jorella Andrews comments on this passage: "The fact that contact with the Other depends, firstly, on our having an appearance for each other and, secondly, on our having an incomplete grasp of our own existence has implications not only for the kind of communications

phenomenology would nourish a philosophy of religion that is more attentive to incarnate embodiment, I also believe the implications of an incarnational phenomenology spill over into other spheres of philosophical concern, particularly questions of intersubjectivity.[5] So as a productive philosophical paradigm, an incarnational phenomenology is not limited to philosophy of religion but would also bear fruit in philosophical explorations of social ontology and ethics.

Finally, as I intimate in the final chapters, I also believe an incarnational phenomenology would be generative in the area of aesthetics.[6] In part because all art is an instance of intersubjectivity, but also insofar as all art (whether visual, performative, or literary) is an embodiment of the invisible, an incarnational phenomenological aesthetics seems poised to provide a rich account of both artistic creation and the experience of being encountered by a work of art. Which is all just to say: this book remains the beginning of a conversation, an intimation of paths to be pursued—some by myself, some, I hope, by others—in the imaginative field opened by the mystery of the Incarnation.

---

we can have with others and the kind of knowledges we can have of them but also for the contexts in which such communications and knowledges must occur" (Jorella Andrews, *The Question of Painting: Re-thinking Thought with Merleau-Ponty* [London: Bloomsbury Academic, 2019], 150).

5   For developments in this direction, see Natalie Depraz, *Trascendence et Incarnation: Le statut de l'intersubjectivité comme altérité à soi chez Husserl* (Paris: Vrin, 1995).

6   For an important trajectory, see Andrews' discussion of "an incarnational logic" in Merleau-Ponty's account of painting in *The Question of Painting*, 41–46.

Author Index

Abraham, William, 28
Adams, Marilyn McCord, 1, 12
Agamben, Giorgio, 30, 55
Alston, William, 1
Andrews, Jorella, 237n4, 238n6
Asad, Talal, 52n62
Auden, W. H., 128
Augustine, 7, 23n31, 35n17, 36n19, 55, 66, 68, 92n58, 96, 103n19, 152, 154–58, 166–75, 185n27, 189–200, 205n6, 232

Badiou, Alain, 3, 55, 61, 68n13
Baker, Deane-Peter, 54n3, 226n2
Batnitzky, Leora, 212, 217–21
Bauckham, Richard, 127n2, 149n79, 150n81, 151n83
Benson, Bruce Ellis, 17n19, 55n8, 56n11, 80n35, 187n30
Berger, Peter, 30, 36, 40
Bergman, Ingmar, 223–24
Blond, Philip, 58n14, 185n26
Blondel, Maurice, 12n4

Bordieu, Pierre, 7, 31n3, 33, 43, 47–49, 69
Boyarin, Daniel, 203, 212n18
Braiterman, Zachary, 215n39
Buber, Martin, 218n48
Burrell, David, 163n14

Camus, Albert, 7
Caputo, John D., 5, 15, 53–91, 96n5, 104–5, 108–9, 130–31, 143–50, 174n11, 189–91, 197–201
Castelli, Elizabeth, 61n19
Chrétien, Jean-Louis, 3n7
Closer, Roy, 21–22
Coakley, Sarah, 19n23
Cohen, Hermann, 213–20
Connolly, William, 22
Courtine, Jean-François, 3n7
Cuneo, Terence, 14n11

Deleuze, Gilles, 53, 61, 82, 117n19
Depraz, Natalie, 238n5

Author Index

Derrida, Jacques, 3–8, 13n10, 17n17, 53–55, 64–198
Descartes, René, 3, 18, 132, 162–64, 177, 226
Dodaro, Robert, 171n2, 189n2
Dooyeweerd, Herman, 20–21, 125n30, 192n9
Dudiak, Jeffrey, 225n13, 232

Farley, Edward, 185n28
Freud, Sigmund, 83, 86, 190n4

Gadamer, Hans-Georg, 13, 21, 54, 113, 171n1
Gallagher, Shaun, 19n23, 43n30
Geertz, Clifford, 68n11
Gilson, Etienne, 12n4, 23, 164, 197n18
Goicoechea, David, 80n35
Gourgouris, Stathis, 31n4, 33n9, 34n11, 35n15, 37n20, 38n22, 43, 52n62
Griffiths, Paul, 45
Gschwandtner, Christina, 14n11

Hadot, Pierre, 19
Harrison, Victoria S., 21n26
Hauerwas, Stanley, 21, 36n19, 41n28, 156n3
Hegel, G. W. F., 1, 100, 113, 125, 143, 171
Heidegger, Martin, 2–3, 7, 13, 15, 17–21, 26, 33, 43–54, 63, 80, 84, 90, 96n8, 100n14, 102–4, 121, 126n32, 133n27, 143n57, 156n6, 158n10, 164, 171n1, 177n17, 192n9, 193–94, 205–6, 213, 224, 226–29
Henry, Michel, 3n7

Husserl, Edmund, 2n2, 18, 20, 29, 31, 43, 53, 55, 80, 87, 101, 132, 134–35, 148, 164, 171–86, 204, 207, 209, 226–29, 236n3, 238n5

Janicaud, Dominique, 3, 174, 230
Johnson, Kristen Deede, 22n30
Johnson, Mark, 43n30, 47n45

Kant, Immanuel, 5, 21, 38, 68, 70, 83, 95–96, 100n14, 111–27, 137–38, 144n64, 163–64, 178, 198–99, 204n2, 217, 226, 232
Kaufman, Gordon, 68n12
Kelsey, David, 186n28
Kenneson, Philip, 41n28
Kierkegaard, Søren, 55, 70n16, 76n30, 80–82, 87, 98, 100n14, 106–7, 115n12, 121, 175, 198n19, 200
King, Martin Luther, 158n8
Kristeva, Julia, 228n23
Kuipers, Ronald, 68n13
Kuyper, Abraham, 20, 125n30

Levinas, Emmanuel, 3, 15, 23, 53–54, 73, 75n28, 82, 98, 100n14, 103–4, 112, 115, 121, 147–48, 156–57, 166, 174, 177, 183, 202, 204, 206n7, 207, 211, 213–15, 217–18n46, 223–36
Lilla, Mark, 67n8
Lindbeck, George, 17n19
Löwith, Karl, 137n36
Lyotard, François, 143n56, 212

MacIntyre, Alasdair, 12–13, 21–27, 36n19, 47n46, 156n3
Mahmood, Saba, 31n4, 33–34, 37–39, 43

Maimonides, 211–12, 215, 217, 220
Marion, Jean-Luc, 3–4, 6n10, 7, 53, 80n35, 87–88, 100, 148n77, 174–77, 183, 201–34
McDannell, Colleen, 210n15
Merleau-Ponty, Maurice, 7, 18, 47, 185n26, 237n4, 238
Milbank, John, 13, 22, 24, 34, 36n19, 69–70, 75, 85, 156n6, 172nn3–4, 174n12, 225–26, 230–31
Miller, J. Hillis, 165n17
Moltmann, Jürgen, 73, 137n6, 138n42, 150n80
Murphy, Francesca Aran, 12n4

Nietzsche, Friedrich, 1, 80–86, 90, 189, 199–200, 204, 225–26

Ochs, Peter, 16n16, 27–28
Olthuis, James, 21n26, 27n41, 58n14, 65n4, 81n39, 85n44, 156n6, 174n11, 223–34

Paffenroth, Kim, 189n1
Pascal, Blaise, 45n38, 121
Peperzak, Adriaan, 3n6, 54n4
Pereboom, Derek, 163n13
Pickstock, Catherine, 26, 172–74
Pieper, Josef, 134nn29–30, 135n33, 136n34, 138nn39–40, 140n49, 150n81, 151
Plantinga, Alvin, 1, 6, 12–13, 20, 23, 58, 60, 236n17
Plato, 1, 124, 169, 171–73, 176, 195, 203, 220
Polanyi, Michael, 21

Rembrandt, 197
Ricoeur, Paul, 2n2, 3, 54, 100n14

Robbins, Jill, 23n31, 103n19
Roberts, Robert C., 45n42
Rorty, Richard, 7, 13n10, 34, 68n13, 127–51, 198
Rosenzweig, Franz, 7, 201–22
Ruskin, John, 77–79

Schleiermacher, Friedrich, 112n6, 215
Schmitz-Perrin, Rudolf, 53n2
Sludds, Kevin, 45, 48nn47–48
Smith, Christian, 32n5, 40n26, 51n61
Steinbock, Anthony J., 55n6, 164n15
Stout, Jeffrey, 34, 36n19
Stump, Eleonore, 12, 16n16

Taylor, Charles, 5, 7, 25–26, 31–39, 43, 47–51, 236n2
Taylor, Mark C., 54, 80
Trakakis, Nick, 54nn3–4

Vandervelde, George, 27n41
Vattimo, Gianni, 53, 61, 71n20, 111n4, 130n14

Ward, Graham, 26–27, 61n19, 172n4
Wesselius, Janet, 21n26
Westphal, Merold, 15n14, 53n2, 54–55, 60, 65n4, 80n35, 125–26, 158n8, 171n1
Wheeler, Samuel C., 2n2
Wirzba, Norman, 55n8
Wittgenstein, Ludwig, 4, 7, 19, 33, 47–48, 235–36
Wolfson, Elliot, 203, 212n18, 212n20, 215n38, 217n43
Wolterstorff, Nicholas, 1, 2, 4, 11n1, 12, 13n6, 20–21, 34